JOHN DRYDEN: A SURVEY AND BIBLIOGRAPHY OF CRITICAL STUDIES, 1895–1974

John Dryden:
A Survey
and Bibliography
of Critical Studies,
1895-1974

David J. Latt

Samuel Holt Monk

UNIVERSITY OF MINNESOTA PRESS,

MINNEAPOLIS

Library of Congress Catalog Card Number 75-36033

ISBN 0-8166-0774-5

Contents

Preface

Samuel Holt Monk's *John Dryden: A List of Critical Studies Published from 1895 to 1948* appeared in 1950. During the intervening twenty-five years the number of studies devoted to Dryden has more than tripled. In updating Professor Monk's list I have generally adopted his approach in format and in the selection of items for inclusion. Accordingly, the bibliography includes items that focus directly on Dryden, those that discuss Dryden's works in the context of the works of other writers and those that investigate material of general importance to Dryden studies. Dissertations from American, German, English and French universities have been added, although master's and honors theses have not. Every reasonable attempt has been made to include all material relevant to the study of Dryden. I have included studies of literary figures who have written on Dryden, such as Samuel Johnson, or who were Dryden's contemporaries, such as Thomas Shadwell, but I have made no attempt to list all such studies or all editions of their works. In updating the bibliography, then, I have been guided by the desire to indicate all the perspectives from which Dryden may be studied.

Following Professor Monk's original design, I have excluded, with few exceptions, trade editions of Dryden's works, as well as editions of separate or selected works prepared solely for classroom use. Complete bibliographic information has been provided for virtually every entry in the bibliography. The annotations and citations are based on my own reading of the publications listed, except in a few instances in which I have relied on the accuracy of the bibliographies noted in Section 1 because the publications were not readily available. As an aid to locating material in the bibliography, the publishing history of each entry has also been provided. Whenever an item has been reprinted, either separately or in a collection, that information has been included; this information is noteworthy because it indicates the relative popularity and thus the influence of

certain studies. Reviews are listed at the end of the entries; no attempt was made to include all the reviews of any item.

The first section of the bibliography contains a listing of *Festschriften* and collections of essays. Each entry in this section has
been assigned an abbreviation which is used for reference purposes
elsewhere in the book. The entries in the balance of the book have
been organized into nine numbered catagories, of which four have sub-
sections. Since not all studies fit neatly into the divisions of the
bibliography, a system of cross-referencing has been provided. Book-
length studies which contain essays on more than one of Dryden's non-
dramatic works or which discuss works from several genres have been
listed in Section 4, General Criticism, and have been cross-referenced to the works that they discuss. Related studies and review articles are also cross-referenced. Studies of Dryden's translations
which originally appeared in miscellanies are to be found in Section
6. The topic index should be consulted for subject listings, while
the author-title index has listings for all of Dryden's works. The
index is a general guide to the material of the bibliography; I have
made every reasonable attempt to indicate the contents of all the
items in the bibliography, but the topic index is not exhaustive.
Brief annotations have been included to indicate the subject or argument of selected entries. The asterisks preceding certain entries
identify works which are of exceptional value or which develop new
points of view. I have used this device only reluctantly, and no
doubt I have sometimes overlooked works of interest, but because of
the size of the bibliography I felt that a general guide to the most
important works would be helpful to many readers.

The compilation of the bibliography was difficult because Dryden's
life and works touched upon a great many areas of seventeenth-century
English culuture, history and literature; and I found it necessary to
go far beyond those studies which have Dryden's name or references to
his works in their titles. For instance, discussions of Dryden's
works occur in virtually all studies of seventeenth- and eighteenth-
century literature, and important analyses often appear in general
studies of drama, criticism, nondramatic poetry and translations.
Most of these have been included in the bibliography.

I have made every effort to ensure that the bibliography is complete, but it is possible that important omissions may come to light.
I would be grateful if reviewers and other readers would bring these
to my attention.

D. J. L.

Acknowledgments

I am most indebted to Samuel Holt Monk, whose original survey and list of Dryden studies were prepared in the late 1940s. Throughout the preparation of the expanded, updated list and survey, Professor Monk has generously given me encouragement and advice. I would also like to thank those who helped me formulate the design of the bibliography and who have read the survey of Dryden studies which precedes the bibliography. Sarah Getty, Paul Maixner, Earl Miner, Jane Yedlin and Steven N. Zwicker have contributed a great deal to the quality of the introduction; Geneva Phillips of the California Dryden and Alan H. Roper have made helpful suggestions about the organization of the index. I would also like to acknowledge the assistance of Angela Bucci, Natalie DiRissio, David J. Gadbois, Susan M. McClelland, Ronald St. Pierre, Sandra Tancredi, Debra Welden and Susan H. Whitmore in the preparation of the manuscript. I should like to thank the staffs of the libraries of the University of California (Los Angeles), Brown University, Columbia University and Rhode Island College, who have cheerfully helped me find items which I wished to read. A grant from the Faculty Research Committee of Rhode Island College made it possible for me to visit a number of other libraries in my search for elusive entries.

D. J. L.

Abbreviations

The function of the asterisk (*) which precedes certain items in the bibliography is explained in the Preface. The abbreviations in brackets which appear in many entries refer to the publications listed in the unnumbered section entitled "Festschriften and Other Collections."

AB-SU   Abstracts of Dissertations, Stanford University

AES   Abstracts of English Studies

AL   American Literature

Anglica   Publication of The Anglica Society of Kansai University, Osaka, Japan

Archiv   Archiv für das Studium der Neueren Sprachen und Literaturen

ARS   Augustan Reprint Society

ASLIB   Association of Special Libraries and Information Bureau, Index to Theses Accepted for Higher Degrees in the Universities of Great Britain and Ireland

AUMLA   Journal of the Australasian Universities Language and Literature Association

BB   Bulletin of Bibliography

BC   Book Collector

BHI   British Humanities Index

BNYPL   Bulletin of the New York Public Library

BSE   Brno Studies in English

BSTCF   Ball State Teachers College Forum

BSUF	Ball State University Forum
BuR	Bucknell Review
CamJ	Cambridge Journal
CathW	Catholic World
CCLC	Cuadernos del Congreso por la Libertad de la Cultura
CE	College English
CEA	CEA Critic
CeS	Cultura e Scuola
CL	Comparative Literature
CLAJ	College Language Association Journal (Morgan State College, Baltimore)
CLS	Comparative Literature Studies (University of Illinois)
CompD	Comparative Drama
ConnR	Connecticut Review
CP	Concerning Poetry (Western Washington State College)
CQ	Cambridge Quarterly
Crit	Critique: Studies in Modern Fiction
CritQ	Critical Quarterly
CSE	Cairo Studies in English
CU-AT	Cornell University, Abstracts of Theses
DA	Dissertation Abstracts
DAI	Dissertation Abstracts International
DDAR-UI	Doctoral Dissertations Abstracts and References, University of Iowa
DownR	Downside Review
DQR	Dutch Quarterly Review of Anglo-American Letters
DR	Dalhousie Review
DSPS	Duquesne Studies, Philological Series
DUJ	Durham University Journal
EA	Etudes Anglaises
EBST	Edinburgh Bibliographical Society Transactions
ECS	Eighteenth-Century Studies (University of California, Davis)
EIC	Essays in Criticism
EigoS	Eigo Seinen (Tokyo)
ELH	Journal of English Literary History
ELN	English Language Notes (University of Colorado)

EM	English Miscellany
EnlE	Enlightenment Essays (Chicago)
ES	English Studies
ESA	English Studies in Africa
EST	Englische Studien
ETJ	Educational Theatre Journal
EUQ	Emory University Quarterly
Expl	Explicator
GR	Germanic Review
HAB	Humanities Association Bulletin
HLB	Harvard Library Bulletin
HLQ	Huntington Library Quarterly
HSL	Hartford Studies in Literature
HTR	Harvard Theological Review
HU-ST	Harvard University Summaries of Theses
HudR	Hudson Review
IER	Irish Ecclesiastical Record
IEY	Iowa English Bulletin: Yearbook
IJES	Indian Journal of English Studies
JAAC	Journal of Aesthetics and Art Criticism
JEGP	Journal of English and Germanic Philology
JHI	Journal of the History of Ideas
JWCI	Journal of the Warburg and Courtauld Institute
Lang&S	Language and Style
LCUT	Library Chronicle of the University of Texas
Macdonald	Macdonald, Hugh. *John Dryden: A Bibliography of Early Editions and of Drydeniana*. Oxford: Oxford University Press, 1939. (Item 1:65.)
MHRA	Modern Humanities Research Association
MiltonQ	Milton Quarterly
MiltonS	Milton Survey
MLN	Modern Language Notes
MLQ	Modern Language Quarterly
MLR	Modern Language Review
MP	Modern Philology
MQR	Michigan Quarterly Review
MusQ	Musical Quarterly

NQ	Notes and Queries
NRam	New Rambler (Johnson Society, London)
NYTBR	New York Times Book Review
OR	Oxford Review
OSU-ADD	Ohio State University, Abstracts of Doctoral Dissertations
PBA	Proceedings of the British Academy
PBSA	Papers of the Bibliographical Society of America
PLL	Papers on Language and Literature
PLPLS	Proceedings of the Leeds Philosophical and Literary Society
PLPLS-LHS	Proceedings of the Leeds Philosophical and Literary Society—Literary and Historical Section
PMLA	Publications of the Modern Language Association
PQ	Philological Quarterly
PSU-ADD	Pennsylvania State University, Abstracts of Doctoral Dissertations
QJS	Quarterly Journal of Speech
QQ	Queens Quarterly
QR	Quarterly Review
RECTR	Restoration and 18th Century Theatre Research
REL	Review of English Literature (Leeds)
RenD	Renaissance Drama
RES	Review of English Studies
RHL	Revue d'Histoire Littéraire de la France
RJ	Romanistisches Jahrbuch
RLC	Revue de Littérature Comparée
RLMC	Rivista di Letterature Moderne e Comparate (Firenze)
RLV	Revue des Langues Vivantes
RMS	Renaissance and Modern Studies
RRestDS	Regents Restoration Drama Series
RS	Research Studies (Washington State University)
RUO	Revue de l'Université d'Ottawa
SAB	South Atlantic Bulletin
SAQ	South Atlantic Quarterly
SB	Studies in Bibliography: Papers of the Bibliographical Society of the University of Virginia
S̆CN	Seventeenth-Century News

SDD–NU	Summaries of Doctoral Dissertations, Northwestern University
SCB	South Central Bulletin
SDD–UW	Summaries of Doctoral Dissertations, University of Wisconsin
SEL	Studies in English Literature, 1500–1900
SM	Speech Monographs
SNL	Satire Newsletter
SoR	Southern Review
SP	Studies in Philology
SQ	Shakespeare Quarterly
SR	Sewanee Review
SSJ	Southern Speech Journal
TA	Theatre Annual
TBS	Transactions of the Bibliographical Society
ThS	Theatre Survey (American Society for Theatre Research)
TLS	Times Literary Supplement
TN	Theatre Notebook
TSE	Tulane Studies in English
TSL	Tennessee Studies in Literature
TSLL	Texas Studies in Literature and Language
UDR	University of Dayton Review
UI–AT	University of Illinois, Abstract of Theses
UNCR–RP	University of North Carolina Record, Research in Progress
UNS	University of Nebraska Studies
UO–AD	University of Oxford, Abstracts of Dissertations
UV–AD	University of Virginia, Abstracts of Dissertations
UTQ	University of Toronto Quarterly
UW–AT	University of Washington, Abstract of Theses
Ward	Ward, Charles E., ed. *The Letters of John Dryden, with Letters Addressed to Him.* Durham: Duke University Press, 1942. (Item 2/4:16.)
WW	Wirkendes Wort
YES	Yearbook of English Studies
YR	Yale Review
YWES	Year's Work in English Studies

JOHN DRYDEN: A SURVEY AND BIBLIOGRAPHY
OF CRITICAL STUDIES, 1895–1974

A Survey of Dryden Studies

To many nineteenth-century writers John Dryden was simply not a reputable figure in English literary history. There seemed to be something unsavory about a man who had changed political parties and religions in an age when such was not done casually and at times when those changes seemed designed to gain him economic advantage. Moreover, Dryden had changed his mind on important critical matters such as the superiority of rhyme over blank verse in the heroic drama. In his definitions of terms such as "nature," "imitation" and "fancy" and in his attitudes about the neoclassic rules, Dryden appeared to be inconsistent, muddled and even deliberately misleading. Reflecting nineteenth-century attitudes, Allan Lubbock (3:110) concluded that Dryden was "a child of a deep enthusiasm, which made him attach but little importance to religion or politics, or even to many aspects of literature itself. What excluded everything else was the love of expression for its own sake. He devoted himself therefore to increasing the efficiency of his instruments." In this, Lubbock simply voiced the popular view that Dryden was an easily excited, somewhat dull artist who had developed a superior technical facility for writing verse. As one of Dryden's defenders summarized his intellectual reputation in the early twentieth century, his mind was thought to be "neither sincere nor significant nor interesting." The problem, then, for serious students and admirers of Dryden's work, was to combat this view and establish Dryden's claims to personal and literary respectability.

A major obstacle in this revaluation was the lack of verifiable evidence with which to investigate his life, particularly the controversial matters of his religious and political conversions. Since little direct information about his life was available, researchers relied on the knowledge and opinions of Dryden's enemies. Accordingly, Dryden's aesthetics and the motivations for his conversions were explained by citing passages from *The Censure of the Rota*, *The Medall*

3

of John Bayes and *The Hind and the Panther Transvers'd*, or far worse, by referring to the views of Langbaine (8/1:110-11) and Macaulay (3:113). At the end of the nineteenth century there was little hope that additional, unbiased information would come to light. George Saintsbury (3:168) despaired: "There is now little chance of fresh information being obtained about the poet, unless it be in a few letters hitherto undiscovered or withheld from publication." To fill the gap, Saintsbury turned to Dryden's works for biographical information; however, he was scrupulous enough to note the limitations of this approach. Since Saintsbury's time, the work of many scholars has made available new information about Dryden's life. Careful investigations of family and public records have revealed new facts about Dryden's life, among them: his genealogy (3:122-29, 3:131-33, 3:136), the date of his birth (3:75), the correction of the notion that he attempted to secure a position at Oxford (3:16, 3:25, 3:52, 3:76, 3:104), the dates of his appointment as poet laureate (3:27, 3:29) and as historiographer royal (3:77) and the truth about his funeral (3:3, 3:5, 3:48, 3:50, 3:87). Moreover, invaluable reference sources for future students of Dryden were provided by Hugh Macdonald (1:65), who established a bibliography of Dryden's works and Drydeniana, and by James M. Osborn (3:144), who identified facts and problems in Dryden's life as he surveyed the Dryden biographies from Thomas Birch's to the biographical notes of George Thorn-Drury and, in a revised edition, the most recent biography by Charles E. Ward. The publication in 1942 of an edition of Dryden's letters by Ward (2/4:16) made available an important source of new material which has yet to be thoroughly exhausted.

It is also useful to study the interaction of Dryden's life and works with those of his contemporaries: Lee (3:79), Etherege (3:28), Rochester (3:154, 3:157, 3:206), Buckingham (3:36, 3:203), Behn (3:182), Settle (3:33), Wycherley (3:181), Shadwell (3:22, 3:179), Tate (3:175), Howard (3:141, 3:159), Sedley (3:155), Dennis (3:149), Davenant (3:139), Tonson (3:43, 3:112) and Congreve (3:70, 3:93, 3:111). The details of these lives and others may yet yield additional information about Dryden's daily activities, about which we know too little. However, even if new facts are not forthcoming, the work of Fredson Bowers (3:23), Vinton A. Dearing (5/6:11) and Edward L. Saslow (5/4:69) indicates that bibliographical investigations can produce important information about Dryden's life, personality and methods of composition. Bower's discovery of the cancellandum leaf A_3 in *King Arthur* shows that Dryden had originally made reference to being offered a restoration of the laureateship, if he would receive the Anglican communion. Since Dryden did not accept the offer, the cancellandum leaf may be regarded as further evidence of the strength of Dryden's convictions and of the sincerity of his conversion. However, while a study of bibliographical information may reveal ways in which Dryden revised his work, Vinton A. Dearing notes that such studies are not practical until detailed, comprehensive collations of manuscript material and of editions published in Dryden's lifetime are readily available. The California edition of *The Works of John Dryden* (2/1:3, 2/2:13, 2/2:21, 2/2:32, 2/3:4, 2/3:9, 2/4:14, 2/5:4, 2/5:5, 2/5:9), of which Dearing is the chief textual editor, is making those collations widely available, so that scholars without immediate access to the original texts will be able to pursue this inquiry more easily.

Another hindrance in Dryden studies had been the lack of an accurate chronology of Dryden's works. As Louis I. Bredvold (4:43) noted in 1934, tracing Dryden's intellectual development was all but impossible because "most of our data remain too vague chronologically to establish any definite stages in the development of his thought." Charles E. Ward's biography (3:193), published in 1961, provided that chronology, and it is not by accident that the majority of studies which analyze Dryden's shifts in thought have appeared since 1961.

Ward also put an end to the attacks on Dryden's character which often had been casually accepted in Dryden studies. The importance of Ward's biography is not, however, simply in its accumulation of verifiable information, important though that was. His work is a model of methodological scrupulousness. Throughout the biography Ward carefully notes the sources of his information, whether from tradition or from documentary evidence. Moreover, he explains not only what has been authenticated about Dryden's life, but what had been mistakenly believed in the past. When confronted with a lack of documentation, Ward takes particular care to indicate the point at which he leaves off analyzing data and begins conjecturing about motivations or reactions. When, for example, the important matter of Dryden's failure to write an epic is considered, Ward notes, "No doubt the reasons for his abandonment of the plan are complex and beyond our interpretation until new sources of information are forthcoming. It may be assumed that the King's lack of tangible encouragement was a factor, but . . . the explanation may eventually be found in his recognition of his own limitations."

If there is a limitation to Ward's biography, it is that he too narrowly sees Dryden as being committed exclusively to literature. In discussing Dryden's responses to the Popish Plot, for instance, Ward argues that Dryden remained "a poet and a playwright: despite the distractions of the political scene, his work was writing." To Ward, Dryden protected his artistic and intellectual integrity by remaining aloof from the turmoil of the Plot. Yet, this view unnecessarily divorces literature and politics in a period in which the two were inseparably joined. Rather than remaining aloof from the turmoil of the Exclusion Crisis and the Popish Plot, Dryden thoroughly immersed himself in those controversies and wrote some twelve works which directly commented on the Crisis and the Plot. Dryden's vision of a providentially mandated political order threatened by forces of degeneration came to maturity at this time. Dryden, like other public poets, refined his ideas about society and about the ways in which literature should function in society by participating in controversies of great importance.

Unfortunately, another limitation of Ward's biography is his acceptance of Louis I. Bredvold's thesis (4:43) that Dryden was a follower of Pyrrhonism. As a result, Ward presents Dryden as not only a fideist, but as an anti-rationalist who denied the ability of reason to participate in religious truth. Yet Ward's acceptance of Bredvold's thesis was in accord with the general critical opinion of the time. It is probably natural that basic ideas developed by certain individuals have set the tone for Dryden studies in general, but the consequences of this fact have been far-ranging and often detrimental. Dryden's supposed licentiousness, self-aggrandizing flattery of the aristocracy, opportunism and hypocrisy became articles of faith in Dryden studies, and thus Macaulay's attacks on Dryden were perpetuated for over a century and a half, even though he had only the scantiest substantiation for his charges. Bredvold's thesis, although it has not enjoyed as long a currency, was as casually accepted, even though his evidence, like Macaulay's, lacked real substance.

In his book, published in 1934, Bredvold responded to a demand, frequently heard in American scholarship of the 1930s, for an improved historiography in the study of seventeenth-century English literature. Many scholars had demonstrated the need to know the historical background of works from the Restoration, given their topical nature. Allardyce Nicoll's discussion of political plays (8/1:67), for example, indicated the need for such historical knowledge. Moreover, as Raymond D. Havens (5/8:2) argued in his discussion of miscellanies, the generalizations of literary history may prove to be abstractions "begotten by Confidence on Inadequate Information." George Williamson (4:544) reproved H. J. C. Grierson (4:187) for having failed adequately to investigate the seventeenth-century meaning of "enthusiasm" before he analyzed trends in the intellectual development of the period, and F. W. Bateson (4:22) characterized his contemporaries as antiquarians rather than historians of English literature. Their concern, he said, was with reproducing the past, not with understanding it. However, Bredvold's historiography differed from that advocated by Havens, Williamson and Bateson, because, like Basil Willey (7:335), he did not seek just to recover contemporary definitions or the facts of topical contexts; rather, he sought to explain Dryden's attitudes and practices by identifying the *milieu* or intellectual background of the age, which, Bredvold maintained, is composed of "representative ideas of the age, growing out of the dominant temper of the age, which happened also to be the temper of Dryden himself."

Yet, Bredvold too hastily attributed Dryden's refusal to dogmatize to Pyrrhonism, and between Dryden's thought and that of others he made connections which were more apparent than real. The points of agreement between Montaigne and Dryden, about which Bredvold made so much, are only those of superficial resemblance. They could both call themselves skeptical, but Montaigne distrusted the New Science and Dryden praised the Royal Society. Although Bredvold investigated some historical material in his search for Dryden's milieu, he did not look closely enough into the immediate context of Dryden's works. Bredvold's thesis was immediately accepted by most Dryden scholars, although George Williamson (4:43), Moody E. Prior (4:43) and R. S. Crane, in a review of an earlier article (3:26), objected that Bredvold had confused "a cautious form of rationalism," in Williamson's words, with anti-rationalism. Only recently, since the important work of Phillip Harth (4:211) and Sanford Budick (5/7:3), has Dryden's skepticism been widely accepted in the context of *scepsis scientifica* rather than in the tradition of Pyrrhonism.

The noble intention of Bredvold's study was to redress three commonly held preconceptions regarding Dryden's intellectual abilities: "that Dryden was a hireling, whose political and religious affiliations were determined by bribes and pensions; that in his most serious work he never rose intellectually above the level of ephemeral journalism; and that the inconsistencies and contradictions with which his work abounds are conclusive evidence of a lack of intellectual character and significance." In resolving the apparent contradiction of Dryden's writing *The Hind and the Panther* after he had written a defense of Anglican orthodoxy in *Religio Laici*, Bredvold

argued that "the earlier poem might be regarded as a sort of prelude
or introduction to the latter; both are basically skeptical and fide-
istic." The link between Dryden's politics and his religious beliefs
in Bredvold's view was that Dryden's distrust of individual reason,
which led him to Catholicism, also led him to political conservatism.
By establishing a philosophical milieu for Dryden, Bredvold success-
fully focused attention on "the content of Dryden's work, his cast of
mind, and his intellectual equipment." With this Bredvold had demonstrated the coherence of Dryden's thought and had repudiated the notion that Dryden was simply a stylist. Yet, in his study there is often a tone of condescension: "His contact with philosophical skepticism enabled him to rationalize his natural diffidence of temper.
Though he has no claim to originality as a thinker, he did possess a
loose group of ideas and philosophical doctrines which he understood
and to which he felt himself affined." Finally, then, Bredvold argued
that while Dryden's intellectual concerns had to be recognized, he
was an artist of only limited intellect who never developed original
ideas. In an important and witty article, Henry Knight Miller (4:336)
points out that early twentieth-century literary historians such as
Bredvold failed to recognize the extent of their debt to post-
Romantic conceptions of art. "Originality" had come to mean something
in modern criticism that was quite different from what it meant to
Renaissance and Restoration writers. However, where Bredvold presented Dryden as slavishly, unimaginatively collecting ideas from
other writers, more recent critics see Dryden as cleverly and aggres-
sively adapting the arguments of others to his own use.

Although Bredvold had intended to sketch the background of Dryden's thought, both religious and political, the greatest influence
of his study was in its arguments about the impact of skepticism on
Dryden's religious beliefs. Although Elias J. Chiasson (5/7:6) and
Thomas H. Fujimura (5/7:9) had pointed out some of Bredvold's errors,
it remained for Phillip Harth (4:211) to provide the authoritative
correction of Bredvold's view. Harth addressed himself to correcting
errors of fact and of method in Bredvold's work. Throughout his book,
published in 1968, Harth demands that Dryden's arguments about the
"respective claims of reason and revelation" be investigated within
their controversialist and poetic contexts. As a result of Harth's
work, the study of Dryden's religious and philosophical thought has
entered a new period of development which is characterized by an improved method in the study of the historical backgrounds of Dryden's
works.

If Dryden's personal reputation did not fare well at the hands of
his contemporaries and his nineteenth-century critics, his artistic
reputation also suffered. Hazlitt, Arnold, Rossetti and Pater denied
Dryden's right to be called a poet, because the subjects and the
style of his verse were not those appropriate for poetry. His work
lacked sublimity, passion and excitement, and he was too preoccupied
with public subjects. Pope shared in this denigration. Together they
were announced as important in the history of English literature for
their refinements of prosody while at the same time they were de-
nounced as perverters of the true poetic spirit. To Arnold they were
"not classics of our poetry, but classics of our prose." Moreover,
they violated the true nature of poetry, for "their poetry is conceived and composed in their wits, [whereas] genuine poetry is composed in the soul." Only in his poems for St. Cecilia's Day was
Dryden said to have achieved something close to the sublime, and ac-

cordingly it was for those poems that he was generally known to the reading public at the turn of the twentieth century. John B. Henneman (4:219), surveying Dryden's reputation in 1901, noted that the odes "make Dryden's name a household word in English poetry," but his other nondramatic works, criticism and plays were virtually unknown, being "largely mere material for the historian and special student of literature." Even after editions of his critical essays and of his poetical works had been made widely available and Mark Van Doren had published his important critical study, Cyrus L. Day (2/2:7) in 1932 lamented the fact that Dryden was still known largely for the two odes on St. Cecilia's Day.

The emphasis given to Dryden's odes reflects a general preference among nineteenth- and early twentieth-century critics for lyric rather than for epic poetry. Henry Knight Miller (4:336) points out that the post-Romantic preference for lyric poetry led to a denigration of Restoration and eighteenth-century poetry. Accordingly, Dryden's narrative poetry was rarely studied except in passing and his satiric poetry was often looked upon unfavorably. To C. W. Previté-Orton (4:395), writing at the beginning of the twentieth century, the satires were simply evidence that Dryden was "but a hireling after all" and were reprehensible because Dryden had placed his superior talents at the disposal of a degenerate, anti-democratic monarch.

A. W. Verrall's *Lectures on Dryden* (4:507), published in 1914, was the first major revaluation of Dryden's work in the twentieth century. Few of Verrall's contemporaries had his acute sense of the breadth of Dryden's achievement. He understood the importance of narrative poetry to Dryden's poetic ambitions, and he was careful to indicate the Restoration response to Dryden's work, even when that response was quite different from his own. Moreover, though his discussions invariably refer to Dryden's life, he does analyze individual works at length. By his careful selection, Verrall ensured that his audience would have a sense of the scope of Dryden's works. His discussions of Dryden's epistles and odes, other than those for St. Cecilia's Day, brought to public attention works which had been ignored by other critics. In considering a poem such as *Absalom and Achitophel*, Verrall appreciated the fact that Dryden's readers would have immediately recognized the comparison between David and Charles II, but given his knowledge of the historical background he could only conjecture that the comparison was "probably common in sermons." Verrall's discussion of Dryden is, however, ultimately disappointing, for while he is a perceptive reader, his lectures are often little more than annotations of obscure references. His fullest discussions are devoted to examinations of prosody. It remained for Mark Van Doren (4:506) to provide a major review of Dryden's works. His book, published in 1920, continued to be the most comprehensive treatment of Dryden's works until the 1960s, and his influence on Dryden studies was substantial.

Van Doren hoped to revitalize Dryden's reputation by presenting a comprehensive view of his experiments, achievements and failures in poetry. Although there is a good deal of biographical material in his study, his focus is on Dryden's artistry and not on his life. He surveys the areas in which Dryden excelled: occasional verse, the lyric, the verse character, narrative. His greatest praise is for Dryden's use of the heroic couplet and for his place in the history of prosodic refinement. Yet although Van Doren looks carefully for the best in

Dryden's work, he as carefully notes the worst as well. Van Doren blames Dryden's faults on his having followed "false lights": Hobbes's separation of reason from fancy, the rhetorical theories of the age, misconceptions about the relationship of painting to poetry, the neo-classic theory of the "general," and a fatuous musicality learned from Waller. Van Doren also agreed with Samuel Johnson that Dryden did not understand human passion and thus made a bathetic mess of heroic action in his plays. Because he always had an eye to Dryden's nineteenth-century critics, Van Doren scrupulously identified areas of weakness in his poetry in order to disarm Dryden's detractors. Though he clearly liked Dryden's work, he did not want to be called a partisan who approved whatever Dryden wrote, regardless of the quality.

Van Doren significantly affected the course of Dryden studies by the summary categorization he gave to Dryden's artistic inclinations: "Dryden was most at home when he was making statements. His poetry was the poetry of statement. At his best he wrote without figures, without transforming power." Moreover, Dryden did not write personal poetry, for he was a "poet of company, a poet of civilizations." In this Dryden was in accord with neoclassic theories of poetry, for to Van Doren "true Augustan verse was to be impersonal." In his treat-ment of events of national importance, such as the Popish Plot, Van Doren presented Dryden as aloof, uncommitted: "He was more than equal to his occasions, few of which moved him. He condescended to them, brought to them richer stores of thought and melody than were ade-quate." The picture of Dryden presented by Van Doren is of a masterly craftsman who lacked commitment, perceptiveness and depth of spirit. Although a recent study by K. G. Hamilton (4:202) seeks to use the term "poetry of statement" to advantage, the wide acceptance of this view inhibited the development of many fruitful areas of investiga-tion which have only recently been pursued. Van Doren accomplished much with his study, yet finally his view of Dryden is neither en-tirely correct nor satisfying. One must wonder at a revaluation which includes the observation that Dryden "was not adept in psychological research, or refined, or especially true; he could be slovenly and gross; but he was never limp or lame." Even though Van Doren repeat-edly notes that Dryden was as "fresh and various as few other poets have been," the weight of his examples would suggest otherwise.

The commendation T. S. Eliot (4:136) afforded Van Doren's study advanced its reputation and lent considerably to its influence. Dry-den's verse appealed to Eliot because he found there a discipline and a sense of tradition which he thought might help reform modern poetry. Yet for all his praise of Dryden, Eliot finally agrees that Dryden's is a poetry of statement, which though it satisfies by the "complete-ness of the statement" is deficient in suggestiveness. Dryden should be read, Eliot says, as his work "is one of the tests of a catholic appreciation of poetry." There is something of a bitter pill rationale in Eliot's revitalization of interest in Dryden.

In the 1930s, 1940s and 1950s valuable research was pursued into the influence of native and foreign writers on Dryden's poetry, his relationship to Milton, and the topical contexts of his occasional verse. There is no need to list all such studies, but in scope they included investigations into the complex problem of dating *Mac Fleck-noe* (5/6:7, 5/6:29, 5/6:37, 5/6:40), the occasions of *Absalom and Achitophel* (5/4:21-22, 5/4:34, 5/4:65), *Annus Mirabilis* (5/3:1-2) and

Of Dramatic Poesy (7:338), the sources of Dryden's comedies (8/1:3, 8/6:5, 8/12:3, 8/12:5, 8/12:12) and heroic plays (8/14:16, 8/4:22, 8/4:29, 8/7:5, 8/12:10), the influence of French neoclassic thought on Dryden's criticism (7:4, 7:6-7, 7:9, 7:16, 7:43, 7:76, 7:85, 7:140, 7:186, 7:227, 7:249) and the quality of Dryden's adaptations of Shakespeare's plays (Section 8/9) and of *Paradise Lost* (Section 8/10). During these important years, scholars who studied the earlier seventeenth century and the Restoration provided much needed information regarding the literary traditions, historical events and intellectual developments which were part of Dryden's world. In particular, historical studies of the cultural, political, religious and economic life of late seventeenth-century England advanced rapidly during this period. The result of these investigations was a perspective which allows Dryden to be seen in terms which he would have recognized.

It might have been expected that close textual readings, advocated by the New Critics, would have been used to examine Dryden's poetry, yet his works did not easily lend themselves to this approach. By their topical nature, Dryden's poems demand an analysis of their extra-textual references. *Mac Flecknoe* has sufficient independence to be considered apart from its historical context, but the unavoidable fact of its topical references proves that there is no good reason for doing so. Before World War II there were few extended analyses of Dryden's imagery, manipulation of tone and use of biblical material. Most studies of his poetry at this time provided annotations of unfamiliar allusions, examined his prosody and investigated questionable attributions to his canon. A number of important historical studies which explored the relationship between individual works and their topical contexts were published during this period. By comparing the conclusion of *Absalom and Achitophel* with Charles II's Oxford speech and *His Majesties Declaration*, Godfrey Davies (5/4:21) argued that the focus and tone of the conclusion, frequently criticized by Samuel Johnson and others, was determined by Dryden's desire to repeat the arguments which Charles II himself had made earlier in the year. In 1945, however, Wallace C. Brown complained in an essay on dramatic tension in neoclassic satire (5/4:8) that the structure of *Absalom and Achitophel* had not yet been analyzed. Brown's examination of the poem's imagery and prosody, for all its insight, fails to consider the historical material which Davies makes clear must be looked at in any explication of the poem. It remained for scholars such as H. T. Swedenberg, Jr. (5/1:4), and W. O. S. Sutherland, Jr. (5/5:9), to combine the historical and close reading approaches. They developed a procedure of explicating Dryden's arguments and use of images, symbols and allusions by referring to the works of his contemporaries, and this procedure became a model for later critics. Swedenberg thus explains Dryden's attacks on the mob in *Astraea Redux* by referring to similar attacks made by Thomas Pecke, Henry Oxenden and Alexander Brome, and Sutherland argues that *The Medall* cannot properly be understood without a prior examination of the images which were "common to the pamphleteers and the poets" of the time. The advantages of this combined approach are amply evidenced in the work of Earl R. Wasserman (5/2:4) on the *Epistle to Dr. Charleton*, Jay Arnold Levine (5/14:11) on the *Epistle to John Driden*, A. E. Wallace Maurer (5/5:6) on *The Medall* and Earl Miner (5/14:12) on *To Sir Godfrey Kneller*.

The work of Bernard N. Schilling (5/4:70), Alan Roper (4:422) and Steven N. Zwicker (4:565) provides some of the best examples of full-

length studies which explicate Dryden's nondramatic works by referring to their historical contexts. Schilling's study of *Absalom and
Achitophel* is the most sustained explication of the poem to date. By
explaining Dryden's use of the conservative myth and the ways in
which Dryden created meanings in the poem, Schilling seeks to defend
it against accusations that it is too drawn out, that there is too
little imagery, that the resolution is too abrupt and that the dispro-
portion between the King's friends and his enemies is unjust. Alan
Roper investigates Dryden's use of metaphoric analogy in his poetry,
while Zwicker focuses on Dryden's use of typology in the political
poetry. Besides providing a very useful survey of the tradition of
seventeenth-century figural exegesis, Zwicker defends Dryden against
those who see his poems as lacking unity. By revealing the ways in
which traditional typological interpretations created connections between contemporary events and providential history, Zwicker demonstrates that a poem such as *Astraea Redux* has a unity which is not
always apparent to the modern eye, but which would have been immediately recognized by Dryden's seventeenth-century reader.

These studies and others have demonstrated Dryden's achievement
in precisely those areas which earlier critics attacked. Macaulay and
Christie had demeaned Dryden's participation in the political controversies of his day as the slavish hackwork of an able writer in the
service of a repressive king. Twentieth-century critics have been
less severe in their strictures on Charles II's court, but Dryden's
service as historiographer royal has still been taken as a sign of an
inferior or, at best, a misused talent. Now, however, as a result of
historically-based studies, Dryden's transformation into art of the
established values of his society is seen to have intellectual vali-
dity and aesthetic power. The book-length studies of Arthur W. Hoffman (4:223) and Earl Miner (4:342) established the quality of that
art and thereby corrected the strictures of Bredvold and Van Doren.

Although some critics have understood Van Doren's thesis that Dryden writes a "poetry of statement" in a nonpejorative way (4:65, 4:
306), many more critics (2/2:11, 4:242, 4:482, 5/7:23, 5/9:2) have
objected to its use. Arthur W. Hoffman in particular saw Van Doren's
view of Dryden as somewhat "defensive and seemingly ungenerous," especially in his pointing out "the worst" in Dryden's work. Hoffman's
book was the first comprehensive survey of Dryden's writings since
Van Doren's. In it Hoffman combined a consideration of the historical
background with a close reading of individual poems and focused on
the complexity of Dryden's imagery as it blends references from classical (especially Virgilian) and biblical (especially messianic) materials.

Earl Miner's book on Dryden's poetry is a work of major importance.
In this lengthy and detailed study, Miner investigates Dryden's view
of history, analyzes individual poems and establishes a public-person-
al paradigm which is at the root of Dryden's concerns. He also considers Dryden's use of metaphor, his rhetorical strategies in complex
works such as *Absalom and Achitophel*, his use of different genres and
his prosodic variations. Miner looks at Dryden's works with the goal
of uncovering his controlling ideas and concerns. Although Bernard
Schilling's examination of Dryden's conservative views provided a pre-
cedent, Miner's study has a much larger scope. Implicitly Miner seeks
to revaluate the older notion which saw Dryden as being, in Arthur
Hoffman's words, "a victim of occasions." Since so much of his poetry

is occasional, the accepted view held that Dryden rarely had control over his materials, but was, instead, forced to treat events as the King or others wished him to. Miner discounts this idea entirely and argues instead that Dryden was an artist of considerable intellect and poetic talent who pursued his concern with the divergence between public and private values through different genres. The influence of this perspective has been substantial. Most recent studies of Dryden's poetry, those of Sanford Budick (5/4:9) and Isabel Rivers (4:417), for example, argue that the events of Restoration life such as the Exclusion Crisis, the Popish Plot and the death of Charles II provided Dryden with backgrounds against which he could continue to work out his ideas about society, politics, literature, religion and the nature of human relationships.

Miner's study marks another shift in Dryden studies. There had been a tendency among those who investigated the contexts of Dryden's works to concern themselves either with the literary traditions or with the intellectual background of the works. Miner synthesizes these two contexts, taking care to explain the topical occasion, the pertinent literary traditions and the intellectual currents which might have influenced his treatment of certain themes or subjects. Paramount to Miner's study is the desire to establish the seventeenth-century nature of Dryden's work. His analysis of the beast fable in *The Hind and the Panther*—an analysis which is continued in Miner's commentary for the third volume of the California Dryden (2/2:21)— demonstrates the advances in knowledge which such a procedure may yield. The guiding principle behind Miner's analysis has been excellently described by Phillip Harth (4:212), whose own work in establishing the doctrinal and controversialist contexts of *Religio Laici* exemplifies the same procedures: "An exact discrimination of the political, as of the religious, ideas in Dryden's poems and plays depends on an acquaintance with the works he is likely to have known when he was writing them, and with the entire range of opinion offered him by those works. Without that knowledge we cannot understand Dryden as his contemporaries once did." Needless to say, such an approach makes the study of Dryden's works a more difficult and time-consuming occupation, but as the work of Miner, Harth, Budick, Rivers, Zwicker, Roper, Schilling, Hoffman and many others now indicates, the rewards of such historical scrupulousness are immense.

The reputation of Dryden's translations has also benefited from the improvement in historiography. The disparagement of Dryden's classicism, long a standard view (2/2:22, 4:429, 4:506, 4:516, 6/2:2, 6/2:22), has been corrected by the efforts of many scholars. Joseph M. Bottkol (6/2:13), Arvid Løsnes (6/2:49) and R. E. Hughes (6/2:41) examined the texts used by Dryden in the preparation of his translations, and Helene Maxwell Hooker (6/2:38) identified those to whom Dryden's translations were indebted in attempts to repudiate the view that Dryden was a sloppy translator. L. Proudfoot (6/2:63) examined the seventeenth-century translations of the *Aeneid* to establish a background for Dryden's *Aeneis*, and William Frost (6/1:8-9, 6/2:28) demonstrated the sophisticated quality of Dryden's classicism by relating Dryden's theories of translation to the seventeenth-century tradition of translation. Those who have accused Dryden of ignorance or of insensitivity in translating Virgil would seem to have lost sight of Dryden's own comments on translation in the preface to *Sylvae*, in which he lays out those elements for which a translator

must be responsible (a comprehensive knowledge of the foreign language and of his own and a thoroughly developed poetic ability). The
most important responsibility and the most difficult task for the
translator is "maintaining the Character of an Author, which distinguishes him from all others, and makes him appear that individual
Poet whom you would interpret." The style, ideas and prosody of the
translation must appropriately reflect those of the original. Dryden's insistence on these responsibilities would suggest that critics
(6/2:60, 6/2:63) who argue that his translation distorts or debases
Virgil have incorrectly appreciated the scrupulousness with which he
pursued his duty as a translator. The superlative work of Norman
Austin (6/2:3) on Dryden's translations of Lucretius and that of
Michael West (6/2:81) on the translations of Homer, Ovid, Boccaccio
and Virgil give substantial evidence that Dryden used the process of
translation to comment on the originals and to make the material and
sentiments of the originals more applicable to the English scene.

Of all Dryden's translations, the *Fables* have recently been the
subject of increased study and appreciation. Until a 1971 article by
Judith Sloman (6/1:20), only Earl Miner (4:342) had considered the
Fables as an original work and not simply as an unconnected series of
translations. In the "connection of the separate fables" Miner found
a design which gave a unity, though not a completely integrated unity,
to the whole. Judith Sloman finds that integration in the fact that
like Ovid's *Metamorphosis* there is a linking of the various parts of
the *Fables* so that the individual poems comment on one another. The
movement through the collection marks a progress from a point of tur-
bulence to a consideration of more ideal modes of behavior and experience and, finally, to a return in *Cymon and Iphigenia* to "the
physical world of unpredictable events and characters swayed by an
arbitrary succession of passions."

Dryden's literary criticism has been the subject of a great many
studies. Given Samuel Johnson's praise of Dryden's critical writings,
that attention is not surprising. Yet, it is surprising that no full-
length study in English of his criticism was published until 1970.
This was the result of a number of complex factors, one of the more
important of which was the influence of William Bohn's (7:30) essay,
written early in the twentieth century. Bohn's concern was largely
defensive. He wanted to correct the view, popularized by Macaulay,
that Dryden's prefaces and dedications were merely evidence of obsequiousness and that the inconsistencies in his critical writings were
unreconcilable and indicative of an inferior intellect. Bohn interpreted the occasional quality of the prefaces and dedications in a
different way. To Bohn the inconsistencies modern critics detected
only affirmed the fact that Dryden was a professional artist who
needed to appeal to the tastes of his audience if he were to be suc-
cessful. The critical opinions advanced by Dryden were those which
would have won favor in the court. Accordingly, Bohn argued, what
Charles II and James II liked, Dryden praised. After 1688 when he was
out of favor, however, Dryden developed a less conservative position,
which actually more accurately reflected his own thinking.

Although Bohn's defense of Dryden can be hardly said to vindicate
him adequately as a critical theorist, it did present a detailed chronology which was persuasive. Only within the past few decades has that
chronology been questioned. The majority of scholars who wrote after
Bohn did not seek to view Dryden's critical writings as a whole (and

thus they implicitly accepted Bohn's five-stage development thesis); instead they concentrated on *aspects* of his criticism: his ideas on satire (7:94-95, 7:240), tragedy (7:104-05, 7:116, 7:163, 7:248), comedy (7:138, 7:163, 7:179, 7:214), translation (7:109, 7:293, 7:333), the heroic poem (7:300-02, 7:335) and farce (7:130-31); definitions of important terms such as "fancy" (7:5, 7:39, 7:73), "imagination" (7:5, 7:13, 7:39, 7:147, 7:303), "wit" (7:5, 7:73, 7:159, 7:208, 7:216, 7:299, 7:321), and "imitation" (4:419, 7:19, 7:135, 7:303); his attitude towards the rules (7:269-71, 7:275, 7:277, 7:300-02, 7:317). So that investigations of particular terms or genres might be pursued more easily, John M. Aden (7:3) published a dictionary and H. James Jensen (7:149) compiled a glossary of Dryden's critical terms.

The extent to which Dryden was indebted to others for his critical ideas has been a subject of continuing concern in Dryden studies. The influence on Dryden's critical writings of Horace, Longinus, Aristotle, Cicero and Quintilian has been studied (7:76, 7:121-22, 7:135, 7:140-41, 7:164, 7:168, 7:231, 7:303-04, 7:306) as has the influence of native English writers (7:76, 7:179, 7:207, 7:242, 7:249, 7:262, 7:283, 7:309, 7:343). In the past it has been a mainstay of modern criticism to emphasize Dryden's indebtedness to French neoclassic critical theory. Dryden's own acknowledgment of his debts to LeBossu, Corneille and Rapin in *The Grounds of Criticism in Tragedy*, for example, indicates that this is a fruitful subject of study. Unhappily, however, the examination of the sources of his critical opinions has too often been conducted in the light of attacks made against Dryden. Martin Clifford's accusation in 1687 that Dryden plagiarized the work of the Abbé d'Aubignac, Mesnardière and Corneille in writing *Of Dramatic Poesy* has frequently been used as a starting point in the analysis of Dryden's indebtedness.

The study of Dryden's use of French criticism has helped place his work in the broad context of European critical thought; yet a simple identification of sources may serve more to obscure than to illuminate Dryden's critical positions. As John M. Aden insisted in a series of articles (7:4, 7:6-9) in the early 1950s, there is a great deal of difference between "influence," meaning the "persuasion to a viewpoint," and "borrowing," meaning plagiarism or the simpleminded use of the ideas of others. Dryden's borrowing from Boileau, St. Evremond and Corneille had long been an axiom of Dryden studies until Aden's articles. The work of Frank L. Huntley (7:141), Richard V. Le-Clerq (7:169) and the editors of the California Dryden (2/4:14) established that Dryden employed the ideas of Corneille, for example, with a great deal more freedom than had been realized in the past. Dryden does not slavishly follow, nor does he simply reject, Corneille's position on the rules. In *Of Dramatic Poesy* all four of the speakers either refer to or employ ideas from Corneille's criticism in support of their arguments.

A concern that Dryden's critical opinions are frequently inconsistent has appeared to motivate some of the investigations into the sources of his ideas, as with the attempts to provide definitions of important terms in his critical vocabulary. One way to account for that inconsistency has been simply to argue that Dryden was not intelligent enough to have formulated a coherent theory of criticism. Another was to argue, with George Watson (2/4:17), that Dryden's lack of a consistently developed view of art was because "his object in his plays and poems was to please, his object in his criticism was to prepare an audience for his plays and poems" and thus Dryden changed his critical ideas to suit his immediate needs. To James Routh (7:249) Dryden is not inconsistent but a conformist who was swayed by the ideas of others or by current fashions, and to Mark Van Doren (4:506) and to Louis I. Bredvold (4:43) "changeableness is beyond dispute one of the dominant characteristics of his mind." Inconsistency was, thus, a personality trait. As John Sherwood (7:269) points out, the question of Dryden's inconsistency actually involved two different areas of concern: "on the one hand, it is supposed that his principles varied from time to time; on the other hand, it is assumed that his judgments on particular works are inconsistent with the neo-classical principles or 'rules' to which he generally adheres."

To Samuel Holt Monk (7:209) Dryden's critical prefaces and dedications are "dialogues he conducted with himself in public," part of his working out of his own questions about the writing of drama. What some have taken as evidence of sloppiness, Monk saw as a sign of Dryden's flexibility. Dryden, unlike Rymer, refused to allow his criticism to harden into a rigid system. Likewise it is true that while there may be inconsistencies in his use of particular terms, "imitation" for one (7:303), in his criticism he is consistent in his larger beliefs and preferences. It should also not be forgotten that when Dryden was writing, literary criticism, as a formal and distinct discipline, was only just beginning.

It was fairly conventional in the past to quote from Dryden's critical writings without specifying the preface or dedication from which the quotation was taken. A citation to W. P. Ker's edition (2/4:8) or to George Watson's (2/4:17) was often all that was provided. Tacitly there was the assumption that Dryden's critical opinions did not change or develop, that his individual works could be discussed collectively. The work of John M. Aden (7:5) and Robert D. Hume (7:135, 7:137) has conclusively demonstrated that Dryden's critical writings can be accurately discussed only if they are considered individually, if they are placed in their topical (historical and biographical) contexts and if they are related to the works they preface.

In the only book-length study of Dryden's criticism, Robert D. Hume (7:135) focuses on topics which have continually plagued discussions of Dryden's criticism. Hume's chapter on the relationship between Dryden and Rymer clarifies a difficult problem of influence. His discussions of the meaning or lack of meaning of the term "neoclassicism" in reference to Dryden's criticism and of the stability of Dryden's critical premises are particularly helpful, both in their isolation of problems and in the solutions presented. Ultimately, however, Hume's book must be seen as a preparatory study, much as James M. Osborn's *Biographical Facts and Problems* (3:144) prepared the way for a full-fledged biography. There is still an evident need for an analysis of Dryden's criticism which would study each of the critical works, as Samuel Holt Monk (4:351) said in 1947, "in relation to the work to which it is attached and to the critical temper of the moment," as well as to Dryden's life and to relevant historical events.

Among his contemporaries Dryden was best known for his dramatic works. His comedies, heroic plays, tragicomedies and operas established trends which others followed, and his plays enjoyed the patronage of Charles II and most of the court. Recent critics have not, however, been enthusiastic about Dryden's dramatic works. Although interest in Restoration comedy has greatly increased in the past

quarter century, Etherege, Wycherley and Congreve have been the ob-
jects of that revival. Dryden's comedies, while still generally respected, have become to many simply a source of *examples* of commonly
used motifs, themes and plots. The absence of Dryden's works from
those numbered as "the first modern comedies" by Norman Holland was
not greatly objected to.

Until Frank Harper Moore's work (8/1:156) there had been no book-
length study of Dryden's comedies as they relate to his theories of
the drama. The comedies had been praised early in the twentieth century by A. W. Ward (8/1:243), George Saintsbury (4:429) and Bonamy
Dobrée (8/1:52), and their importance in the history of English drama
had been noted by John B. Henneman (4:219), Joseph Wood Krutch (8/1:
109), Kathleen M. Lynch (8/1:130) and Allardyce Nicoll (8/1:164, 8/1:
166); but Moore was the first to subject the comedies to systematic
study. Apparently their reputation as mere hackwork and, even on
Dryden's own authority, as being inferior to his other plays and non-
dramatic work had led scholars to neglect them.

Important work has also been done on the sources of Dryden's plays.
Ever since the accusations of Gerard Langbaine, scholars have been
faced with the difficult problem of identifying the extent of Dryden's
indebtedness to other dramatists. The early work of Allison Gaw (8/1:
63) and the more comprehensive investigations of Ned Bliss Allen (8/1:
3) corrected many of the errors about the extent to which Dryden used
the works of others in writing his plays. More recently, John Loftis
(8/1:127) has taken up the complicated question of Dryden's indebtedness to Calderón's *El principe constante* in writing *The Indian Emperour*, and in the pursuit of that question he has carefully examined
the relationship between English and Spanish drama in the seventeenth
century. These studies have yielded helpful results. By comparing
Dryden's plays with those from which he borrowed we are better able
to understand Dryden's methods of composition. There are also in-
sights to be gained from knowing which elements Dryden excised and
which he expanded.

The placement of Dryden's dramatic works in their literary and
historical contexts has been a major area of study. This approach was
encouraged by Dryden himself, who in his critical prefaces and dedications often made connections between his own work and dramatic traditions in England and those on the continent. The background of the
heroic play, in particular, has been studied by many scholars. In the
early part of the twentieth century, a debate began about the origin
of the heroic play, whether it was a native English form, indebted to
Beaumont and Fletcher and the Cavalier drama, or a derivative of Continental forms, indebted to the French romances and the heroic poem.
It is rather generally agreed that the heroic play has native English
origins, going back as far as Marlowe, as Eugene Waith has demonstrated (8/2:88-89), and that it was also influenced by French dramatic
conventions and by theories of the epic. As a result of the analyses
of Moody E. Prior (8/2:66) we now have a clearer sense about the effective intentions of the heroic play, which, unlike Shakespearean
tragedy, seeks to evoke admiration rather than pity or fear from the
audience and is thus closer in design to the heroic poem. Sarup Singh
(7:277) sees the heroic play as not only different from Elizabethan
tragedy but as a reaction against it. Whether or not Singh is correct,
it does appear clear that analyses which seek to interpret or evaluate the heroic play using Elizabethan criteria will surely not do

justice to this important dramatic form. Whatever the modern view
might be, the Restoration did not see the heroic play as "a colossal
joke," in Norman Holland's phrase (8/1:88). By Dryden's own estima-
tion, repeatedly voiced in his prefaces and dedications, the heroic
play had a tremendous potential to reform as well as to entertain.

Not all critics see the heroic plays as Dryden apparently did. Explaining the heroic drama in terms of a "comic" thesis, D. W. Jefferson (4:242, 8/2:37) hypothesizes that while Dryden's plays are apparently serious, they may be modified by a "lurking comic intention."
Rather than expecting his audiences to admire Almanzor, for example,
Jefferson suggests that Dryden ridiculed him. Bruce King (8/2:38) has
refined Jefferson's thesis, in that he sees Dryden as satirizing the
pomposity and the Hobbesian pretensions of his characters. The problem with this view is that it can only be completely accepted if we
are willing to take Dryden's critical prefaces and dedications as
disingenuous. Robert D. Hume (7:135), on the other hand, along with
others, has related Dryden's use of the heroic play to his commitment
to heroic values. In fact, Hume speculates that Dryden stopped writing heroic plays precisely because they had become debased by authors
such as Elkanah Settle. Dryden had hoped that the spectacle of the
heroic play would encourage his audience to emulate the noble acts
and sentiments of his characters, but by the mid-1670s, around the
time of *Aureng-Zebe*, he realized that the spectacle itself had cap-
tured his audience's attention.

As might be expected, Dryden's *All for Love*, his adaptation of
Shakespeare's *Antony and Cleopatra*, has received a great deal of attention from modern critics. Considered by many to be his best play,
although *Don Sebastian* and *Aureng-Zebe* are now respected as its ri-
vals, *All for Love* has been the subject of continuous discussion from
Verrall's lectures to Earl Miner's *Dryden's Poetry*. Unfortunately,
only recently has Dryden's play been considered separately from
Shakespeare's. As R. J. Kaufmann notes (2/5:26), it has been "conventional to make set comparisons of the two plays, to the predictable
disadvantage of Dryden." Kaufmann, for one, has carefully noted the
excellencies of Dryden's play, which had all too often been overlooked. Limitations of space prevent a more detailed summary of all
the works which had added to our understanding of Dryden's best adaptation, but those works in the present bibliography which have asterisks placed before them should be consulted with particular attention.
It should also be added that although *All for Love* has most frequently been compared with *Antony and Cleopatra*, it has also been compared
with Milton's *Samson Agonistes* (4:155) and with those versions of
Antony and Cleopatra written by Charles Sedley (8/9:9, 8/9:25), Thomas May (8/9:17) and Samuel Daniel (3:188). Jean H. Hagstrum (4:197)
has profitably considered the play in the context of the *ut pictura
poesis* tradition, as he argues that the play is a "speaking picture"
in which the audience is presented with a "gallery" of heroic portraits. Countering the accusation that the play's language is merely
decorative and fustian, Derek W. Hughes (8/9:36) has offered an in-
genious and detailed explication which illustrates Dryden's complex
use of imagery to reinforce the statement of the play.

The improvement of Dryden's modern reputation has been effected as
much by the availability of reliable, well-annotated editions as it
has been by advancements in his biography and the publication of important critical works. At the beginning of the twentieth century,

several editions appeared which remained the standard texts for over
half a century. The textually unreliable Oxford Standard Author's edition of Dryden's poems by John Sargeaunt (2/2:26) followed by one
year the publication of George R. Noyes's *The Poetical Works of Dryden* (2/2:22). Noyes had taken care to provide good texts and sufficient annotations to make Dryden accessible to twentieth-century students. Sargeaunt's edition was eventually replaced by James Kinsley's
excellent four-volume edition (2/2:18). Kinsley published the most
accurate texts then available, and he arranged the poems chronologically by date of publication, thereby allowing Dryden's development
and shifting concerns to be readily seen. Dryden's prose has
presented formidable editorial problems. The great bulk of his critical writings has made a complete edition of his prose works an ex-
pensive and difficult project. W. P. Ker (2/4:8) aided Dryden studies immensely when he published his two-volume edition of selections
from Dryden's criticism. George Watson's edition (2/4:17), published
in 1962, has replaced Ker's, yet both leave something to be desired.
They often provide only excerpts and their texts are modernized. The
more recent editions by Arthur Kirsch (2/4:10) and by James Kinsley
and George Parfitt (2/4:9) have similar limitations although all four
editions have made Dryden's critical writings more widely available,
and they are, thus, invaluable.

Editions of individual plays have been plentiful. *All for Love*,
The Tempest, *Troilus and Cressida*, *Marriage A-la-Mode* and *Aureng-Zebe*
have been frequently published. The only complete edition of Dryden's
plays in the twentieth century, by Montague Summers (2/5:12), proved
to be a disappointment. It did not improve upon the excellent nineteenth-century edition of Sir Walter Scott, as revised by George
Saintsbury (2/1:11). In 1967 L. A. Beaurline and Fredson Bowers published four of Dryden's comedies and four tragedies in a two-volume
companion set. The texts and annotations are well prepared and readily adaptable to classroom use.

Facsimile editions of individual poems and plays and *Of Dramatic
Poesy* have also allowed students to experience Dryden's works as they
appeared in his own lifetime.* Yet, with all the editions which have
thus far been published, there is still an evident need for a modern,
complete edition of his works. At present, about half of the projected twenty volumes of *The Works of John Dryden* have been published.
It has been contemplated that after all twenty volumes have become
available a computer-produced concordance will be prepared. The critical and textual commentaries in these volumes continue to maintain
the exceedingly high standards established for the series by its orig-
inators, Edward Niles Hooker and H. T. Swedenberg, Jr. By his pains-
taking meticulousness, the chief textual editor, Vinton A. Dearing,
has ensured that the texts present as accurately as possible Dryden's
originals.

As this survey has shown, we have learned a great deal about Dryden in the past three-quarters of a century. Yet much work must still

---

*In addition to facsimile editions of Dryden's works, seventeenth-
century documents important for Dryden studies have been made more
widely available through photographic reproduction. For information
about facsimile editions, the topical index and the Addendum should
be consulted.

be done before we will have a comprehensive understanding of his intellectual and aesthetic development and of his true place in English
literary history. Many have pointed out the way by which that view
will be obtained: Frank Harper Moore (8/1:156) and John Loftis (8/1:
123) on Dryden's comedies, Eugene M. Waith on Dryden's heroes (8/2:
87-89), Robert D. Hume on the critical writings (7:135), Phillip
Harth (4:211) and Sanford Budick (5/7:3) on *Religio Laici* and *The
Hind and the Panther* and Earl Miner on Dryden's use of the public
mode (4:348). These critics and others have shown that Dryden's works
must be placed in their literary, historical and biographical contexts if they are to be fully understood and appreciated. Moreover,
it has also become increasingly evident that all of Dryden's works
must be considered together. Too much of twentieth-century criticism
has compartmentalized Dryden's work in the different genres. David
Nichol Smith (4:455) and George R. Wasserman (4:520) attempted to
survey all of Dryden's works, and they made an effort to interrelate
his work in the various genres, but their studies are too brief and
could not adequately treat a subject of such tremendous complexity.
Should a comprehensive study of Dryden's career ever be completed, we
will surely learn a great deal not only about John Dryden but about
the nature of literature in general and about its uses in a literate
society.

THE BIBLIOGRAPHY

Festschriften and Other Collections

[Boys] Boys, Richard C., ed. *Studies in the Literature of the Augustan Age: Essays Collected in Honor of Arthur Ellicott Case*. New York: Gordian Press, 1966. *See* items 1:84, 4:305, 5/3:1, 5/4:34, 7:301.

[Cambridge History] Ward, A. W., and A. R. Waller, eds. *The Cambridge History of English Literature*. 8: *The Age of Dryden*. New York: G. P. Putnam; Cambridge: At the University Press, 1912. Reprinted in a condensed form as *The Concise Cambridge History of English Literature*, ed. George Sampson. Cambridge: At the University Press; New York: Macmillan, 1941. *See* items 1:11, 3:198, 4:394, 4:431, 4:516, 7:311, 8/1:194, 8/1:250, 8/2:11.

[Clark Library] Miner, Earl, ed. *Stuart and Georgian Moments: Clark Library Seminar Papers on Seventeenth and Eighteenth Century English Literature*. (The 17th and 18th Centuries Studies Group, U.C.L.A., Clark Memorial Library.) Berkeley, Los Angeles, London: University of California Press, 1972. *See* items 1:105, 3:192, 5/12:2, 5/12:23, 7:298.

[Clifford] Clifford, James L., and Louis A. Landa, eds. *Pope and His Contemporaries: Essays Presented to George Sherburn*. New York: Oxford University Press, 1949. *See* items 4:6, 4:277, 4:306, 4:376, 5/9:9.

[Critical Essays] Schilling, Bernard N., ed. *Dryden: A Collection of Critical Essays*. (Twentieth Century Views.) Englewood Cliffs, N.J.: Prentice-Hall, 1963. *See* items 2/5:26, 3:144, 4:43, 4:55, 4:136, 4:223, 4:226, 4:349, 4:356, 4:554, 5/2:4, 5/7:13, 5/10:8, 8/2:66.

[Culture and Society] Swedenberg, H. T., Jr., ed. *England in the Restoration and Early Eighteenth Century: Essays on Culture and Society*. (The 17th and 18th Centuries Studies Group, U.C.L.A., Clark Memorial Library.) Berkeley, Los Angeles, London: University of California Press, 1972. *See* items 4:52, 4:198, 4:245, 8/1:125.

[Keast] Keast, William R., ed. *Seventeenth-Century English Poetry: Modern Essays in Criticism*. Rev. ed. London, Oxford, New York: Oxford University Press, 1971. *See* items 4:55, 4:385, 4:506, 5/6: 20, 5/10:10, 7:208.

[King] King, Bruce, ed. *Dryden's Mind and Art*. (Essays Old and New 5.) Edinburgh: Oliver and Boyd, 1969. *See* items 4:217, 4:223, 4:242, 5/4:38, 5/7:6, 5/10:3, 5/14:11, 6/2:36, 7:62, 7:95.

[Loftis] Loftis, John, ed. *Restoration Drama: Modern Essays in Criticism*. New York: Oxford University Press, 1966. *See* items 8/1:16, 8/1:106, 8/1:154, 8/2:37, 8/2:45, 8/7:4.

[Miner] Miner, Earl, ed. *John Dryden* (Writers and their Background.) Athens, Ohio: Ohio University Press; London: G. Bell, 1972. Includes chronological tables which corollate the main events of Dryden's life with those events of literary, intellectual and historical importance. *See* items 4:222, 4:344, 4:346, 5/4:49, 6/2:28, 7:113, 8/1:74, 8/1:123, 8/2:87.

[Rest. Dramatists] Miner, Earl, ed. *Restoration Dramatists: A Collection of Critical Essays*. (Twentieth Century Views.) Englewood Cliffs, N.J.: Prentice-Hall. 1966. *See* items 8/2:37, 8/2:88, 8/7: 4.

[Rest. Theatre] Brown, John Russell, and Bernard Harris, eds. *Restoration Theatre*. (Stratford-Upon-Avon Studies 6.) London: Edward Arnold, 1965. *See* items 4:446, 8/1:78, 8/1:98, 8/2:68, 8/9:59, 8/12:8.

[Schilling] Schilling, Bernard N., ed. *Essential Articles: for the Study of English Augustan Backgrounds*. Hamden, Conn.: Archon Books, 1961. *See* items 4:549, 7:31, 7:36, 7:152, 7:153, 7:240, 7:301, 7:343.

[17th Century] Jones, Richard Foster, and Others. *The Seventeenth Century: Studies in the History of English Thought and Literature from Bacon to Pope*, eds. Francis R. Johnson, Marjorie H. Nicolson, George B. Parks, George Sherburn and Virgil K. Whitaker. Stanford: Stanford University Press, 1951. *See* items 4:254, 7:125, 7:152, 7:153, 7:312.

[Swedenberg] Swedenberg, H. T., Jr., ed. *Essential Articles for the Study of John Dryden*. Hamden, Conn.: Archon Books, 1966. *See* items 3:26, 3:77, 3:114, 3:146, 4:57, 4:154, 4:218, 4:269, 4:351, 5/3:1, 5/4:21, 5/4:34, 5/6:7, 5/6:23, 5/6:40, 5/7:6, 5/7:13, 5/7:26, 5/10:10, 5/12:1, 6/2:13, 7:78, 7:139, 7:142, 7:317, 7:338, 8/1:229, 8/2:97, 8/6:2, 8/9:87.

[20th Century Interpretations] King, Bruce, ed. *Twentieth Century Interpretations of "All for Love": A Collection of Critical Essays*. Englewood Cliffs, N.J.: Prentice-Hall, 1968. *See* items 4:197, 4: 455, 8/2:42, 8/2:88, 8/9:4, 8/9:20, 8/9:23, 8/9:63, 8/9:74, 8/9:84.

1. Bibliography and Canon

1:1 *Abstracts of English Studies*. Boulder, Colorado: National Council of Teachers of English. A monthly (excepting July and August) abstract of journal publications.

1:2 Alden, John. *The Muses Mourn: A Checklist of Verse Occasioned by the Death of Charles II*. Charlottesville: Bibliographical Society of the University of Virginia, 1958.

1:3   Alleman, Gellert S., et al., comps. *English Literature 1660-1800: A Bibliography of Modern Studies Founded by Ronald S. Crane Compiled for "Philological Quarterly".* 5: *1961-1965.* Foreword by Curt A. Zimansky. Princeton: Princeton University Press, 1972.

1:4   *Annual Bibliography of English Language and Literature.* Cambridge: Modern Humanities Research Association. An annual bibliography.

1:5   Archer, Stanley. "Some Early References to Dryden." *NQ* 17(1970): 417-18. Addenda to Macdonald.

1:6   Barnard, John. "John Dryden." *The New Cambridge Bibliography of English Literature,* ed. George Watson. 2:439-63. Cambridge: At the University Press, 1971.

1:7   Bartlett, Henrietta C. *Mr. William Shakespeare: Original and Early Editions of His Quartos and Folios.* New Haven: Yale University Press, 1922.

1:8   Bond, Donald F. *The Age of Dryden.* (Goldentree Bibliographies in Language and Literature.) New York: Appleton-Century-Crofts, 1970.

1:9   Bowers, Fredson. "Bibliography and Restoration Drama." *Bibliography (Papers Read at a Clark Library Seminar, May 7, 1966),* introd. Hugh G. Dick, pp. 1-25. Los Angeles: Clark Memorial Library, University of California, 1966.

1:10 ———. "Current Theories of Copy-Text, with an Illustration from Dryden." *MP* 68(1950):19-36. Reprinted in *Bibliography and Textual Criticism: English and American Literature, 1700 to the Present,* eds. O. M. Brack, Jr., and Warner Barnes, pp. 59-72. Chicago, London: University of Chicago Press, 1969. *The Indian Emperour. See* item 8/4:26.

1:11 ———. "Established Texts and Definitive Editions." *PQ* 41(1962): 1-17. *See* item 8/4:26.

1:12 Boys, Richard C. "A Finding-List of English Poetical Miscellanies 1700-48 in Selected American Libraries." *ELH* 7(1940):144-62. Includes Dryden's *Miscellanies.*

1:13 Bredvold, Louis I., and Hugh Macdonald. "John Dryden." *Cambridge Bibliography of English Literature,* ed. F. W. Bateson. 2: 262-75. Cambridge: At the University Press, 1940. *See* item 1:6.

1:14 *British Humanities Index* [formerly known as *Subject Index to Periodicals*]. London: The Library Association. An annual bibliography of materials published in journals.

1:15 Cameron, W. J. *John Dryden in New Zealand: An Account of Early Editions Found in Various Libraries Throughout New Zealand.* (Library School Bulletin 1.) Wellington: Library School, 1960.

1:16 Case, Arthur E. *A Bibliography of English Poetical Miscellanies 1521-1750.* (Bibliographical Society.) Oxford: At the University Press, 1935.

1:17 Chapman, R. W. "Cancels in Malone's *Dryden*." *Library* (4th ser.) 23(1942):131.

1:18 Clark Memorial Library. *Report of the Second Decade 1945-1955.* Los Angeles: Clark Memorial Library, University of California, 1956.

1:19 Cox, E. H. M., ed. *The Library of Edmund Gosse.* London: Dulau, [1924]. Includes Gosse's collection of Dryden materials.

1:20 Crane, Ronald S., et al., comps. *English Literature 1660-1800: A Bibliography of Modern Studies Compiled for "Philological Quarterly."* 1: *1926-1938.* Foreword by Louis A. Landa. Princeton: Princeton University Press, 1950. 2: *1939-1950.* Princeton: Princeton University Press, 1952.

1:21   Crum, Margaret. *First-line Index of English Poetry, 1500-1800, in Manuscripts of the Bodleian Library.* 2 vols. Oxford: At the Clarendon Press, 1969.

1:22   Davies, Godfrey, and Mary Frear Keeler, eds. *Bibliography of British History: Stuart Period, 1603-1714.* 2nd rev. ed. Oxford: At the Clarendon Press [for the American Historical Association and the Royal Historical Society of Great Britain], 1970.

1:23   ———, and Mary Isabel Fry. "Supplements to the Short-Title Catalogue, 1641-1700." *HLQ* 16(1953):393-436. Reprinted San Marino: Huntington Library, 1953. *See* item 1:114.

1:24   Day, Cyrus L., and Eleanore Boswell Murrie. *English Song-Books, 1651-1702: A Bibliography with a First-Line Index of Songs.* London: Printed for the Bibliographical Society at the University Press, Oxford, 1940 (for 1937).

1:25   ———, and ———. "English Song-Books, 1651-1702, and Their Publishers." *Library* 16(1936):356-401.

1:26   Dearing, Vinton A. *A Manual of Textual Analysis.* Berkeley, Los Angeles: University of California Press, 1959.

*1:27   ———. "Computer Aids to Editing the Text of Dryden." *Art and Error: Modern Textual Editing*, eds. Ronald Gottesman and Scott Bennett, pp. 254-278. Bloomington, London: Indiana University Press, 1970.

*1:28   ———. *Methods of Textual Editing.* (Clark Memorial Library Seminar Paper.) Los Angeles: Clark Memorial Library, University of California, 1962. Reprinted in *Bibliography and Textual Criticism: English and American Literature, 1700 to the Present*, eds. O. M. Brack, Jr., and Warner Barnes, pp. 73-101. Chicago, London: University of Chicago Press, 1969. An explanation of the eight-step process used in preparing the texts for the California Dryden.

1:29   Dobell, Percy John. *Books of the Time of the Restoration: Being a Collection of Plays, Poems and Prose Works Produced Between the Years 1660 and 1700, by the Contemporaries of John Dryden.* With Annotations. London: P. J. and A. E. Dobell, 1920.

1:30   ———. "A Dryden Library." *The Book-Collector's Quarterly* 2 (1931):36-39. *See* item 1:117.

1:31   ———, comp. *John Dryden: Bibliographical Memoranda.* London: P. J. and A. E. Dobell, 1922.

1:32   ———. *The Literature of the Restoration: Being a Collection of the Poetical and Dramatic Literature Produced Between the Years 1660 and 1700, with Particular Reference to the Writings of John Dryden.* With Annotations. London: P. J. and A. E. Dobell, 1918. Includes Tonson's accounts with Dryden in the Preface.

1:33   ———, and A. E. Dobell. *A Catalogue of the Works of John Dryden and Drydeniana.* London: P. J. and A. E. Dobell, 1940.

1:34   "Dryden First Editions." *TLS* 7 April 1927, p. 256. A note on Sotheby's sale of the Britnell Library.

1:35   "The Eighteenth Century: A Current Bibliography" [incorporates "English Literature, 1660-1800"]. *Philological Quarterly.* Iowa City: University of Iowa. An annotated bibliography appearing annually in the third issue.

1:36   Falle, George. "Sir Walter Scott as Editor of Dryden and Swift." *UTQ* 36(1967):161-80. *See* items 2/1:11, 4:207.

1:37   Faulkner, Thomas C. "Dryden and *Great and Weighty Considerations*: An Incorrect Attribution." *SEL* 11(1971):417-25. Argues against attributing the pamphlet to Dryden.

1:38 "First Collation of an Interesting Dryden Item." *Bookman's Journal* 12(1925):163–64. *The Character of St. Evremond.*

1:39 Ford, H. L. *Shakespeare 1700-1740: A Collation of the Editions and Separate Plays.* Oxford: Oxford University Press, 1935.

1:40 Freeman, Phyllis. "Two Fragments of Walsh Manuscripts." *RES* 8 (1957):390–401. Possibly a portion of Walsh's Preface to *Love Triumphant.*

1:41 Friedman, Arthur, et al., comps. *English Literature 1660-1880: A Bibliography of Modern Studies Founded by Ronald S. Crane Compiled for "Philological Quarterly."* 3: *1951-1956.* Foreword by Gwin J. Kolb and Curt A. Zimansky. Princeton: Princeton University Press, 1962.

1:42 Genova, A. Obertello, ed. *Un Dramma Inglese Inedite del Secolo Diciassettesimo, "The Lover's Strategem, or Virtue Rewarded."* Genova: Instituto Universitario di Magistero, 1952. Attributed to Dryden. *See SCN* 18:25–26.

1:43 Graham, John. "'Ut Pictura Poesis': A Bibliography." *BB* 29 (1972):13–15, 18.

1:44 Grolier Club. *Catalogue of Original and Early Editions of Some of the Poetical and Prose Works of English Writers from Wither to Prior* [1900]. Vol. I. New York: Cooper Square, 1963.

1:45 ———. *Exhibition of First and Other Editions of the Works of John Dryden (1631-1700), Together with a Few Engraved Portraits and Two Oil Paintings.* New York: The DeVinne Press, 1900.

1:46 ———. *An Exhibition of Selected Works of the Poets Laureate of England.* New York: The DeVinne Press, 1901.

1:47 Grose, Clyde Leclare. *A Select Bibliography of British History 1660-1760.* Chicago: University of Chicago Press, 1939. Reprinted New York: Octagon Books, 1967.

1:48 Habicht, Werner, ed. *English and American Studies in German: Summaries of Theses and Monographs.* (Supplement to *Anglia* 1969.) Tübingen: Niemeyer, 1970.

1:49 Haraszti, Zoltán. "A List of Dryden's Plays in the Boston Public Library, Including his Adaptations and Operas." *More Books* 8(1933):100.

1:50 Harbage, Alfred, and S. Schoenbaum. *Annals of English Drama 975-1700: An Analytical Record of All Plays, Extant or Lost, Chronologically Arranged and Indexed by Authors, Titles, Dramatic Companies.* 2nd rev. ed. Philadelphia: University of Pennsylvania, 1964. *See* A. H. Carter, *MP* 40:201–12.

1:51 ———. "Elizabethan and Seventeenth-Century Play Manuscripts." *PMLA* 50(1935):687–99. *See* addenda, ibid., 52(1937):905–07.

1:52 Harris, Brice. "Dorset's Poem, 'On the Young Statesmen'." *TLS* 4 April 1935, pp. 227–28.

1:53 Hiscock, W. G. "A Poem Attributed to Dryden." *TLS* 18 April 1936, p. 340. *The Triumphs of Levy. See* correspondence, W. G. Hiscock, ibid., 25 April 1936, p. 360; E. S. de Beer, ibid., 16 May 1936, p. 420; W. G. Hiscock, ibid., 23 May 1936, p. 440; E. S. de Beer, ibid., 30 May 1936, p. 460; W. G. Hiscock, ibid., 10 October 1936, p. 815. *See also* item 1:91.

1:54 Howard-Hill, T. H. *Bibliography of British Literary Bibliographies.* Oxford: At the Clarendon Press, 1969.

1:55 Hustvedt, Sigurd B. "The Age of Dryden." *William Andrews Clark Memorial Library: Report of the First Decade, 1934-1944.* Berkeley, Los Angeles: Clark Memorial Library, University of California, 1946.

1:56   Jackson, Allan S. "Bibliography of 17th & 18th Century Play Editions in the Rare Book Room of the Ohio State University Library." *RECTR* 8, i(1969):30–58.

1:57   Janssens, G. "Critical Bibliography of English Literature." *DQR* 3(1972):97–103.

1:58   Keast, W. R. "Dryden Studies, 1895–1948." *MP* 48(1951):205–10. Rev. art. *See* item 1:74.

1:59   Kennedy, Arthur G., Donald B. Sands, and William E. Colburn. *A Concise Bibliography for Students of English.* Rev. ed. Stanford: Stanford University Press, 1972.

1:60   Kinsley, James. "Dryden, 1631–1700." *English Poetry: Select Bibliographical Guides*, ed. with introd. A. E. Dyson, pp. 111–27. London, New York: Oxford University Press, 1971. A descriptive summary of commentary on Dryden, together with a bibliographical list.

1:61   Langhans, Edward A. "Restoration Theatre Scholarship 1960–66: A Resumé and Suggestion for Future Work." *RECTR* 6,i(1967):8–11.

1:62   Legouis, Pierre. "Editions savantes d'Outre-Atlantique et d'Outre-Manche." *EA* 6(1953):35–40. Rev. art. *See* item 2/2:10.

1:63   Love, Harold., Mary Lord, et al., comp. *John Dryden in Australian Libraries: A Checklist of Pre-1800 Holdings.* (Monash University English Department Bibliography Checklists 1.) Melbourne: Monash University, 1972.

1:64   Lowe, Robert W. *A Bibliographical Account of English Theatrical Literature from the Earliest Times to the Present Day* [1888]. Detroit: Gale Research Company, 1966.

*1:65 Macdonald, Hugh. *John Dryden: A Bibliography of Early Editions and of Drydeniana.* Oxford: Oxford University Press, 1939. *See* James M. Osborn, *MP* 39:313–19; Louis I. Bredvold, *PQ* 19:196–97; Edward N. Hooker and H. T. Swedenberg, Jr., *MLN* 56:74–75; G. R. Potter, *RES* 16:221–23; V. de Sola Pinto, *MLR* 25:238–39. *See also* items 1:83, 1:96.

1:66   ———. "Some Poetical Miscellanies, 1672–1716." *Essays and Studies by Members of the English Association* 26(1940):106–12.

1:67   MacMillan, Dougald. "The William Andrews Clark Edition of Dryden—the Plays." *SAB* 15,i(1950):10–11. Describes the plan for the projected edition of Dryden's plays.

1:68   McNamee, Lawrence F. *Dissertations in English and American Literature: Theses Accepted by American, British, and German Universities, 1865–1964.* Supplements: *1964–1968*; *1969–1973*. New York, London: R. R. Bowker, 1968–1974.

1:69   Metzdorf, Robert F. "Three States of 'The Revolter'." *PBSA* 45 (1951):362. Macdonald 242.

1:70   Milne, Alexander Taylor, comp. *Writings on British History 1901–1933.* 3: *The Tudor and Stuart Periods 1485–1714.* London: Jonathan Cape [for Royal Historical Society], 1968.

1:71   ———, comp. *Writings on British History 1940–1945.* vol. 1. New York: Barnes and Noble [for Royal Historical Society], 1961.

1:72   Modern Humanities Research Association. *Annual Bibliography of English Language and Literature.* Cambridge: Bowes and Bowes; Leeds: Maney. An annual bibliography.

1:73   Modern Language Association. *International Bibliography of Books and Articles on the Modern Languages and Literatures.* New York: Modern Language Association of America. An annual bibliography.

1:74   Monk, Samuel Holt. *John Dryden: A List of Critical Studies Published from 1895 to 1948*. Minneapolis: University of Minnesota
Press; London: Oxford University Press, 1950. *See TLS* 6 April
1952, p. 214; *NQ* 196:352; James M. Osborn, *PQ* 30:267-68. *See also*
item 1:58.

*1:75   Montgomery, Guy, ed. *Concordance to the Poetical Works of John
Dryden*. Assisted by Mary Jackman and Helen S. Agoa. Preface by
Josephine Miles. Los Angeles, Berkeley: University of California
Press, 1957. *See* Curt A. Zimansky and Robert A. Edberg, *PQ* 37:323-
25; G. Blakemore Evans, *JEGP* 57:344; Pierre Legouis, *EA* 11:253-54;
TLS 4 July 1959, p. 378 and correspondence, S. M. Parrish, ibid,
8 August, p. 477.

1:76   Mummendey, Richard. *Language and Literature of the Anglo-Saxon
Nations as Presented in German Doctoral Dissertations: 1885-1950*.
Bonn, Charlottesville, Va.: Bibliographical Society of the Univer-
sity of Virginia, 1954.

1:77   Murrie, Eleanore Boswell. "Notes on the Printers and Publishers
of English Song-Books 1651-1702." *EBST* 1,iii(1937-38):241-76.

1:78   Needham, Francis, ed. *A Collection of Poems by Several Hands*.
(Welbeck Miscellany 2.) London: Dobell, 1934. A song for *Martin
Mar-All*?

1:79   Newton, Evelyn. "Poem Attributed to Dryden." *NQ* (12th ser.) 12
(1923):12. "The Conquest of England."

1:80   Nicholls, Norah. "Some Early Editions of John Dryden." *Bookman*
(London) 80(1931):266-67.

1:81   Noyes, George R. "An Unnoticed Edition of Dryden's *Virgil*." *MLN*
19(1904):125-27. *See* retraction, *MLN* 24(1909):31.

1:82   ———, and Herman Ralph Mead, eds. *An Essay Upon Satyr (1680)*.
(University of California Publications in English 7.) Berkeley,
Los Angeles: University of California Press, 1948. Attributed to
Dryden by his contemporaries.

*1:83   Osborn, James M. "Macdonald's Bibliography of Dryden: An An-
notated Check List of Selected American Libraries." *MP* 39(1941):
69-98, 197-212, 313-19. *See* items 1:65, 8/4:26.

1:84   ———. "The Search for English Literary Documents." *English
Institute Annual 1939* (1940):31-55. Reprinted in [Boys]: 232-57.

1:85   Perrin, Michel P. "Theses and Dissertations in Restoration and
18th Century Theatre: Further Addenda." *RECTR* 7,i(1968):1-6. *See*
items 1:99, 1:109.

1:86   Pettit, Henry. "Dryden's Works in Dryden, New York." *BB* 18(1946):
198.

1:87   Pinto, V. de Sola. *The English Renaissance 1510-1688*. London:
Cresset, 1939. Rev. ed. 1952.

1:88   Purpus, Eugene R. "Some Notes on a Deistical Essay Attributed
to Dryden." *PQ* 29(1950)347-49.

1:89   "Recent Studies in the Restoration and Eighteenth Century."
Studies in English Literature 1500-1900. Houston: Rice University.
A review article appearing annually in the summer issue which
surveys recent work.

1:90   "Restoration and 18th Century Theatre Research Bibliography."
Restoration and 18th Century Theatre Research. Chicago: Loyola
University of Chicago. An annotated bibliography appearing an-
nually in the second issue.

1:91   S. "Dryden's Satire 'The Tribe of Levi'." *NQ* (10th ser.) 11
(1909):229. *See* item 1:53.

1:92   S., C. "A Check-List of Dryden's Plays." *Bibliographer* (New York) 1(1902):374-78. A list of 27 plays by or attributed to Dryden.

1:93   Sachse, William L., comp. *Restoration England 1660-1689*. Cambridge: Cambridge University Press for the Conference on British Studies, 1971.

1:94   Schmitt, Albert R. "The Programmschriften Collection." *Library Chronicle* (University of Pennsylvania) 25(1959):29-42. Lists Philipp Ott's paper on Dryden's relationship to Molière.

1:95   Sotheby and Co. *Catalogue of the Very Extensive and Well-Known Library of English Poetry, Drama and Other Literature, Principally of the Seventeenth and Early Eighteenth Centuries, Formed by the Late George Thorn-Drury, Esq., K. C.* London: J. Davy, 1931.

1:96   Steck, James S. "Dryden's *Indian Emperour*: The Early Editions and their Relation to the Text." *SB* 2(1949):139-52. *See* item 1:65.

1:97   Strachan, L. R. M. "Reputed Song by Dryden." *NQ* (12th ser.) 11 (1922):341-42. "What Shall I Do to Show How Much I Love Her?" music reputed to be by Purcell.

*1:98   Stratman, Carl J., C. S. V., ed. "John Dryden." *Bibliography of English Printed Tragedy 1565-1900*, pp. 165-85. Carbondale: Southern Illinois University Press; London, Amsterdam: Feffer and Simons, 1966. Extensively annotated.

1:99   ———. "Theses and Dissertations in Restoration and 18th Century Theatre." *RECTR* 2,ii(1963):20-45. *See* items 1:85, 1:109.

1:100   ———. "Unpublished Dissertations in the History and Theory of Tragedy, 1889-1957." *BB* 22(1958-59):161-64, 190-92, 214-16, 237-40; 23(1960-62):15-20, 162-65, 187-92.

1:101   ———, ed., Edmund A. Napieralski and Jean E. Westbrook, comps. *Restoration and Eighteenth Century Theatre Research Bibliography: 1961-1968*. Troy, New York: Whitston, 1969.

*1:102   ———, David G. Spencer and Mary Elizabeth Devine, eds. *Restoration and Eighteenth Century Theatre Research: A Bibliographical Guide, 1900-1968*. Carbondale: Southern Illinois University Press, 1971.

1:103   "Summary of Periodical Literature." *Review of English Studies: A Quarterly Journal of English Literature and the English Language*. Oxford: At the Clarendon Press. Recent publications are listed by the journals in which they appear; published quarterly.

1:104   Summers, Montague. *A Bibliography of the Restoration Drama*. London: The Fortune Press, 1934. Includes a list of Dryden's plays.

*1:105   Swedenberg, H. T., Jr. "Challenges to Dryden's Editor." *John Dryden: Papers Read at a Clark Library Seminar, February 25, 1967*, introd. John Loftis, pp. 23-40. Los Angeles: Clark Memorial Library, University of California, 1967. Reprinted in [Clark Library]:93-108.

1:106   ———. "Literature: 1640-1750." *Report of the Third Decade 1956-1966*. Los Angeles: Clark Memorial Library, University of California, 1966.

1:107   ———. "On Editing Dryden's Early Poems." *Essays Critical and Historical Dedicated to Lily B. Campbell*, pp. 73-84. Berkeley, Los Angeles: University of California Press, 1950.

1:108   Tobin, James E. *Eighteenth Century English Literature and Its Cultural Background: A Bibliography*. New York: Fordham University Press, 1939.

1:109 Vernon, P. F. "Theses and Dissertations in Restoration and
18th Century Theatre: Addenda." *RECTR* 6,i(1967):55–56. All those
listed are in the University of London Library. *See* items 1:85,
1:99.

1:110 Watson, George, ed. *The Cambridge Bibliography of English Literature. 5: Supplement: A. D. 600–1900.* Cambridge: At the University Press, 1957.

1:111 Wheatley, Henry B. "A Dryden [Bibliography]." [Cambridge His-
tory]:447–62.

1:112 ———. "Post-Restoration Quartos of Shakespeare's Plays." *Library* (3rd ser.) 4(1913):237–69.

1:113 Wikelund, Philip. "Restoration Literature: An Annotated Bibliography." *Folio* 19,ii(1954):135–55.

1:114 Wing, Donald G., comp. *Short-Title Catalogue of Books Printed
in England, Scotland, Ireland, Wales, and British America and of
English Books Printed in Other Countries 1641–1700. 1: A–England.*
New York: Columbia University Press, 1945. 2nd ed., rev. and enl.
New York: Index Committee, MLA, 1972. *See* item 1:23.

1:115 Wise, Thomas J. *The Ashley Library: A Catalogue of Printed
Books, Manuscripts and Autograph Letters.* 11 vols. London:
Printed for private circulation, 1922–36. Dryden and Drydeniana
items in vols. 10–11.

1:116 ———. *A Catalogue of the Library of the Late John Henry Wrenn.*
Austin, Texas: University of Texas, 1920.

1:117 ———. *A Dryden Library: A Catalogue of Printed Books, Manuscripts and Autograph Letters by John Dryden.* London: Printed for
private circulation only, 1930.

1:118 Woods, Charles B., et al., comps. *English Literature 1660–1800:
A Bibliography of Modern Studies Founded by Ronald S. Crane Com-
piled for "Philological Quarterly." 4: 1957–1960.* Princeton:
Princeton University Press, 1962.

1:119 Woodward, Gertrude L., and James G. McManaway, comps. "Dryden,
John." *A Check List of English Plays 1641–1700*, pp. 42–54. Chicago: The Newberry Library, 1945. *Supplement* by Fredson Bowers.
Charlottesville, Va.: Bibliographical Society of the University
of Virginia, 1949.

1:120 *Year's Work in English Studies.* London: John Murray for The
English Association. Review articles which appear annually.

1:121 Zamonski, John A. *An Annotated Bibliography of John Dryden:
Texts and Studies, 1949–1973.* New York, London: Garland, 1975.

1:122 Zimansky, Curt A., et al., comps. *English Literature 1660–1800:
A Bibliography of Modern Studies Founded by Ronald S. Crane Com-
piled for "Philological Quarterly." 6: 1966–1970.* Princeton:
Princeton University Press, 1972.

See also items 3:140, 3:146, 3:188, 4:23, 4:301, 5/4:56, 5/4:69, 5/6:
11, 5/6:16, 5/14:6, 6/2:48, 6/2:73–74, 7:98, 8/1:30, 8/3:3, 8/4:6,
8/4:17, 8/4:26, 8/9:83, 8/10:1, 8/10:3, 8/10:8–10.

2. Editions

2/1. COLLECTIONS

2/1:1 Arundell, Dennis D., ed. *Dryden and Howard 1664–1668: The Text* of "An Essay of Dramatic Poesy," "The Indian Emperor," and "The Duke of Lerma" with Other Controversial Matter. Cambridge: Cambridge University Press, 1929. See item 7:292.

2/1:2 Bredvold, Louis I., ed. The Best of Dryden. With an Introd. and Notes. (English Series.) New York: Ronald Press, 1933.

*2/1:3 Chambers, A. B., and William Frost, eds.; Vinton A. Dearing, textual ed. The Works of John Dryden. 4: Poems 1693-1696. With Commentary and Textual Notes. Berkeley, Los Angeles, London: University of California Press, 1974.

2/1:4 Crump, Galbraith M., ed. Poems on Affairs of State: Augustan Satirical Verse, 1660-1714. 4: 1685-1688. New Haven, London: Yale University Press, 1968. "Prologue and Epilogue" to Albion and Albanius; Britannia Rediviva; also includes attacks on The Hind and the Panther.

2/1:5 Ellis, Frank H., ed. Poems on Affairs of State: Augustan Satiric Verse, 1660-1714. 6: 1697-1704. New Haven, London: Yale University Press, 1970. "Prologue" to The Pilgrim; "The Fourth Pastoral of Virgil"; also includes the "Epitaph upon Mr. John Dryden" (11 June 1700).

2/1:6 Elloway, D. R., ed. Dryden's Satire. London: Macmillan; New York: St. Martin's Press, 1966.

2/1:7 Frost, William, ed. Selected Works of John Dryden. New York: Rinehart, 1953. 2nd ed. San Francisco: Rinehart, 1971. Uses Noyes's texts.

2/1:8 Grant, Douglas, ed. Dryden: Poetry, Prose and Plays. Cambridge, Mass.: Harvard University Press, 1952. See TLS 1 February 1952, p. 94.

2/1:9 Kallich, Martin, Andrew MacLeish, and Gertrude Schoenbohm, eds. Oedipus: Myth and Drama. New York: Odyssey, 1968. Oedipus the King; "The Grounds of Criticism in Tragedy." Includes the texts of Oedipus by Sophocles and by Hugo von Hofmannsthal, as well as ancient and modern criticism.

2/1:10 Miner, Earl R., ed. Selected Poetry and Prose of John Dryden. With an Introd. and Notes. (Modern Library College Editions.) New York: Random House, 1969.

*2/1:11 Scott, Sir Walter, ed. The Works of John Dryden. Illustrated with Notes, Historical, Critical, and Explanatory, and A Life of the Author. Revised and Corrected by George Saintsbury. 8 vols. Edinburgh: William Paterson, 1882-84. "The Life of Dryden" ed. and reprinted by Bernard Kreissman. Lincoln: University of Nebraska Press, 1963. See Pierre Legouis, EA 17:155-56. See also items 1:36, 4:207, 7:294.

2/1:12 Smith, D. Nichol, ed. Poetry and Prose. With an Introd. Oxford: Oxford University Press, 1925.

2/1:13 Thomas, Donald, ed. A Selection from John Dryden. (Longman English Series.) Harlow: Longman, 1972.

2/1:14 Zesmer, David, ed. John Dryden: Poems, Plays, and Essays. (Bantam Classics.) New York: Bantam, 1967.

2/2. NONDRAMATIC POEMS

Collected Works

2/2:1 Auden, W. H., ed. A Choice of Dryden's Verse. London: Faber, 1973.

2/2:2 Boas, Frederick S., ed. *Songs and Lyrics from the English Playbooks*. London: Cresset Press, 1945.

2/2:3 Brower, Reuben A., ed. *Dryden*. (Laurel Poetry Series.) With an Introd. and Notes. New York: Dell, 1962.

2/2:4 Christie, W. D., ed. *Dryden: Select Poems*. With a "Biographical Introduction [1871]." 5th ed., rev. by Charles Harding Firth. Oxford: Oxford University Press, 1901.

2/2:5 ———, ed. *The Poetical Works of John Dryden*. With a "Memoir of Dryden." (The Globe Edition.) London, New York: Macmillan, 1925. Based on the 1871 ed. *See* item 4:298.

2/2:6 Collins, John Churton, ed. *The Satires of Dryden*. With Memoir, Introd., and Notes. London: Macmillan, 1897. *Absalom and Achitophel, I and II*; *The Medall*; *Mac Flecknoe*.

2/2:7 Day, Cyrus L., ed. *The Songs of John Dryden*. Cambridge, Mass.: Harvard University Press, 1932. Reprinted New York: Russell and Russell, 1967. Songs to be accompanied by music.

2/2:8 Dobrée, Bonamy, ed. *Dryden's Poems*. With an Introd. London: J. M. Dent; New York: E. P. Dutton, 1934.

2/2:9 Elloway, D. R., ed. *Dryden's Satire*. With an Introd. London: Macmillan; New York: St. Martin's, 1966.

2/2:10 Gardner, William Bradford, ed. *The Prologues and Epilogues of John Dryden: A Critical Edition*. New York: Published for the University of Texas by Columbia University Press, 1951. *See* Hoyt Trowbridge, *MLN* 68:428-29; James Kinsley, *RES* 3:397-98; V. de Sola Pinto, *MLR* 47:224; *TLS* 13 July 1952, p. 432; Henry Hitch Adams, *PQ* 31:267-69.

2/2:11 Grigson, Geoffrey, ed. *Selected Poems: John Dryden*. London: Grey Walls Press, 1950. *See* V. de Sola Pinto, *TLS* 22 September 1951, p. 603.

2/2:12 Hadfield, John, ed. *Restoration Love Songs*. Preston, Hertfordshire: Cupid Press, 1950.

*2/2:13 Hooker, Edward Niles, and H. T. Swedenberg, Jr., eds; Vinton A. Dearing, textual ed. *The Works of John Dryden*. 1: *Poems 1649-1680*. Assoc. eds. Frederick M. Carey, Hugh G. Dick, Godfrey Davies, Samuel Holt Monk and John Harrington Smith. With Commentary and Textual Notes. Berkeley, Los Angeles: University of California Press, 1956. *See TLS* 30 November 1956, p. 712; James M. Osborn, *PQ* 36:358-61; G. Blakemore Evans, *JEGP* 56:490-92; James Kinsley, *RES* 8:445-48; Alfred Harbage, *NYTBR* 15 July 1956, p. 4; Douglas M. Knight, *CE* 18:290; V. de Sola Pinto, *MLR* 52:590-92; Charles E. Ward, *MP* 55:129-32; Pierre Legouis, *EA* 11:54-56. *See also* item 4:422.

2/2:14 Hooper, Richard, ed. *Poetical Works*. With a "Life of Dryden." 5 vols. (The Aldine edition of the British poets.) Rev. ed. London: G. Bell, 1891.

2/2:15 Jones, Gwyn, ed. *Songs and Poems of John Dryden*. Drawings by Lavinia Blythe. London: The Golden Cockerel Press, 1957. *See TLS* 23 August 1957, p. 509.

2/2:16 Kinsley, James, ed. *Dryden: Selected Poems*. (New Oxford English Series.) London: Oxford University Press, 1963.

2/2:17 ———, ed. *The Poems and Fables of John Dryden*. (Oxford Standard Authors.) London, New York: Oxford Univeristy Press, 1962.

*2/2:18 ———, ed. *The Poems of John Dryden*. 4 vols. (Oxford English Texts.) Oxford: Clarendon Press, 1958. *See* John Butt, *RES* 11:213-

15; *Listener* 60:389; Curt A. Zimansky, *PQ* 38:320-21; Pierre Legouis, *EA* 12:353-54; V. de Sola Pinto, *MLR* 54:592-94; David M. Vieth, *MP* 56:279-82; George Watson, *JEGP* 58:530-33. *See also* items 4:7, 4:123.

2/2:19 Legouis, Pierre, ed. *Dryden: Poèmes Choisis*. With an Introd. and Notes. (Collection bilingue des classiques étrangers.) Paris: Aubier, 1946.

2/2:20 Mengel, Elias F., Jr. *Poems on Affairs of State: Augustan Satirical Verse, 1660-1714*. 2: *1678-1681*. New Haven, London: Yale University Press, 1965. *Absalom and Achitophel*; "Prologue" to *The Loyal Brother*.

*2/2:21 Miner, Earl, ed.; Vinton A. Dearing, textual ed. *The Works of John Dryden*. 3: *Poems 1685-1692*. Assoc. eds. Norman Austin, Samuel Holt Monk, Thomas G. Rosenmeyer. With Commentary and Textual Notes. Berkeley, Los Angeles: Univeristy of California Press, 1969. *See* George McFadden, *PQ* 69:340-42; *TLS* 4 September 1970, p. 977; Colin J. Horne, *RES* 25:205-06; *YWES* 50:244-45.

2/2:22 Noyes, George R., ed. *The Poetical Works of Dryden*. (The Cambridge Edition of the Poets.) With a "Biographical Sketch." Boston: Houghton-Mifflin, 1909. 2nd, rev. ed. 1950. *See* item 6/2:44.

2/2:23 Oswald, Norman H. "The Satires of John Dryden: A Critical Edition." Diss. Calif., Berkeley, 1946.

2/2:24 *The Poetical Works of John Dryden*. With Memoir and Introd. (Gladstone Edition.) New York, Boston: Cromwell [1906].

2/2:25 Reed, Edward Bliss, ed. *Songs from the British Drama*. New Haven: Yale University Press, 1925.

2/2:26 Sargeaunt, John. *Poems of John Dryden*. With an Introd. (Oxford Standard Authors.) London: Oxford University Press, 1910. *See* George R. Noyes, *MLR* 7:117-23.

2/2:27 Schless, Howard H., ed. *Poems on Affairs of State: Augustan Satirical Verse, 1660-1714*. 3: *1682-1685*. New Haven, London: Yale University Press, 1968. *The Medall*; "Prologue" to *The Duke of Guise*; *The Second Part of Absalom and Achitophel*; "Prologue to the King and Queen at the Opening of their Theater"; *Threnodia Augustalis*.

2/2:28 Sharrock, Roger, ed. *Selected Poems of John Dryden*. With an Introd. and Notes. London: Heinemann, 1963. *See* Pierre Legouis, *EA* 17:157-58.

2/2:29 Stead, Philip John, ed. *Songs of the Restoration Theatre: Edited from the Printed Books of the Time*. London: Methuen, 1948. Modernized ed. *See TLS* 17 April 1949, p. 220.

2/2:30 Strachey, J. St. Loe, ed. *John Dryden*. With an Introd. London, Edinburgh: Nelson, 1925. Reprinted as *Poems of Dryden*. 1929.

2/2:31 Summers, Montague, ed. *Covent Garden Drollery*. London: The Fortune Press, 1927.

*2/2:32 Swedenberg, H. T., Jr., ed.; Vinton A. Dearing, textual ed. *The Works of John Dryden*. 2: *Poems 1681-1684*. With Commentary and Textual Notes. Berkeley, Los Angeles: University of California Press, 1972. *See* Phillip Harth, *PQ* 52:492-93; Colin J. Horne, *RES* 25:205-08; D. I. B. Smith, *MP* 72:422-27; *TLS* 14 December 1973, p. 1530; George deF. Lord, *Scriblerian* 5:101-02. *See also* item 5/4: 69.

2/2:33 Thorp, Willard, ed. *Songs from the Restoration Theater*. Princeton: Princeton University Press, 1934.

Individual Works

2/2:34 *Absalom and Achitophel, 1681; The Second Part of Absalom and Achitophel, 1682.* Menston: Scolar Press, 1970. Facsimile ed.

2/2:35 *Alexander's Feast; or, The Power of Music: A Song in Honour of St. Cecilia, 1697.* London: E. Arnold, 1904.

2/2:36 *Alexander's Feast; or the Power of Musique* (1697). [London: H. Milford, 1925]. Facsimile of first ed.

2/2:37 *Annus Mirabilis: The Year of Wonders, 1666.* Oxford: At the Clarendon Press, 1927. A facsimile reprint of first ed. with bibliographical preface.

2/2:38 Christie, W. D., ed. *Absalom and Achitophel.* 5th ed., rev., Charles Harding Firth. Oxford: Oxford University Press, 1911.

2/2:39 Frye, B. J., ed. *MacFlecknoe.* (Merrill Casebooks.) Columbus, Ohio: Charles E. Merrill, 1970. Includes selections from the criticism.

2/2:40 Handel, George Frederich. *Alexander's Feast or the Power of Music. The Works.* Vol. 12. (The German Handel Society.) Ridgewood, N.J.: Gregg Press, 1965. Contains a text of Dryden's poem, a German translation and Handel's score.

2/2:41 Hiscock, Walter George, ed. "Epilogue . . . 1681." *A Christ Church Miscellany,* pp. 113-15. Oxford: At the University Press, 1946. Photographic reproduction.

2/2:42 ———, ed. *Epilogue Spoken to the King March the Nineteenth 1681.* Oxford: At the Clarendon Press, 1932.

2/2:43 Kinsley, James, and Helen Kinsley, eds. *Absalom and Architophel.* London: Oxford University Press, 1961.

2/2:44 ———, introd. *Sylvae, 1685.* Menston: Scolar Press, 1973. Facsimile ed.

2/2:45 ———, and James T. Boulton, eds. *English Satiric Poetry: Dryden to Byron.* With an Introd. on satire. (Arnold's English Texts.) London: Edward Arnold, 1966. *Mac Flecknoe.*

2/2:46 Lord, George deF., ed. *Poems on Affairs of State: Augustan Satirical Verse, 1660-1714.* 1: *1660-1678.* New Haven, London: Yale University Press, 1963. *Mac Flecknoe.*

2/2:47 *MacFlecknoe 1682.* Oxford: At the Clarendon Press, 1924. Facsimile ed. with textual notes.

2/3. TRANSLATIONS

Collected Works

2/3:1 Kinsley, James, introd. *Fables Ancient and Modern: Translated into Verse from Homer, Ovid, Boccace & Chaucer: With Original Poems, 1700.* London: Scolar Press, 1973.

2/3:2 ———, ed. *The Works of Virgil: Translated by John Dryden.* With an Introd. London: Oxford University Press, 1961. Modernized ed.

2/3:3 *Metamorphoses: In Fifteen Books, Translated into English Verse Under the Direction of Sir Samuel Garth by John Dryden and Others.* New York: Heritage, 1961.

*2/3:4 Noyes, George Rapall, and George Reuben Potter, eds. *Hymns Attributed to John Dryden.* (University of California Publications in English 6.) Berkeley: University of California Press, 1937. *See* item 6/3:5.

2/3:5 Whicher, George F., introd. *The Georgics: Translated into English Verse by John Dryden*. Verona: Limited Editions Club, 1952; New York: Heritage, 1953.

Individual Works

2/3:6 Brewster, William Tenney, ed. *Palamon and Arcite*. With an Introd. (Longman's English Classics.) New York, London: Longmans, 1898.

2/3:7 Cook, Albert S., ed. "Boileau's Art of Poetry." *The Art of Poetry: The Poetical Treatises of Horace, Vida, and Boileau* [1892], pp. 159-222. New York: Stechert, 1926.

2/3:8 Elledge, Scott, and Donald Schier, eds. "The Art of Poetry." *The Continental Model: Selected French Critical Essays of the Seventeenth Century, in English Translation*, pp. 207-68. With the French text. Rev. ed. Ithaca, London: Cornell University Press, 1970. The Dryden-William Soame translation.

*2/3:9 Roper, Alan, ed.; Vinton A. Dearing, textual ed. *The Works of John Dryden*. 18: *Prose: The History of the League 1684*. With Commentary and Textual Notes. Berkeley, Los Angeles: University of California Press, 1974.

2/4. CRITICAL WRITINGS AND PROSE

Collected Works

2/4:1 Adams, Henry Hitch, and Baxter Hathaway, eds. *Dramatic Essays of the Neoclassic Age*. New York: Columbia University Press, 1950. *Heads of an Answer to Rymer; An Essay of Dramatic Poesy*; modernized eds.

2/4:2 Boulton, James T., ed. *Dryden: Of Dramatick Poesie, An Essay, with Sir Robert Howard's Preface to The Great Favourite and Dryden's Defence of an Essay*. With an Introd. and Notes. Oxford, London: Oxford University Press, 1964. Allows the Howard-Dryden argument to be seen from both sides. *See YWES* 45:255.

2/4:3 Collins, J. Churton, introd. *Critical Essays and Literary Fragments*. New York: E. P. Dutton, [1905]. "Dedicatory Epistle" to the *Rival Ladies; Of Dramatic Poesy*.

2/4:4 Dennis, John, ed. *Letters Upon Several Occasions (1696)*. Westmead, England: Greeg, 1971. Includes letters by Dryden.

2/4:5 Flower, Desmond, comp. *The Pursuit of Poetry: A Book of Letters about Poetry Written by English Poets: 1550-1930*. London: Cassell, 1939. Etherege to Dryden; Dryden to Tonson.

2/4:6 Hudson, William Henry, ed. *Dramatic Essays by John Dryden*. With an Introd. (Everyman's Library 568.) London: J. M. Dent; New York: E. P. Dutton, 1912.

2/4:7 Johnson, Reginald Brimley, ed. *Poetry and the Poets*. London: Faber and Gwyer, [1926]. *Heads of an Answer to Rymer*; *Essay of Dramatick Poesie*; *A Parallel betwixt Painting and Poetry*.

2/4:8 Ker, W. P. ed. *Essays of John Dryden*. 2 vols. Oxford: At the Clarendon Press, 1900. Reprinted New York: Russell and Russell, 1961.

2/4:9 Kinsley, James, and George Parfitt, eds. *John Dryden: Selected Criticism*. Oxford: Clarendon Press, 1970. *See* Roger Lonsdale, *NQ* 20:197-99.

2/4:10 Kirsch, Arthur C., ed. *Literary Criticism of John Dryden*. With an Introd. (Regents Critics Series.) Lincoln: Nebraska University Press, 1966.

2/4:11 Mahoney, John L., ed. *An Essay of Dramatic Poesy. A Defence of an Essay of Dramatic Poesy. Preface to the Fables.* With an Introd. and Notes. (Library of Liberal Arts.) Indianapolis, Indiana: Bobbs-Merrill, 1965.

2/4:12 McCollum, John I., ed. *The Restoration Stage.* (Houghton Mifflin Research Series 8.) Boston: Houghton Mifflin, 1961. Selections from Dryden's criticism.

2/4:13 Mirizzi, Piero, ed. *John Dryden: Saggi critici.* Scelta, introd. e note. (Biblioteca Italiana di Testi Inglesi 14.) Bari: Adriatica Editrice, 1968.

*2/4:14 Monk, Samuel Holt, and A. E. Wallace Maurer, eds.; Vinton A. Dearing, textual ed. *The Works of John Dryden.* 17: *Prose 1668-1691: An Essay of Dramatick Poesie and Shorter Works.* Assoc. eds. R. V. LeClercq and Maxmillian E. Novak. With Commentary and Textual Notes. Berkeley, Los Angeles: University of California Press, 1971. *See* Phillip Harth, *PQ* 51:672-74; John R. Clark, *SCN* 31:3, Hoyt Trowbridge, *MP* 72:197-202; Robert D. Hume, *Scriblerian* 5:32-33.

2/4:15 Rajan, B., and A. G. George, eds. "John Dryden." *Makers of Literary Criticism.* 1:179-242. (Literary Perspectives 4.) New York: Asia, 1965. *Of Dramatic Poesy*; Preface to *Fables, Ancient and Modern.*

*2/4:16 Ward, Charles E., ed. *The Letters of John Dryden, with Letters Addressed to Him.* Durham, N.C.: Duke University Press, 1942. Reprinted New York: AMS Press, 1965. *See* George R. Noyes, *JEGP* 43: 124-27; Hugh Macdonald, *RES* 19:308-09; Louis Bredvold, *PQ* 22:157; Rae Blanchard, *MLN* 59:200-01. *See also* item 3:98.

*2/4:17 Watson, George, ed. *Of Dramatic Poesy and Other Critical Essays.* 2 vols. (Everyman's Library 568-69.) New York: E. P. Dutton; London: J. M. Dent, 1962. *See TLS* 8 June 1962, p. 430. Modernized text, using first eds.

Individual Works

2/4:18 Arnold, Thomas, ed. *An Essay of Dramatic Poesy* [1889]. 3rd ed. Oxford: At the Clarendon Press, 1903.

2/4:19 Davies, Godfrey, introd. *His Majesties Declaration Defended (1681).* (ARS 23.) Los Angeles: Clark Memorial Library, University of California, 1950. A facsimile ed.

2/4:20 Enright, D. J., and Ernst de Chickera, eds. "John Dryden: An Essay of Dramatic Poesy." *English Critical Texts 16th Century to 20th Century*, pp. 50-110. London: Oxford University Press, 1962.

2/4:21 LeClercq, Richard V. "John Dryden: *An Essay of Dramatic Poesy.*" *DA* 29(1968):1901A(U.C.L.A.). An ed. of the 1668 text with notes. *See* items 7:22, 7:274.

2/4:22 Leech, Clifford, ed. "Preface" to *Troilus and Cressida. Shakespeare: The Tragedies: A Collection of Critical Essays*, pp. 1-9. Chicago: Chicago University Press, 1965.

2/4:23 Novak, Maximillian E., introd. *Notes and Observations on The Empress of Morocco (1674). The Empress of Morocco and Its Critics: Settle, Dryden, Shadwell, Crowne, Duffet.* (ARS Spec. Pubs.) Los Angeles: Clark Memorial Library, University of California, 1968. A facsimile ed.

2/4:24 *Of Dramatick Poesie: An Essay 1668; Preceded by a Dialogue on Poetic Drama by T. S. Eliot.* London: Frederick Etchells and Hugh Macdonald, 1928. A facsimile ed.

2/4:25 *Of Dramatic Poesie (1668)*. Menston: Scolar Press, 1969. A
   facsimile ed. of the British Museum copy of Wing D2327/Macdonald
   127a.
2/4:26 Smith, David Nichol, ed. *Essay of Dramatic Poesy*. With an Introd. and Notes. London: Blackie, 1900.

See also item 7:67.

2/5. DRAMATIC WORKS

Collected Works

*2/5:1 Beaurline, L. A., and Fredson Bowers, eds. *John Dryden: Four
   Comedies*. With an Introd. and Notes. (Curtain Playwrights.) Chicago, London: University of Chicago Press, 1967. *Secret Love*; *Sir
   Martin Mar-All*; *An Evening's Love*; *Marriage A-la-Mode*. *See* Robert
   Folkenflik, *SCN* 27:28; John Holloway, *Spectator* 220:669-70; Philip Roberts, *NQ* 16:393-94; Phillip Harth, *MP* 67:379-82; *PQ* 47:370-
   71; *YWES* 48:135-36, 235-36.
*2/5:2 ———, eds. *John Dryden: Four Tragedies*. With an Introd. and
   Notes. (Curtain Playwrights.) Chicago, London: University of Chicago Press, 1967. *The Indian Emperour*; *Aureng-Zebe*; *All for Love*;
   Don Sebastian.
2/5:3 Bentley, Gerald Eades, ed. *The Development of English Drama:
   An Anthology*. New York: Appleton-Century-Crofts, [1950]. *The Indian Queen*; *All for Love*.
*2/5:4 Loftis, John, ed.; Vinton A. Dearing, textual ed. *The Works
   of John Dryden*. 9: *Plays: The Indian Emperour; Secret Love; Sir
   Martin Mar-All*. With Commentary and Textual Notes. Berkeley, Los
   Angeles: University of California Press, 1966. *See* Arthur C.
   Kirsch, *PQ* 46:340-41; Pierre Legouis, *EA* 22:193-94; William Myers,
   RES 23:357-60.
*2/5:5 Novak, Maximillian E., ed.; George Robert Guffey, textual ed.
   The Works of John Dryden. 10: *Plays: The Tempest; Tyrannick Love;
   An Evening's Love*. With Commentary and Textual Notes. Berkeley,
   Los Angeles: University of California Press, 1970. *See* Eric Roth-
   stein, *ECS* 5:608-14; Arthur C. Kirsch, *PQ* 50:426-27; William
   Myers, *RES* 23:357-60, *TLS* 30 July 1971, p. 916.
2/5:6 Noyes, George R., ed. *Selected Dramas of John Dryden with The
   Rehearsal*. With "Dryden as Dramatist," pp. ix-lv. Chicago, New
   York: Scott, Foresman, 1910. *The Conquest of Granada*, pts. I and
   II; *Marriage A-la-Mode*; *All for Love*; *The Spanish Fryar*.
2/5:7 Saintsbury, George, ed. *John Dryden*. With an Introd. and Notes.
   2 vols. (The Mermaid Series.) London: Unwin, [192-]. *The Conquest
   of Granada*; *Marriage A-la-Mode*; *Aureng-Zebe*; *The Spanish Fryar*;
   Albion and Albanius; *Don Sebastian*.
2/5:8 ———, ed. *Plays*. With an Introd. [reprinted in *A Saintsbury
   Miscellany*, pp. 74-88. New York: Oxford University Press, 1947].
   London, New York, 1904. Reprinted as *John Dryden (Three Plays)*.
   (Mermaid Dramabook.) New York: Hill and Wang, 1957. *The Conquest
   of Granada*, I and II; *Marriage A-la-Mode*; *Aureng-Zebe*.
*2/5:9 Smith, John Harrington, and Dougald MacMillan, eds.; Vinton
   A. Dearing, textual ed. *The Works of John Dryden*. 8: *Plays: The
   Wild Gallant, The Rival Ladies, The Indian Queen*. Assoc. eds.
   Samuel Holt Monk and Earl Miner. With Commentary and Textual
   Notes. Berkeley, Los Angeles: University of California Press,
   1962. *See* V. de Sola Pinto, *PQ* 42:342-44; William Myers, *RES* 23:

357-60; *TLS* 22 March 1963, p. 196; Clarence Tracy, *QQ* 70:286-87. *See also* item 5/13:22.

2/5:10 Stroup, Thomas B., and Arthur L. Cooke, eds. *Oedipus: A Tragedy. The Works of Nathaniel Lee.* 1: 369-449. *The Duke of Guise.* 2: 389-476. New Brunswick, N.J.: Scarecrow Press, 1954-55. Old spelling texts.

2/5:11 Strunk, William, Jr., ed. *"All for Love" and "The Spanish Fryar."* (The Belles-Lettres Series Section 3 The English Drama.) Boston, London: Heath, 1911.

2/5:12 Summers, Montague, ed. *Dryden: The Dramatic Works.* With Notes, Introd. and Chronology. 6 vols. London: The Nonesuch Press, 1931-32. *See TLS* 4 February 1932; William S. Clark, ibid., 12 May 1932, p. 351; Montague Summers, ibid., 19 May 1932, p. 368; John Hayward, *Criterion* 11:519-23; Bonamy Dobrée, *Spectator* 24 September 1932, pp. 376-77; E. S. de Beer, *RES* 8:453-56; ibid., 9:203; Montague Summers, ibid., 9:202. *See also* item 8/1:184.

Individual Works

2/5:13 *All for Love (1678).* Menston: Scolar Press, 1969. A facsimile ed.

2/5:14 Arundell, Dennis, introd. *King Arthur, or The British Worthy: A Dramatic Opera as Performed at the New Theatre Cambridge 14-18 February, 1928, with the Alterations Adopted by Henry Purcell.* Cambridge: At the University Press, 1928.

2/5:15 Brossman, Sidney W. "A Critical Edition of Dryden's *Cleomenes, The Spartan Heroe.*" Diss. U.S.C., 1955.

2/5:16 Clark, William A., Jr., ed. *All for Love* [1678]. San Francisco: Nash, 1929. Facsimile ed. with notes of the first ed.

2/5:17 Crinò, Anna Maria, ed. *Aureng-Zebe.* Verona: Fiorini, 1971.

2/5:18 Davison, Dennis, ed. *Marriage à la Mode (1672). Restoration Comedies*, pp. 135-215. With an Introd. London, Oxford, New York: Oxford University Press, 1970. Modernized text.

2/5:19 Dobrée, Bonamy, ed. *All for Love. Five Restoration Tragedies*, pp. 1-107. With an Introd. (World's Classics 313.) London, New York, Toronto: Oxford University Press, 1928.

2/5:20 ———, ed. *Aureng-Zebe. Five Heroic Plays*, pp. 317-417. With an Introd. (World's Classics 576.) London, New York: Oxford University Press, 1960.

2/5:21 Enck, John J., ed. *All for Love; or, The World Well Lost.* (Crofts Classics.) New York: Appleton-Century-Crofts, 1966.

2/5:22 Fiorino, Salvatore, ed. *John Dryden: The Mock Astrologer, Fonti e Pseudo-Fonti.* Palermo: Bassi, 1959.

2/5:23 Griffith, Benjamin W., Jr., ed. *All for Love.* New York: Barron, 1960.

2/5:24 Guffey, George R., introd. *After "The Tempest": "The Tempest, or The Enchanted Island" (1670); "The Tempest, or The Enchanted Island" (1674); "The Mock-Tempest: or The Enchanted Castle" (1675): "The Tempest. An Opera" (1756).* (ARS Spec. Pubs.) Los Angeles: Clark Memorial Library, University of California, 1969. A facsimile ed.

2/5:25 *The Indian Emperor, 1667.* Menston: Scolar Press, 1971. A facsimile ed.

*2/5:26 Kaufmann, R. J., ed. *All for Love.* San Francisco: Chandler, 1962. With an Introd. ("On the Poetics of Terminal Tragedy: Dryden's *All for Love*") reprinted in [Critical Essays]:86-94.

2/5:27 Kilbourne, Frederick W., ed. *The Tempest (The Text of the Folio of 1623 with that as revised finally by John Dryden in his Second Edition of 1676)*. (The Bankside-Restoration Shakespeare.) New York: Shakespeare Society of New York, 1908.

2/5:28 Link, Frederick M., ed. *Aureng-Zebe*. (RRestDS.) Lincoln: University of Nebraska Press, 1971.

2/5:29 Smith, Francis A., ed. *Anthony and Cleopatra (The Text of the Folio of 1623, with That of All for Love. . . .)*. New York: Shakespeare Society, 1908.

2/5:30 Spencer, Christopher, ed. *The Tempest, or The Enchanted Island (1674)*. *Five Restoration Adaptations of Shakespeare*, pp. 109-99. With an Introd. and Textual Notes. Urbana: University of Illinois Press, 1965. *See YWES* 46:127.

2/5:31 Summers, Montague, ed. *The Tempest; or, The Enchanted Island. Shakespeare Adaptations*, pp. 1-103. With a lengthy Introd. London: J. Cape, 1922. Reprinted New York: Blom, 1966.

2/5:32 Sutherland, James R., ed. *Marriage à la Mode*. With an Introd., Notes and Glossary. London: J. M. Dent, 1934.

2/5:33 *The Tempest (1670)*. London: Cornmarket Press, 1969. A facsimile ed.

2/5:34 *Troilus and Cressida, 1679*. London: Cornmarket Press, 1969.

2/5:35 Vickery, Willis, ed. *The Tempest, A Comedy by William Shakespeare (Reprinted from the Folio of 1623) together with the Text Revised and Rewritten by John Dryden and William D'Avenant*. Cleveland: The Rowfant Club, 1911.

2/5:36 Vieth, David M., ed. *All for Love*. (RRestDS.) Lincoln: University of Nebraska Press, 1972.

2/5:37 Waith, Eugene M., ed. *All for Love. Restoration Drama*. Preface by John Gassner. Toronto, New York: Bantam, 1968.

2/5:38 Ward, A. W., ed. *The Spanish Fryar. Representative English Comedies*, eds., Charles Mills Gayley and Alwin Thaler. 4: *Dryden and His Contemporaries: Cowley to Farquhar*, pp. 133-240. New York, London: Macmillan, 1936. Reprinted New York: AMS Press, 1969. Modernized text.

2/5:39 Wilson, John Harold, ed. *All for Love; or, The World Well Lost (1678)*. *Six Restoration Plays*, pp. 169-243. (Riverside Editions.) Boston: Houghton Mifflin, 1959.

3. Biography

3:1 Adams, Henry Hitch. "A Note on the Date of a Dryden Letter." *MLN* 64(1949):528-31. Ward #25, to Walsh.

3:2 Albraugh, Ralph M. "Dryden's Literary Relationships, 1689-1700." *OSU-ADD* 56(1947-48):173-78. Doubts whether Dryden held court at Will's Coffee House as has been suggested by Spence (4:376) and Johnson (4:250); identifies those with whom Dryden would have been friendly at this time.

3:3 Allen, Robert J. *The Clubs of Augustan London*. Cambridge, Mass.: Harvard University Press, 1933. Discusses Dryden at Will's Coffee House, the attacks of the Rota on Dryden, the Kit-Cat Club and Dryden's funeral.

3:4 ———. "Two Wycherley Letters." *TLS* 18 April 1935, p. 257. Reference to Dryden's disapproval of Rymer.

3:5 Allen, T. "The Kit-Cat Club and the Theatre." *RES* 7(1931):56-61. Dryden's funeral.

3:6 Alssid, Michael W. *Thomas Shadwell*. New York: Twayne, 1967.

3:7 Archer, Stanley. "A Dryden Record." *NQ* 211(1966):264-65. A possible reference to John Dryden, Jr.

3:8 ———. "John Dryden and the Earl of Dorset." *DA* 26(1965):1018-19(Miss.). Patronage and Dryden's relationship with his chief patron.

3:9 ———. "Some Early References to Dryden." *NQ* 17(1970):417-18.

3:10 ———. "Two Dryden Anecdotes." *NQ* 20(1973):177-78. Concerns Dryden's relations with the Earl of Dorset.

3:11 Barker, G. F. Russell. *Memoir of Sir Richard Busby, D. D. (1606-1695)*. London: Lawrence and Bullen, 1895.

3:12 Barnard, John. "The Dates of Six Dryden Letters." *PQ* 42(1963): 396-403. Ward #32-37. *See* item 3:21.

3:13 ———. "Dryden, Tonson, and Subscriptions for the 1697 *Virgil*." *PBSA* 57(1963):129-51. Dryden's profit from the translation is evidence of the increased importance of the bookseller and indicative of a movement away from the reliance on patrons.

3:14 Barron, M. "Dryden the Catholic." *Dominicana* 24(1939):111-15.

3:15 Bayley, A. R. "Dryden's Portraits." *NQ* (10th ser.) 1(1904):435. *See* correspondence, ibid., 2(1904):18; ibid., 3(1905):114; ibid., 4(1905):389. The Kneller portraits.

3:16 Bennett, J. A. W. "Dryden and All Souls." *MLN* 52(1937):115-16. *See* items 3:76, 3:81, 3:104.

3:17 Birrell, T. A. "Dryden's Library." *NQ* 203(1958):409.

3:18 ———. "James Maurus Corker and Dryden's Conversion." *ES* 54 (1973)461-68.

3:19 ———. "John Dryden's Purchases at Two Book Auctions, 1680 and 1682." *ES* 42(1961):193-217. *See* James M. Osborn, *PQ* 41:580.

3:20 Boddy, Margaret. "Contemporary Allusions in Lauderdale's *Aeneid*." *NQ* 9(1962):386-88. *See* item 6/2:63.

3:21 ———. "Dryden-Lauderdale Relationships. Some Bibliographical Notes and a Suggestion." *PQ* 42(1963):267-72. Redates six of Dryden's letters (Ward #32-#37). *See* item 3:12.

3:22 Borgman, Albert S. *Thomas Shadwell: His Life and Comedies*. New York: New York University Press, 1928.

3:23 Bowers, Fredson. "Dryden As Laureate: The Cancel Leaf in 'King Arthur'." *TLS* 10 April 1953, p. 244. *See* item 3:210.

3:24 Boyce, Benjamin. *Tom Brown of Facetious Memory: Grub Street in the Age of Dryden*. (Harvard Studies in English 21.) Cambridge, Mass.: Harvard University Press, 1939.

3:25 Bredvold, Louis I. "Dryden and the University of Oxford." *MLN* 46(1931):218-24. *See* items 3:16, 3:81.

3:26 ———. "Dryden, Hobbes, and the Royal Society." *MP* 25(1928):417-38. Reprinted in [Swedenberg]:314-40. *See* R. S. Crane, *PQ* 8:188-89.

3:27 ———. "Notes on John Dryden's Pension." *MP* 30(1933):267-74.

3:28 Brett-Smith, H. F. B. "Introduction." *The Dramatic Works of Sir George Etherege*, pp. xi-lxxxiii. Oxford: Basil Blackwell, [1927]. Reprinted St. Clair Shores, Mich.: Scholarly Press, 1971.

3:29 Broadus, E. K. "The Date of Dryden's Appointment as Poet-Laureate." *Nation* 98(1941):751-52.

3:30 ———. "The Laureateship." *London Mercury* 22(1930):127-36.

3:31 ———. *The Laureateship: A Study of the Office of Poet Laureate in England with Some Account of the Poets*. Oxford: Clarendon Press, 1921.

3:32   Brooks, H. F. "The Complete Works of John Oldham (1653-83): Edited with an Introduction, Biographical and Critical, Textual Apparatus, and Explanatory Notes." *UO-AD* 12(1940):71-78.

3:33   Brown, Frank C. *Elkanah Settle: His Life and Works*. Chicago: University of Chicago Press, 1910.

3:34   Brown, Gillian Fansler. "'The Session of the Poets to the Tune of Cock Lawrel': Playhouse Evidence for Composition Date of 1664." *RECTR* 13,i(1974):19-26, 62. An attack on Dryden and *The Wild Gallant*.

3:35   Bryant, Arthur, *King Charles II*. London, New York, Toronto: Longmans, Green, 1932.

3:36   Burghclere, Lady Winifred. *George Villiers, Second Duke of Buckingham, 1628-1687*. London: Murray, 1903. Reprinted New York, London: Kennikat Press, 1971.

3:37   Calder-Marshall, Arthur. "Dryden and the Rise of Modern Publishing." *History Today* 2(1952):641-45.

3:38   Cameron, William J. "John Dryden and Henry Heveningham." *NQ* 4 (1957):199-203. The Knights of the Toast.

3:39   Carnie, R. H. "Lord Hailes's Notes on Johnson's 'Lives of the Poets'." *NQ* 3(1956):73-75, 106-08.

3:40   Casey, Lucian T. "The Biographies and Biographers of John Dryden." Diss. Niagara, 1945.

3:41   Chesterton, G. K. "The Don and the Cavalier." *The Well and the Shallows*, pp. 152-59. London: Sheed and Ward, 1935. *See* item 3:94.

3:42   Churchill, Winston S. *Marlborough: His Life and Times: 1688-1702*. Vol. 2. New York: Scribner, 1933. Dryden's hand in James II's memoirs.

3:43   Clapp, Sarah Lewis Carol, ed. *Jacob Tonson in Ten Letters By and About Him*. Austin: The University of Texas Press, 1948.

3:44   Clark, William S. "Dryden's Relations with Howard and Orrery." *MLN* 42(1927):16-20. *See* items 3:194, 8/3:13.

3:45   Colby, Elbridge. "John Dryden." *English Catholic Poets: Chaucer to Dryden*, pp. 176-90. Milwaukee: Bruce, 1936. Reprinted (Essay Index Reprint Series) Freeport, New York: Books for Libraries Press, 1967.

3:46   Collinson, Joseph. "Vanishing London." *NQ* (8th ser.) 10(1896): 154. Dryden's house at 16 Fetter Lane. *See* W. F. Prideaux, ibid., 212-13; Ralph Thomas, ibid., 364; W. F. Prideaux, ibid., 525-26.

3:47   Connely, Willard. *Brawny Wycherly: First Master in English Modern Comedy*. New York: Scribner, 1930.

3:48   Couper, Ramsay W. "John Dryden's First Funeral." *Athenaeum* 4005 (30 July 1904):145-46. *See* reply, W. J. Harvey, ibid., 4009 (27 August 1904):271.

3:49   Cunningham, Robert N. *Peter Anthony Motteux 1663-1718: A Biographical Study*. Oxford: At the Clarendon Press, 1933.

3:50   Cushing, Harvey. "Dr. Garth: The Kit-Kat Poet." *Bulletin of the Johns Hopkins Hospital* 17(1906):1-17. On Dryden's funeral.

3:51   Davies, Godfrey. "Charles II in 1660." *HLQ* 19(1956):245-75. References to Dryden as Poet Laureate and Historiographer.

3:52   de Beer, E. S. "Dryden's Anti-Clericalism." *NQ* 179(1940):254-57. *See* item 8/9:2.

3:53   Dick, Hugh G. "The Dryden Almanac Story: A Further Analogue." *PQ* 18(1939):222-24.

3:54   Dodds, John W. *Thomas Southerne Dramatist*. (Yale Studies in English 81.) New Haven: Yale University Press, 1933.

3:55   "Dryden's Conversion: The Struggle for Faith." *TLS* 17 April 1937, p. 281-82.

3:56   "Eighteenth Century Reminiscences." *QR* 185(1897):94-116. Rev. art.

3:57   Empson, William. "Dryden's Apparent Scepticism." *EIC* 20(1970): 172-81. Initiates a debate on a dead issue: the sincerity of Dryden's conversion. *See* correspondence, Phillip Harth, ibid., 446-50; Robert D. Hume, ibid., 492-95; William Empson, ibid., 21 (1971):111-15; Earl Miner, ibid., 410-11. *See also* item 5/7:6.

3:58   Esdaile, K. A. "Cousin to Pepys and Dryden: A Note on the Works of Mrs. Elizabeth Creed of Tichmarsh." *Burlington Magazine* 77 (1940):24-27.

3:59   Farley-Hills, David, ed. *Rochester: The Critical Heritage*. London: Routledge, 1972. Snippets from Dryden about Rochester.

3:60   Fletcher, Edward G. "A Dryden Anecdote." *MLN* 50(1935):366.

3:61   Freedman, Morris. "Dryden's 'Memorable Visit' to Milton." *HLQ* 18(1955):99-108.

3:62   ———. "Dryden's Reported Reaction to *Paradise Lost*." *NQ* 5 (1958):14-16.

3:63   Freeman, Phyllis. "William Walsh and Dryden: Recently Recovered Letters." *RES* 24(1948):195-202.

3:64   ———. "William Walsh's Letters and Poems in MS Malone 9." *Bodleian Quarterly Record* 7(1934):503-07. *See* item 2/4:16.

3:65   Geduld, Harry M. "Dryden's Publisher." *Prince of Publishers: A Study of the Work and Career of Jacob Tonson*, pp. 51-86. Bloomington: Indiana University Press, 1969.

3:66   "George Villiers, Second Duke of Buckingham." *QR* 187(1898):86-111. Rev. art.

3:67   Glazier, George E. *John Dryden's Associations with Northamptonshire: A Tercentenary Recapitulation*. Northampton: [n.p.], 1931.

3:68   Gomme, G. J. L. "Elizabeth Dryden and Dr. Busby." *TLS* 10 May 1941, p. 227.

3:69   Goodison, J. W. "Cambridge Portraits II: Later Seventeenth and Eighteenth Centuries." *Connoisseur* 140(1957):231-36.

3:70   Gosse, Edmund. *Life of William Congreve* [1888]. (Great Writers.) New York: Scribner, 1924.

3:71   Gray, W. Forbes. "John Dryden (1670-89)." *The Poets Laureate of England: Their History and Their Odes*, pp. 55-78. New York: E. P. Dutton, 1915.

3:72   Greene, Graham. *British Dramatists.* London: William Collins, 1942. Color reproduction of the James Maubert portrait of Dryden.

3:73   Gumbley, W. "Dryden's Dominican Son." *Blackfriars* 32(1951):263-68.

3:74   Ham, Roswell G. "The Authorship of *A Session of the Poets* (1677)." *RES* 9(1933):319-22. Claims authorship of the poem for Elkanah Settle. *See* D. M. Walmsey, *RES* 8:484-87.

3:75   ———. "The Date of Dryden's Birth." *TLS* 20 August 1931, p. 633. *See* correspondence, Duncan MacNaughton, ibid., 3 September 1931, p. 664; Roswell G. Ham, ibid., 17 September 1931, p. 706; Duncan MacNaughton, ibid., 24 September 1931, p. 730; Edward G. Fletcher, ibid., 21 November, p. 894.

3:76   ———. "Dryden and the Colleges." *MLN* 49(1934):324-32. The post at Oxford. *See* items 3:16, 3:25, 3:81, 3:104.

3:77 ———. "Dryden as Historiographer-Royal: The Authorship of *His Majesties Declaration Defended*, 1681." *RES* 11(1935):284-98. Reprinted in [Swedenberg]:135-53.

3:78 ———. "Dryden Versus Settle." *MP* 25(1928):409-16. *See* items 3: 74, 3:205.

3:79 ———. *Otway and Lee: Biography from a Baroque Age*. New Haven: Yale University Press; London: Oxford University Press, 1931.

3:80 ———. "Shadwell and 'The Tory Poets'." *NQ* 152(1927):6-8.

3:81 ———. "Some Uncollected Verse of John Dryden." *London Mercury* 21(1930):421-26. *See* items 3:16, 3:25.

3:82 Hamer, Douglas. "Some Spenser Problems." *NQ* 180(1941):206-09. Sir Erasmus Dryden and Spenser.

3:83 Hamilton, Walter. "John Dryden." *The Poets Laureate of England, Being a History of the Office of Poet Laureate* [1879], pp. 81-111. Reprinted New York: Burt Franklin, 1970. Accuses Dryden of being licentious and bigoted.

3:84 Handasyde, Elizabeth. *Granville the Polite: The Life of George Granville Lord Lansdowne, 1666-1735*. London: Oxford University Press, 1933.

3:85 Harbage, Alfred. *Sir William Davenant Poet Venturer 1606-1668*. Philadelphia: University of Pennsylvania Press, 1935.

3:86 Harris, Brice. *Charles Sackville Sixth Earl of Dorset: Patron and Poet of the Restoration*. (Illinois Studies in Language and Literature 26, iii-iv.) Urbana: University of Illinois Press, 1940.

3:87 Harvey, William J. "John Dryden's First Funeral." *Athenaeum* 4017(22 October 1904):271.

3:88 Havens, Raymond D. "Dryden's Visit to Milton." *RES* 1(1925):348-49.

3:89 Hayward, John, ed. "Introduction." *Collected Works of John Wilmot Earl of Rochester*, pp. xix-1. London: The Nonesuch Press, 1926.

3:90 Higbame, Frederick T. "Dryden's House in Soho." *NQ* (9th ser.) 8(1901):262. 43 Gerrard Street.

3:91 Hinchman, Walter S., and Francis B. Gummere. "John Dryden." *Lives of Great English Writers from Chaucer to Browning*, pp. 128-39. Boston, New York: Houghton Mifflin, 1908.

3:92 Hodges, John C., ed. *William Congreve: Letters & Documents*. New York: Harcourt, Brace, 1964.

3:93 ———. *William Congreve the Man: A Biography from New Sources*. (The Modern Language Association of America General Series 9.) New York: Modern Language Association of America; London: Oxford University Press, 1941.

3:94 Hollis, Christopher. *Dryden*. London: Duckworth, 1933. *See* Louis I. Bredvold, *PQ* 13:117-18. *See also* item 3:41.

3:95 ———. "Dryden's Conversion." *Tablet* 177(1941):470-71.

3:96 Hooker, Edward Niles "The Dryden Almanac-Story." *PQ* 13(1934):295.

3:97 Hopkins, Kenneth. *The Poets Laureate*. London: The Bodley Head, 1954.

*3:98 Howarth, R. G. "Dryden's Letters." *ESA* 1(1958):184-94. *See* item 2/4:16.

3:99 Howland, Frances Louis (Morse)/Kenyon West (pseud.). "John Dryden." *The Laureates of England from Ben Jonson to Alfred Tennyson*, pp. 31-51. New York, London: Stokes, [1895]. An anecdotal survey.

3:100   Irvine, Maurice, "Identification of Characters in Mulgrave's *Essay Upon Satire*." *SP* 34:(1937):533-51.

3:101   Jordan, Arnold. "The Conversion of John Dryden." *Month* 158 (1931):18-25.

3:102   Leech, Clifford. "Thomas Southerne and *On the Poets and Actors in King Charles II's Reign*." *NQ* 164(1933):401-03.

3:103   Legouis, Pierre. "A Journal from Parnassus." *EA* 2(1938):151-55. Rev. art. *See* item 3:116.

3:104   ———. "Dryden and Eton." *MLN* 52(1937):111-15. *See* items 3:16, 3:25, 3:76, 3:81.

3:105   ———. "Dryden's Letter to 'Ormond'." *MLN* 66(1951):88-92. Ward #56.

3:106   Leo, Brother. "How Dryden Became a Catholic." *CathW* 105(1917): 483-94.

3:107   Lloyd, Claude. "John Dryden and the Royal Society." *PMLA* 45 (1930):967-76. *See* correspondence, Ella Theodora Riske, ibid., 46 (1931):951-54; Louis I. Bredvold, ibid., 954-57; Thomas B. Stroup, ibid., 957-61; Claude Lloyd, ibid., 961-62. *See also* Louis I. Bredvold, *PQ* 10:198.

3:108   Logan, Terence P. "John Dennis's *Select Works, 1718, 1721*." *PBSA* 65(1971):155-56. Dennis's letters to Dryden and others.

3:109   Love, Harold. "The Satirised Characters in *Poeta De Tristibus*." *PQ* 47(1968):547-62. A 1682 attack on Dryden and others.

3:110   Lubbock, Alan. *The Character of John Dryden*. London: The Hogarth Press, 1925.

3:111   Lynch, Kathleen M. *A Congreve Gallery*. Cambridge, Mass.: Harvard University Press, 1951.

3:112   ———. "Dryden and Tonson." *Jacob Tonson: Kit-Cat Publisher*, pp. 17-36. Knoxville: University of Tennessee Press, 1971.

3:113   Macaulay, Thomas Babington Macaulay, 1st Baron. "Dryden." *The History of England*, ed. Charles Harding Firth. 2:850-52. London: Macmillan, 1914. Dryden was an opportunist and a hypocrite in religion and politics.

*3:114   Macdonald, Hugh. "The Attacks on Dryden." *Essays and Studies* 21(1936):41-74. Reprinted [Swedenberg]:22-53.

3:115   ———. "'A Journal from Parnassus': An Unpublished Satire on Dryden." *TLS* 17 October 1936, p. 844.

3:116   ———, introd. *A Journal from Parnassus Now Printed from A Manuscript circa 1688*. London: P. J. Dobell, 1937. *See* item 3:103.

3:117   McKeithan, D. M. "The Authorship of 'The Medal of John Bayes'." *Studies in English* (University of Texas) 12(1932):92-97. Attributed to Shadwell.

3:118   Miller, C. William. "Henry Herringman, Restoration Bookseller-Publisher." *PBSA* 42(1948):292-306.

3:119   Mizener, Arthur. "George Villiers, Second Duke of Buckingham." Diss. Princeton, 1934.

3:120   Mundy, Percy Dryden. "The Baptism of John Dryden." *NQ* 173(1937): 225 and 184(1943):286, 352.

3:121   ———. "The Brothers and Sisters of John Dryden, the Poet." *NQ* 193(1948):120-24, 186, 217.

3:122   ———. "Cope, Dryden, Throckmorton, Oxenbridge and Allied Puritan Families." *NQ* 180(1941):182-83.

3:123   ———. "The Cumberland Ancestry of John Dryden." *NQ* 180(1941): 290-91, 409.

3:124   ——. "Dryden and Swift." *NQ* (11th ser.) 11(1915):257-58. *See* item 3:125.

3:125   ——. "Dryden and Swift: Their Relationship." *NQ* 147(1924): 243-44, 279-80, 334. Corrects item 3:124.

3:126   ——. "Dryden's and Swift's Snuff-Boxes." *NQ* 197(1952):62.

3:127   ——. "Dryden Baronetcy (Extinct 1770)—Additions to 'G. E. C.'" *NQ* 198(1953):435-36.

3:128   ——. "The Dryden-Swift Relationship." *NQ* 193(1948):470-74. Includes a Dryden family pedigree.

3:129   ——. "Dryden's Dominican Son—Sir Erasmus Henry Dryden, 5th Bart." *NQ* 196(1951):442-43. *See* item 3:73.

3:130   ——. "Dryden's Hermitage." *NQ* 174(1938):102.

3:131   ——. "Dryden's Sisters." *NQ* (10th ser.) 3(1950):377. *See* correspondence, Leopold A. Violer, ibid., 498.

3:132   ——. "Drydon Leach, 1708." *NQ* 164(1933):209.

3:133   ——. "Henry Dryden, Goldsmith." *NQ* 193(1948):217.

3:134   ——. "John Dryden's Character." *NQ* 152(1927):152. *See* item 3:159.

3:135   ——. "John Dryden's Widow." *NQ* 1(1954):272. *See* reply, J. B. Whitmore, ibid., 363; Charles A. Toase, ibid., 547.

3:136   ——. "The Pickerings of Aldwincle All Saints, Northants." *NQ* 197(1952):490-92.

3:137   ——. "Portraits of Dryden." *NQ* (11th ser.) 10(1914):28; ibid., 164(1933):423-24; ibid., 165(1933):194; ibid., 170(1396):318-19. *See* correspondence, ibid., 165(1933):33, 160, 377.

3:138   Murrie, Eleanore Boswell. "Chaucer, Dryden and the Laureateship: A Seventeenth-Century Tradition." *RES* 7(1931):337-39.

3:139   Nethercot, Arthur H. *Sir William D'Avenant: Poet Laureate and Playwright-Manager*. Chicago: University of Chicago, 1938. Reprinted with additional notes New York: Russell and Russell, 1967. Chronicles Dryden's early days in London and Davenant's influence on him.

3:140   Nicoll, Allardyce. "Dryden, Howard, and Rochester." *TLS* 13 January 1921, p. 27.

*3:141   Oliver, H. J. *Sir Robert Howard (1626-1698): A Critical Biography*. Durham: Duke University Press, 1963. Views the controversy over rhyme from Howard's point of view.

3:142   Ogg, David. *England in the Reign of Charles II*. 2 vols. Oxford: At the Clarendon Press, 1956.

3:143   Osborn, James M. "Edmond Malone and the Dryden Almanac Story." *PQ* 16(1937):412-14; ibid., 17(1938):84-86.

*3:144   ——. *John Dryden: Some Biographical Facts and Problems*. New York: Columbia University Press, 1940. Rev. ed. Gainesville: University of Florida Press, 1965. *"The Medal of John Bayes"* is reprinted in [Critical Essays]:31-42. *See* Brice Harris, *JEGP* 40:419-23; Geoffrey Tillotson, *MLR* 37:214-16; René Wellek, *MP* 40:104-07; Richard H. Perkinson, *MLQ* 2:650-51; Hugh Macdonald, *RES* 17:482-83; Edward N. Hooker, *MLN* 58:566-67; Philip Roberts, *NQ* 14:239-40.

3:145   ——. "A Lost Portrait of Dryden." *HLQ* 36(1973):341-45. By John Riley.

3:146   ——. "Macdonald's Bibliography of Dryden." *MP* 39(1942):313-19. Reprinted in [Swedenberg]:54-62.

3:147   Parsons, Coleman O. "Dryden's Letter of Attorney." *MLN* 50(1935): 364-65. 14 December 1680.

3:148   Paul, Francis. "John Dryden." *American Catholic Quarterly Review* 42(1917):454-62. *See* item 3:161.

3:149   Paul, H. G. *John Dennis, His Life and Criticism*. New York: Columbia University Press, 1911.

3:150   Perromat, Charles. *William Wycherley sa vie—son oeuvre*. Paris: Librairie Félix Alcan, 1921.

3:151   Perry, Henry Ten Eyck. *The First Duchess of Newcastle and Her Husband as Figures in Literary History*. (Harvard Studies in English 4.) Boston, London: Ginn, 1918. Reprinted New York, London: Johnson Reprint, 1968.

3:152   Pinto, V. de Sola, ed. *Poems by John Wilmot, Earl of Rochester*. With an Introd. Cambridge, Mass.: Harvard University Press; London: Routledge and Kegan Paul, 1953. The Rose Alley affair.

3:153   ———. "Rochester, Dryden, and the Duchess of Portsmouth." *RES* 16(1940):177-78. The Duchess not Rochester was responsible for the Rose Alley affair. *See* item 3:204.

3:154   ———. *Rochester, Portrait of a Restoration Poet*. London: The Bodley Head, 1935.

3:155   ———. *Sir Charles Sedley, 1639-1701: A Study in the Life and Literature of the Restoration*. London: Constable, 1927.

3:156   Praz, Mario. "Poets and Wits of the Restoration." *ES* 10(1928): 41-53.

3:157   Prinz, Johannes. *John Wilmot Earl of Rochester, His Life and Writings*. (Palaestra 154.) Leipzig: Mayer and Müller, 1927.

3:158   ———. *Rochesteriana: Being Some Anecdotes Concerning John Wilmot, Earl of Rochester*. Leipzig: Mayer and Müller, 1926.

3:159   Richardson, Ethel M. *The Lion and the Rose (the Great Howard Story)*. 2:331-42. London: Hutchinson, [1923]. *See* item 3:134.

3:160   Riske, Ella Theodora, Louis I. Bredvold, Thomas B. Stroup, and Claude Lloyd. "Dryden and Waller as Members of the Royal Society." *PMLA* 46(1931):951-62.

3:161   Root, Robert K. "Dryden's Conversion to the Roman Catholic Faith." *PMLA* 22(1907):298-308. *See* item 3:148.

3:162   Roscioni, Gian Carlo. "Sir Robert Howard's 'Skeptical Curiosity'." *MP* 65(1967):53-59. Howard's influence on Dryden.

3:163   Rosenfeld, Sybil, ed. *The Letterbook of Sir George Etherege*. Oxford: At the Clarendon Press, 1928. Letters to, from and about Dryden.

3:164   Rupert-Jones, John A. "Sir Gilbert Pickering, of Titchmarsh." *NQ* (10th ser.) 5(1906):82-84. *See* J. T. Page, ibid., p. 151.

*3:165   Russell, Doris A. "Dryden's Relations with His Critics." *DA* 11(1951):117-18(Columbia).

3:166   S., E. "Dryden's Conversion to Catholicism." *More Books* 13 (1938):437.

3:167   Saillens, Emile. *John Milton: Man, Poet, Polemicist*. Oxford: Blackwell, 1964.

*3:168   Saintsbury, George. *Dryden*. (English Men of Letters.) New York: Harper, 1881. Reprinted New York: AMS Press, 1969. Combines a biography with a survey of Dryden's works.

3:169   Schumacher, Edgar. *Thomas Otway* [1924]. New York: Burt Franklin, 1970.

3:170   Seymour-Smith, Martin. "Dryden." *Poets Through Their Letters*. 1:146-56. London: Constable, 1969.

3:171   Smith, David Nichol. "Edmond Malone." *HLQ* 3(1939):23-36.

3:172   Smith, John Harrington. "Dryden and Buckingham: The Beginnings of the Feud." *MLN* 69(1954):242-45.

3:173   Souers, Philip Webster. *The Matchless Orinda*. (Harvard Studies in English 5.) Cambridge: Harvard University Press, 1931. Katherine Philips.

3:174   Späth, Eberhard. "Dryden als Poeta Laureatus." *Literatur im Dienste der Monarchie*, pp. 195-205. (Erlanger Beiträge zur Sprach- und Kunstwissenschaft 36.) Nürnberg: H. Carl, 1969. *See YWES* 50: 242-43.

3:175   Spencer, Christopher. *Nahum Tate*. (Twayne's English Authors.) New York: Twayne, 1972.

3:176   Stauffer, Donald A. *The Art of Biography in Eighteenth Century England*. Princeton: Princeton University Press; London: Oxford University Press, 1941.

3:177   Steeves, Harrison Ross. "'The Athenian Virtuosi' and the 'Athenian Society'." *MLR* 7(1912):358-71. *The Censure of the Rota*.

3:178   S[tephen], L[eslie]. "John Dryden." *Dictionary of National Biography*. 16:64-75. New York, London: Macmillan, 1888.

3:179   Summers, Montague, ed. *The Complete Works of Thomas Shadwell*. With an Introd. 5 vols. London: Fortune Press, 1927. Reprinted New York: Blom, 1968.

3:180   ———. "John Dryden." *Great Catholics*, ed. Claude Williamson, pp. 204-16. London: Macmillan, 1938.

3:181   ———. "Introduction." *The Complete Works of William Wycherley*. 1:3-64. Soho: The Nonesuch Press, 1924. *See* 4:63-69, 154, 155-60 for poems addressed to Dryden.

3:182   ———. "Memoir of Mrs. Behn." *The Works of Aphra Behn*. 1:xv-lxi. London: Heinemann, 1915.

3:183   Sweney, John R. "Political Attacks on Dryden, 1681-1683." *DA* 29(1968):915A(Wis.).

3:184   ———. "The Religion of Lady Elizabeth Howard Dryden." *NQ* 19 (1972):365.

3:185   Tanner, Lawrence E. "Dryden's Monument in Westminster Abbey." *NQ* 158(1930):191. *See* correspondence, Percy Dryden Mundy, ibid., 1934.

3:186   Taylor, Daniel Crane. *William Congreve*. London: Oxford University Press, 1931. Reprinted New York: Russell and Russell, 1963.

3:187   Thorn-Drury, George, ed. *The Poems of Edmund Waller* [1893]. With an Introd. New York: Greenwood Press, 1968.

*3:188   ———. "Some Notes on Dryden." *RES* 1(1925):79-83, 187-97, 324-30.

3:189   Treadway, Thomas J. "The Religious Sincerity of John Dryden." *Ecclesiastical Review* 85(1931):277-90.

3:190   Turner, W. Arthur. "Milton, Marvell and 'Dradon' at Cromwell's Funeral." *PQ* 28(1949):320-23. Dryden attended the funeral.

3:191   Ward, Charles E. "A Biographical Note on John Dryden." *MLR* 27 (1932):206-10. Dryden's finances.

*3:192   ———. "Challenges to Dryden's Biographer." *John Dryden: Papers Read at a Clark Library Seminar, February 25, 1967*, introd. John Loftis, pp. 1-21. Los Angeles: Clark Memorial Library, University of California, 1967. Reprinted in [Clark Library]:73-91.

*3:193   ———. *The Life of John Dryden*. Chapel Hill: University of North Carolina Press, 1961. *See* James M. Osborn, *PQ* 41:585-86; Aubrey Williams, *YR* 51:615-20; *TLS* 14 September 1963, p. 688; Pierre Legouis, *EA* 17:148-58; V. de Sola Pinto, *MLR* 58:408-11. *See also* item 3:144.

3:194 ———. "Some Notes on Dryden." *RES* 13(1937):297–306. *See* correspondence, W. S. Clark, ibid., 14(1938):330–32. Henley's reference to selling "the serge Bed Mr Dreidon useth." *See also* items 3:44, 8/3:13.

3:195 ———. "An Unpublished Dryden Letter." *TLS* 29 October 1938, p. 700. 1677 letter to Danby.

3:196 ———. "Was John Dryden Collector of Customs?" *MLN* 47(1932): 246–49.

3:197 Wheatley, Henry B. "Dryden's Publishers." *TBS* 11(1909–11):17–38. Herringman and Tonson.

3:198 Whibley, Charles. "The Court Poets." [Cambridge History]:224–52.

3:199 White, Arthur F. *John Crowne: His Life and Dramatic Works.* Cleveland: Western Reserve University Press, 1922.

3:200 Wild, Josef B. *Dryden und die römische Kirche.* Leipzig: Noske, 1928. *See PQ* 8:190.

3:201 W[illiamson], H. R. "Portrait of a Man of Letters: The Career of Mr. John Dryden." *Bookman* (London) 80(1931):239–42.

*3:202 Wilson, John Harold. *The Court Wits of the Restoration.* Princeton: Princeton University Press, 1948. Reprinted New York: Octagon, 1967. Dryden's relationship with the courtier poets of the Restoration court.

3:203 ———. *A Rake and His Times: George Villiers 2nd Duke of Buckingham.* New York: Farrar, Straus and Young, 1954.

3:204 ———. "Rochester, Dryden, and the Rose-Street Affair." *RES* 15 (1939):294–301. *See* item 3:153.

3:205 ———. "Rochester's 'A Session of the Poets'." *RES* 22(1946): 109–16. *See* item 3:78.

3:206 ———, ed. *The Rochester-Savile Letters: 1671–1680.* Columbus, Ohio: Ohio State University Press, 1941. Denies that Rochester was involved in the Rose Alley affair.

3:207 Wise, Thomas J. *A Dryden Library. A Catalogue of Printed Books, Manuscripts, and Autograph Letters by John Dryden.* London: Printed for private circulation only, 1930.

3:208 Woodcock, George. *The Incomparable Aphra.* London: T. V. Boardman, 1948.

3:209 Wright, J. C. *The Poets Laureate from the Earliest Times to the Present.* London, 1896.

3:210 Young, Kenneth. "Dryden As Laureate." *TLS* 8 May 1953, p. 301. *See* item 3:23.

3:211 ———. *John Dryden: A Critical Biography.* London: Sylvan Press, 1954. Reprinted New York: Russell and Russell, 1969. *See* John Harrington Smith, *PQ* 34:285–86; V. de Sola Pinto, *English* 10:190–92; *TLS* 4 February 1956, p. 74; Pierre Legouis, *EA* 9:57–58.

See also items 2/1:11, 2/2:5–6, 2/2:14, 2/2:22, 2/2:24, 4:29–30, 4:43, 4:56, 4:79, 4:104–05, 4:243, 4:250, 4:303, 4:371, 4:348, 4:404, 4: 506, 4:516, 4:520, 4:522, 5/11:13, 5/11:26, 5/12:19, 6/2:78, 7:30, 7:139, 8/6:2, 8/10:18.

4. General Criticism

4:1 Adams, Percy G. "'Harmony of Numbers': Dryden's Alliteration, Consonance, Assonance." *TSLL* 9(1967):333–43.

4:2   Aden, John M. "Dryden and Swift." *NQ* 2(1955):239-40.

4:3   Adrian, Daryl B. "Changing Attitudes Toward the English Puritans, 1660-1740: A Study of Major Non-Dramatic Works." *DA* 28(1968): 4113A(Missouri).

4:4   Alden, Raymond M. *The Rise of Formal Satire in England Under Classical Influence*. (University of Pennsylvania Publications, Series in Philology, Literature and Archaeology 7, ii.) Philadelphia: University of Pennsylvania, 1899.

4:5   Allen, John D. *Quantitative Studies in Prosody*. Johnson City, Tenn.: East Tennessee State University Press, 1968.

4:6   Allen, Robert J. "Pope and the Sister Arts." [Clifford]:78-88.

4:7   Alvarez, A. "Public Poet." *New Statesman* 57(3 January 1959):18-19. Rev. art. *See* item 2/2:18.

*4:8   Amarasinghe, Upali. *Dryden and Pope in the Early Nineteenth Century: A Study of Changing Literary Taste, 1800-1830*. Cambridge: Cambridge University Press, 1962. *See* Pierre Legouis, *EA* 17:155-56.

4:9   Anselment, Raymond A. "Satiric Strategy in Marvell's *The Rehearsal Transpros'd*." *MP* 68(1970):137-50.

4:10   Anthony, Geraldine M. "Divine Imagery in Dryden's Lyric Poetry." Diss. St. John's, 1963.

4:11   Archer, Stanley. "A Dryden Critic of the Romantic Period." *SCB* 33(1973):192-93. Thomas Green.

4:12   Arnold, Matthew. *The Complete Prose Works*, ed. R. H. Super. 10 vols. Ann Arbor: University of Michigan Press, 1960-74. Comments on the quality of Dryden's verse.

4:13   Arthos, John. *The Language of Natural Description in Eighteenth-Century Poetry*. (University of Michigan Publications Language and Literature 24.) Ann Arbor: University of Michigan Press, 1949.

4:14   Artz, Frederick B. *From the Renaissance to Romanticism: Trends in Style in Art, Literature, and Music, 1300-1830*. Chicago: University of Chicago Press, 1962. *See* Jean H. Hagstrum, *PQ* 42:314-15.

4:15   Ashley, Maurice. *England in the Seventeenth Century*. Baltimore, Maryland: Penguin, 1952.

4:16   Atkins, George D. "Dryden and the Clergy." *DAI* 30(1970):4396A (Va.).

4:17   Bady, David M. "The Exact Balance of True Virtue: John Dryden and the Tradition of Epideictic Comparison." *DAI* 33(1973):5712A-13A(Columbia). *See* item 4:178.

4:18   Baker, Herschel. *The Wars of Truth*. Cambridge, Mass.: Harvard University Press, 1952.

4:19   Baker, Van R. "Dryden's Military Imagery." *DAI* 32(1971):3290A (Columbia).

4:20   Banks, Theodore Howard, Jr. "Introduction." *The Poetical Works of Sir John Denham*, pp. 1-57. New Haven: Yale University Press, 1928.

4:21   Bate, Walter Jackson. *The Burden of the Past and the English Poet*. Cambridge, Mass.: Harvard University Press, 1970.

4:22   Bateson, F. W. *English Poetry and the English Language: An Experiment in Literary History*. Oxford: At the Clarendon Press, 1934. Reprinted New York: Russell and Russell, 1961.

4:23   ——. *A Guide to English Literature*. Rev. ed. Chicago: Aldine, 1968.

4:24   Bawcutt, N. W. "More Echoes in Pope's Poetry." *NQ* 5(1958):220-21.

4:25 Belanger, Terry. "Booksellers' Sales of Copyright: Aspects of the London Book Trade, 1718-1768." *DAI* 32(1971):379A(Columbia). Discusses Tonson's 1767 sale of his copyrights on the works of Dryden and others.

*4:26 Beljame, Alexandre. *Men of Letters and the English Public in the Eighteenth Century, 1660-1744: Dryden, Addison, Pope* [1897], ed. Bonamy Dobrée. Trans. E. O. Lorimer. London: Kegan Paul, 1948. Reprinted St. Clair Shores, Mich.: Scholarly Press, 1971.

4:27 Bensly, Edward. "Pope's 'Rape of the Lock'." *MLR* 7(1912):94-97. Comparisons of lines from *Tyrannic Love* and *Conquest of Granada*.

4:28 Benson, Donald R. "Halifax and the Trimmers." *HLQ* 27(1964):115-34.

4:29 ———. "John Dryden and the Church of England: The Conversion and the Problem of Authority in the Seventeenth Century." *DA* 20 (1960):4106-07(Kansas).

4:30 ———. "Theology and Politics in Dryden's Conversion." *SEL* 4 (1964):393-412. Sees the conversion as the result of political rather than theological concerns. *See* item 4:211.

4:31 Bentley, G. E. "Seventeenth-century Allusions to Ben Jonson." *HLQ* 5(1941):65-113.

4:32 Bernard, Sister Rose. "The Character of Dryden in the Twentieth Century." *Catholic Educator* 25(1955):423-25.

4:33 Bethell, S. L. *The Cultural Revolution of the Seventeenth-Century.* London: Dobson, 1951.

4:34 Birrell, T. A. *Catholic Allegiance and the Popish Plot: A Study of Some Catholic Writers of the Restoration Period.* Utrecht: Dekker, 1950.

4:35 Blair, Joel. "Dryden and Fanciful Poetry." Diss. Harvard, 1965.

*4:36 ———. "Dryden's Ceremonial Hero." *SEL* 9(1969):379-93. Dryden's changing attitude toward the heroic figure.

4:37 Bolgar, R. R. *The Classical Heritage and Its Beneficiaries.* Cambridge: At the University Press, 1958.

4:38 Bollough, Geoffrey. "Changing Views of the Mind in English Poetry." *PBA* 41(1955):61-83.

4:39 Borinski, Ludwig. *Englischen Geist in der Geschichte seiner Prosa.* Freiburg: Herder, [1951].

4:40 Born, Lester K. "The Perfect Prince According to the Latin Panegyrists." *American Journal of Philology* 55(1934):20-35. The tradition of the *specula principum.*

4:41 Bowler, Elizabeth A. "The Augustan Heroic Idiom in Dryden, Rowe, and Pope." Diss. Bristol, 1973.

4:42 Bradham, Jo Allen. "English Lucilian Satire: The Augustan Mode." *DA* 25(1964):450-51(Vanderbilt).

*4:43 Bredvold, Louis I. *The Intellectual Milieu of John Dryden: Studies in Some Aspects of Seventeenth Century Thought.* (University of Michigan Publications Language and Literature 12.) Ann Arbor: University of Michigan Press, 1934. Reprinted London: Oxford University Press, 1957. Chap. 1 ("Introduction") and Chap. 6 ("Conclusion") reprinted in [Critical Essays]:17-30. *See* Moody E. Prior, *MP* 32:324-29; George Williamson, *MLN* 51:195-96; Roswell G. Ham, *RES* 12:353-55; V. de Sola Pinto, *MLR* 31:429-31; Alan D. McKillop, *PQ* 14:375; Arthur Secord, *JEGP* 34:402-04; *TLS* 24 June 1935, p. 50. *See also* items 5/4:3, 5/7:6, 8/1:229, 8/2:32.

4:44 ———. "The Literature of the Restoration and the Eighteenth Century 1660-1798." *A History of English Literature*, ed. Hardin Craig, pp. 343-459. New York: Oxford University Press, 1950.

4:45 ──── . "The Rise of English Classicism: Study in Methodology."
    CL 2(1950):253-68. Calls for a revaluation of common assumptions
    about the importance of French thought in the development of En-
    glish classicism.
4:46 Brereton, John C. "Heroic Praise: Dryden and the State Panegy-
    ric." DAI 34(1973):306A(Rutgers).
4:47 Brett, R. L. "Thomas Hobbes." The English Mind: Studies in the
    English Moralists Presented to Basil Willey, ed. Hugh Sykes Da-
    vies and George Watson, pp. 30-54. Cambridge: At the University
    Press, 1964. The influence of Hobbes on Dryden's poetry.
4:48 Brett, Richard D. "Ironic Harmony: Poetic Structure in Donne,
    Marvell and Dryden." DA 22(1962):2783-84(Cornell).
4:49 Bridges, Robert. "Dryden on Milton" [1903]. Collected Essays,
    Papers, &c. 10:271-82. London: Oxford University Press, 1932.
4:50 Brinkley, Roberta Florence, ed. and Louis I. Bredvold, introd.
    Coleridge on the Seventeenth Century. Durham: Duke University
    Press, 1955.
4:51 Deleted.
4:52 Bronson, Bertrand H. "The Trough of the Wave." [Culture and So-
    ciety]:197-226. Dryden and Pope's influence on early eighteenth-
    century poetic modes. See item 4:334.
4:53 Brooke, Stopford A. "Dryden and Pope." Naturalism in English
    Poetry, pp. 1-21. New York: E. P. Dutton, 1920.
4:54 Brooks, Harold F. "Dryden and Cowley." TLS 19 April 1957, p.
    245. See correspondence, Agnes Arber, ibid., 7 June, p. 349; W.
    K. Scudamore, ibid., 14 June, p. 365. Echoes of Cowley.
*4:55 Brower, Reuben A. "An Allusion to Europe: Dryden and Poetic
    Tradition." ELH 19(1952):38-48. Reprinted in Alexander Pope: Po-
    etry of Allusion, pp. 1-14. Oxford: At the Clarendon Press, 1959.
    Also in Essential Articles: for the Study of Alexander Pope, ed.
    Maynard Mack, pp. 122-35. Hamden, Connecticut: Archon Books, 1964.
    And in [Keast]:414-24; and [Critical Essays]:43-54. Dryden reaf-
    firmed the public role of the poet and the importance of the Eu-
    ropean tradition.
*4:56 ──── . "Dryden and the 'Invention' of Pope." Restoration and
    Eighteenth-Century: Essays in Honor of Alan Dugald McKillop, ed.
    Carroll Camden, pp. 211-33. Chicago, London: University of Chica-
    go Press for William Marsh Rice University, 1963. Dryden's antic-
    ipation of Pope and later poets.
*4:57 ──── . "Dryden's Epic Manner and Virgil." PMLA 55(1940):119-38.
    Reprinted in [Swedenberg]:466-92. The importance of Virgil in Dry-
    den's appreciation of the epic.
4:58 ──── . "Dryden's Poetic Diction and Virgil." PQ 18(1939):211-17.
4:59 ──── . The Fields of Light: An Experiment in Critical Reading.
    New York: Oxford University Press, 1951.
*4:60 ──── . "Form and Defect of Form in Eighteenth-Century Poetry:
    A Memorandum." CE 29(1968):535-41. A warning against overenthusi-
    astic revaluations which find continuity in Dryden's imagery
    where none exists. See items 4:185, 4:490.
4:61 ──── . "John Dryden's Use and Criticism of Virgil." HU-ST 12
    (1936):310-12.
4:62 Brown, Wallace Cable. The Triumph of Form: A Study of the Later
    Masters of the Heroic Couplet. Chapel Hill: University of North
    Carolina Press, 1948.
4:63 Browne, Ray B. "Dryden and Milton in Nineteenth-Century 'Popu-
    lar' Songbooks." BB 22(1958):143-44.

4:64 Bryan, Arthur. *Literature and the Historian*. Cambridge: At the University Press, 1953.

*4:65 Budick, Sanford. "The Demythological Mode in Augustan Verse." *ELH* 37(1970):389-414. The poet as *keryx*, the herald of divinely sanctioned authority.

4:66 Buhtz, Georg. "Drydens moralische Gedankenwelt." Diss. Hamburg, 1958.

4:67 Bullough, Geoffrey. "The Grand Style in English Poetry." *Cairo Studies in English* (1959):9-25.

4:68 Burke, Margaret J. "Dryden and Eliot: A Study in Literary Criticism." Diss. Niagara, 1945.

4:69 Burton, K. M. P. "John Dryden" and "Apologia: John Dryden." *Restoration Literature*, pp. 126-35 and pp. 223-26. London: Hutchinson University Library, 1958.

4:70 Bush, Douglas. *English Poetry: The Main Currents from Chaucer to the Present*. New York: Oxford University Press, 1952.

4:71 ———. *Mythology and the Renaissance Tradition in English Poetry*. Minneapolis: University of Minnesota Press, 1932. Rev. ed. New York: Norton, 1960.

4:72 ———. *Science and English Poetry: A Historical Sketch, 1590-1950*. (The Patten Lectures, Indiana University, 1949.) New York: Oxford University Press, 1950. Science helped nourish Dryden's distrust of reason.

4:73 Busson, Henri. *Les Sources et le Développement du Rationalisme dans la Littérature Française de la Renaissance (1533-1601)*. Paris: Letouzey, 1922.

4:74 Butt, John. "Dryden." *The Augustan Age*, pp. 9-27. New York, London: Hutchinson, 1950. Reprinted New York: Norton, 1966.

4:75 ———. "A Plea for More English Dictionaries." *DUJ* 43(1951):96-102. Dryden's vocabulary has been inadequately·recorded in the *OED*.

4:76 Butterworth, Richard. "Dryden and the Methodist Hymn-Book." *Proceedings of the Wesley Historical Society* 10(1916):159-62.

4:77 Cable, Chester. "Methods of Non-Dramatic Verse Satire, 1640-1700." Diss. Chicago, 1948.

*4:78 Cameron, Allen Barry. "Donne and Dryden: Their Achievement in the Verse Epistle." *Discourse* 11(1968):252-56.

*4:79 Cameron, William J. "John Dryden's Jacobitism." *Restoration Literature: Critical Approaches*, ed. Harold Love, pp. 277-308. London: Methuen, 1972.

4:80 ———, ed. *Poems on Affairs of State: Augustan Satirical Verse, 1660-1714*. Vol. 5: *1688-1697*. New Haven, London: Yale University Press, 1971. Dryden did not participate in the partisan controversies of the period, but he was nonetheless attacked in lampoons.

4:81 Carritt, E. F. *A Calendar of British Taste from 1600 to 1800: Being a Museum of Specimens and Landmarks Chronologically Arranged*. London: Routledge and Kegan Paul, [1949]. *See TLS* 16 December 1949, p. 820.

4:82 Carroll, J. T. "Dryden and the Great Chain of Being." *ASLIB* 11 (1960-61):10(Ireland, National Univ.).

4:83 Casson, T. E. "John Dryden." *Poetry Review* 23(1932):47-51.

4:84 Cazamian, Louis. *L'Evolution Psychologique et la Littérature en Angleterre (1660-1914)*. Paris: Librairie Félix Alcan, 1920.

4:85 ———, and Emile Legouis. "Dryden and Lyrical Poetry." *A History of English Literature*, trans. from the French by Helen Douglas

Irvine and W. D. MacInnes, pp. 605–23. Rev. ed. London: J. M. Dent, 1957.

4:86 Geis, Walter. "Die Anschauungen von den religiösen und politi- schen Ordnungen in der Dichtung John Drydens, dargestellt vornehm- lich auf Grund der Interpretation der Lehrgedichte in Zusammen- hang des Gesamtwerkes." Diss. Frankfurt/Main, 1950.

4:87 Chesterton, G. K. "The Last Taboo." *G. K.'s Weekly* 17(1933):391– 92.

4:88 Chubb, Edwin Watts. "Dryden." *Masters of English Literature*, pp. 82–101. Chicago: McClurg, 1914. Reprinted (Essay Index Reprint Series) Freeport, N.Y.: Books for Libraries Press, 1967.

4:89 Clapp, Sarah L. C. "Jacob Tonson Eminent Hand." *LCUT* 3(1949): 136–45.

4:90 Clark, Sir George. *The Later Stuarts: 1660–1714.* (*Oxford His- tory of England.*) Oxford: At the Clarendon Press, 1934.

4:91 Clark, J. Scott. "Dryden, 1631–1700." *A Study of English and American Poets: A Laboratory Method*, pp. 131–62. New York: Scrib- ner, 1909.

4:92 Clarke, George Herbert. "Christ and the English Poets." *QQ* 55 (1948):292–307. *Veni Creator Spiritus* and *The Hind and the Pan- ther.*

4:93 Clough, Arthur Hugh. "Dryden and His Times." *Selected Prose Works*, ed. Buckner B. Trawick, pp. 85–106. University: Alabama University Press, 1964.

4:94 Clough, Ben C. "Notes on the Metaphysical Poets." *MLN* 35(1920): 115–17.

4:95 Cohen, Ralph. "The Augustan Mode in English Poetry." *ECS* 1 (1967):3–32.

4:96 Collins, John Churton. "Waller, Cowley, and Dryden." *Poets' Country*, ed. Andrew Lang, pp. 133–39. London, Edinburgh: T. C. and E. C. Jack, 1913. Dryden was uninterested in nature.

4:97 Congleton, James E. "The Effect of the Restoration on Poetry." *TSL* 6(1961):93–101.

4:98 Cook, Elizabeth C. *Literary Influence in Colonial Newspapers 1704–1750.* (Columbia University Studies in English and Compara- tive Literature.) New York: Columbia University Press, 1912. Re- printed with an Introd. by Donald H. Stewart. Port Washington, N.Y.: Kennikat, 1966.

4:99 Cooper, Lane. "Dryden and Shelley on Milton." *MLN* 23(1908):93.

4:100 Cope, Jackson I. "Dryden *vs.* Hobbes: An Adaptation from the Platonists." *JEGP* 57(1958):444–48. *See* item 7:309.

4:101 Cornelius, David K. "The Caustic Muse: A Study in Seventeenth- Century Verse Satire." *DA* 16(1956):747(Columbia).

4:102 Courthope, W. J. "John Dryden and the Satirists of the Country Party." *A History of English Poetry.* 3:482–533. London: Macmillan, 1903. Reprinted New York: Russell and Russell, 1962.

4:103 Crinò, Anna Maria. *Dryden: Poeta Satirico.* (Biblioteca dell' "Archivum Romanicum." Ser. 1: Storia-letteratum-paleografia 55.) Firenze: Olschki, 1958. *See* Jackson I. Cope, *MLN* 74:636–40; Anne- Marie Imbert, *Anglia* 76:559–60.

4:104 ———. *John Dryden.* Florence: Olschki, 1957.

4:105 ———. *L'opera letteraria di John Dryden.* Verona: Fiorini, 1971. A general survey of all of Dryden's major works, together with a biographical sketch and a bibliography of critical studies.

4:106 ——. *Il Popish Plot nelle Relazioni Inedite dei Residenti Granducali alla Corte di Londra (1678-1681)*. Roma: Edizioni di Storia e Letteratura, 1954.

4:107 ——. "Ritorno al Dryden." *CeS* 1,iv(1962):65-71.

4:108 Cubbage, Virginia C. "The Reputation of John Dryden, 1700-1779." *SDD-NU* 12(1944):10-15.

4:109 Daiches, David. *A Critical History of English Literature*. 2 vols. New York: Ronald Press, 1960.

4:110 Dandridge, Rita B. "Satire Against the Catholic Tendencies of the Stuart Kings, 1603-1688." *DAI* 31(1971):6006A(Howard).

4:111 Davies, Godfrey. *Essays on the Later Stuarts*. San Marino: Huntington Library, 1958.

4:112 ——. *The Restoration of Charles II, 1658-1660*. San Marino: Huntington Library, 1955.

4:113 Davies, Hugh Sykes, comp. "Dryden." *The Poets and Their Critics: Chaucer to Collins*, pp. 157-84. New York: Penguin Books, 1943. Rev. ed. London: Hutchinson, 1960.

4:114 Davies, Paul C. "Restoration Liberalism." *EIC* 22(1972):226-28.

4:115 Davison, Dennis. *Dryden*. (Literature in Perspective.) London: Evans Brothers, 1968. A general introduction.

4:116 DeArmond, Anna J. "Some Aspects of Character-Writing in the Period of the Restoration." *Delaware Notes* 16th ser. (1943):55-89.

4:117 Dewitt, Susan Vera. "Ben Jonson and the English Verse Letter." *DAI* 33(1973):6868A(Wash.).

4:118 Dick, Hugh G. "John Dryden's Conception of Tides." *Isis* 42 (1952):266. *See* reply, C. W. Adams, ibid., 44(1953):100-01.

4:119 Dicks, George W. "Dryden's Use of Scripture in His Nondramatic Poetry." *DAI* 30(1970):4405A(Vanderbilt).

4:120 Dierberger, Josef. *John Drydens Reime: Ein Beitrag zur Geschichte der englischen Tonvokale*. Freiburg: Lehmann, 1895.

4:121 Dixon, W. MacNeile. *English Epic and Heroic Poetry*. (The Channels of English Literature.) London: J. M. Dent; New York: E. P. Dutton, 1912.

4:122 Dobrée, Bonamy. *The Broken Cistern: The Clark Lectures 1952-53*. London: Cohen and West, 1954; Bloomington: Indiana University Press, 1955.

4:123 ——. "Dryden's Poems." *SR* 67(1959):519-26. Rev. art. *See* item 2/2:18.

4:124 ——. "John Dryden." *Fifteen Poets*, pp. 141-44. Oxford: At the University Press, 1941.

4:125 ——. "John Dryden." *Variety of Ways: Discussions on Six Authors*, pp. 1-16. Oxford: At the Clarendon Press, 1932. Reprinted (Essay Index Reprint Series) Freeport, New York: Books for Libraries Press, 1967. Considers the uses of poetry.

4:126 ——. *John Dryden*. London, New York: Longmans, 1956. Rev. ed. 1961.

4:127 ——. "Milton and Dryden: A Comparison in Poetic Ideas and Poetic Method." *ELH* 3(1936):83-100. Reprinted in *Milton to Ouida: A Collection of Essays*, pp. 1-21. London: Frank Cass, 1970.

4:128 Doughty, Oswald. *The English Lyric in the Age of Reason*. London: Daniel O'Connor, 1922.

4:129 Draper, John W. *The Funeral Elegy and the Rise of English Romanticism*. New York: New York University Press, 1929.

4:130 Duncan, Carson S. *The New Science and English Literature in the Classical Period*. Menasha, Wis.: Banta, 1913.

4:131 Dunne, J. W. "John Dryden: Catholic Apologist." *Clergy Review* 21(1942):15-22.

4:132 Dykema, K. W. "Samuel Sewell Reads John Dryden." *AL* 14(1942): 157-58.

4:133 Ehrenpreis, Irvin. "Lecture on a Master Mind: Jonathan Swift." *PBA* 54(1968):149-64. Dryden's praise of science is contrasted with Swift's ridicule of the Royal Society.

4:134 Ehrman, Madeline. *The Meanings of the Modals in Present-Day American English*. The Hague: Mouton, 1966. Modals in Dryden are used to compare with those in present-day American English.

4:135 Eliot, T. S. "The Age of Dryden." *The Use of Poetry and the Use of Criticism: Studies in the Relation of Criticism to Poetry in England*, pp. 53-65. (The Charles Eliot Norton Lectures 1932- 33.) Cambridge, Mass.: Harvard University Press, 1933. Reprinted London: Faber, 1948.

*4:136 ———. "John Dryden." *TLS* 9 June 1921, pp. 361-62. Reprinted in *Homage to John Dryden: Three Essays on Poetry of the Seven- teenth Century*. (The Hogarth Essays 1,iv.) London: Leonard and Virginia Woolf, 1927. Also in *Selected Essays*, pp. 264-74. New, rev. ed. New York: Harcourt, Brace, 1950. Also in [Critical Es- says]:8-16. Reading Dryden is an important test of a catholic ap- preciation of poetry.

4:137 ———. "John Dryden: The Poet, the Dramatist, the Critic." *Listener* 5(1931):621-22, 681-82, 724-25. Published in an expanded form New York: Holliday, 1932.

4:138 Elkin, P. K. "Dryden as Intellectual, Playwright and Critic." *AUMLA* 36(1971):210-16. Rev. art. *See* items 2/5:1, 2/5:2, 4:211, 7:136.

4:139 Elton, Oliver. *The Augustan Ages*. (Periods of European Litera- ture 8.) New York: Scribner, 1899.

4:140 ———. "Dryden and Others." *The English Muse: A Sketch*, pp. 250-71. London: G. Bell, 1933. Impressionistic comparisons of a number of poets.

4:141 Emery, John P. "Restoration Dualism of the Court Writers." *RLV* 32(1966):238-65.

4:142 Empson, William. *Seven Types of Ambiguity*. Norfolk, Conn.: New Directions, 1930. 2nd rev. ed. 1947. 3rd rev. ed. 1953.

4:143 Emslie, McD. "Dryden's Couplets: Imagery Vowed to Poverty." *CQ* 2(1960):51-57.

4:144 ———. "The Relationship Between Words and Music in the En- glish Secular Song, 1622-1700." *ASLIB* 8(1957-58):9(Cambridge, Pembroke).

4:145 Erskine-Hill, Howard. "Augustans on Augustanism: England, 1655- 1759." *RMS* 11(1967):53-83.

4:146 ———. "John Dryden." *Dryden to Johnson*, ed. Roger Lonsdale. (Sphere History of Literature in the English Language 4.) London: Sphere, 1971.

4:147 ———. "Rochester: Augustan or Explorer?" *Renaissance and Mod- ern Essays Presented to Vivian de Sola Pinto in Celebration of his Seventieth Birthday*, ed. G. R. Hibbard, assisted by George A. Panichas and Allan Rodway, pp. 51-64. London: Routledge and Kegan Paul, 1966.

4:148 "*Et caetera*." *Tablet* 158(1931):183.

4:149 Evans, B. Ifor. "Dryden and Pope." *Tradition and Romanticism: Studies in English Poetry from Chaucer to W. B. Yeats*, pp. 61-75.

London: Methuen, 1940. Reprinted London: Archon Books, 1964. Dryden's awareness of the strength of the English tradition com-
pelled him to develop a sense of classicism different from that
of the French.

4:150 Evans, Betty D. "Dryden's Imagery in His Nondramatic Poetry."
DA 17(1957):1749(Okla.).

4:151 Evans, G. Blakemore. "A Seventeenth-Century Reader of Shakespeare." *RES* 21(1945):271-79. Contemporary criticism of Dryden.

4:152 Fairclough, H. R. "The Influence of Virgil Upon the Forms of
English Verse." *CJ* 26(1930):74-94.

4:153 Feder, Lillian. "John Dryden's Interpretation and Use of Latin
Poetry and Rhetoric." Diss. Minn., 1952.

*4:154 ———. "John Dryden's Use of Classical Rhetoric." *PMLA* 69
(1954):1258-78. Reprinted in [Swedenberg]:493-518.

*4:155 Ferry, Anne Davidson. *Milton and the Miltonic Dryden*. Cam-
bridge, Mass.: Harvard University Press, 1968. Chaps. on *All for
Love*, *State of Innocence*, *Absalom and Achitophel*. See Anthony
Low, *SCN* 26:72-73; *YWES* 49:211.

4:156 Field, P. J. C. "Authoritative Echo in Dryden." *DUJ* 62(1970):
137-51. The Bible and the classics were indispensible in providing Dryden with a scheme of values.

4:157 Fink, Zera Silver. *The Classical Republicans: An Essay in the
Recovery of a Pattern of Thought in Seventeenth Century England*.
Evanston: Northwestern University Press, 1945.

4:158 Fisch, Harold. *Jerusalem and Albion: The Hebraic Factor in
Seventeenth Century Literature*. New York: Schocken, 1964.

4:159 Fisher, Alan S. "The Form, History, and Significance of the
Augustan Literary Portrait." *DAI* 31(1970):386A(Berkeley). *See*
item 4:198.

4:160 Fisher, Mary. "Dryden." *Twenty-five Letters on English Authors*.
Chicago: Griggs, 1895.

4:161 Fleischmann, Wolfgang Bernard. *Lucretius and English Literature 1680-1740*. Paris: A. G. Nizet, 1964. Dryden accepted Lucretius the poet, but rejected the Epicurean metaphysics with which
he was usually associated.

4:162 Fornelli, Guido. *La Restaurazione inglese nell' opera di John
Dryden*. Firenze: La Nuova Italia, 1932.

4:163 Fosberry, M. W. "The Case of John Dryden." *OR* 8(1968):65-72;
ibid., 9(1968):75-81.

4:164 Foss, Michael. *The Age of Patronage: The Arts in England,
1660-1750*. Ithaca: Cornell University Press, 1972.

4:165 Fowler, Alastair. *Triumphal Forms: Structural Patterns in Elizabethan Poetry*. Cambridge: At the University Press, 1970. Numerological approach.

4:166 Fox, Adam. "Dryden: the Poet at Work." *Oxford Magazine* 57(1937):
644-45.

4:167 Freedman, Morris. "Milton and Dryden." *DA* 14(1954):109(Columbia).

*4:168 ———. "A Note on Milton and Dryden as Satirists." *NQ* 1(1954):
26-27.

4:169 Frye, Northrop. *Anatomy of Criticism*. Princeton: Princeton University Press, 1957.

4:170 ———. "The Nature of Satire." *UTQ* 14(1945):75-89.

*4:171 Frye, Posser Hall. "Dryden and the Critical Canons of the
Eighteenth Century." *University Studies (University of Nebraska)*

7(1907):1-39. Dryden lacked creative power and had a "prose spirit."

*4:172 Fujimura, Thomas H. "The Personal Element in Dryden's Poetry." *PMLA* 89(1974):1007-23.

4:173 Fussell, Paul. *The Rhetorical World of Augustan Humanism*. Oxford: At the Clarendon Press, 1965.

4:174 Gaines, Ervin J. "Merchant and Poet: A Study of Seventeenth Century Influences." *DA* 14(1954):110(Columbia).

4:175 Gardner, Helen. "The Historical Approach." *The Business of Criticism*, pp. 25-51. Oxford: At the Clarendon Press, 1959. The various liabilities of different critical approaches.

4:176 Gardner, William Bradford. "John Dryden's Interest in Judicial Astrology." *SP* 47(1950):506-21.

4:177 Garnett, Richard. *The Age of Dryden*. London: G. Bell, 1895. Reprinted (Essay Index Reprint Series) Freeport, N.Y.: Books for Libraries Press, 1971. A prosaic age and a prosaic poet.

4:178 Garrison, James D. "Dryden and Verse Panegyric." *DAI* 33(1972): 752A(Calif., Berkeley). *See* items 4:17, 4:65, 4:534.

4:179 Golladay, Gertrude. "Dryden's Rhetoric and Poetic." Diss. Smith, 1967.

4:180 Gordon, R. K. "Dryden and the 'Waverley Novels'." *MLR* 34(1939): 201-06.

4:181 Gosse, Edmund. *From Shakespeare to Pope: An Inquiry Into the Causes and Phenomena of the Rise of Classical Poetry in England* [1885]. (Research and Source Works Series 292. Selected Essays in Literature and Criticism 15.) New York: Burt Franklin, 1968.

4:182 Grant, Douglas. "Samuel Johnson: Satire and Satirists." *NRam* Ser. C 3(1967):5-17.

4:183 Graves, Robert. "The Age of Obsequiousness." *The Crowning Privilege*, pp. 25-44. (The Clark Lectures 1954-55.) London: Cassell, 1955.

4:184 Greene, Donald. "Augustinianism and Empiricism: A Note on Eighteenth-Century English Intellectual History." *ECS* 1(1967):33-68.

*4:185 ———. "'Logical Structure' in Eighteenth-Century Poetry." *PQ* 31(1952):315-36. *See* items 4:60, 4:482, 4:490.

4:186 Greenleaf, W. H. *Order, Empiricism and Politics: Two Traditions of English Political Thought 1500-1700*. London, New York, Toronto: Oxford University Press for the University of Hull, 1964.

4:187 Grierson, H. J. C. "John Dryden." *Cross-Currents in English Literature of the Seventeenth Century*, pp. 311-40. London: Chatto and Windus, 1929. Reprinted New York: Harper, 1958. *See* item 4: 544.

4:188 ———, and J. C. Smith. "Cowley to Dryden." *A Critical History of English Poetry*, pp. 172-90. London: Chatto and Windus, 1944. Rev. ed. 1947.

4:189 Griffith, R. H. "Dryden in the *Dunciad*." *Nation* 98(1914):568.

4:190 Griffith, Richard R. "Science and Pseudo-Science in the Imagery of John Dryden." *DA* 17(1957):1072-03(Ohio St.). Metallurgy and astrology.

4:191 Groom, Bernard. "Dryden." *The Diction of Poetry from Spenser to Bridges*, pp. 95-111. Toronto: University of Toronto Press, 1955. *See* Ralph Cohen, *PQ* 36:323-24.

4:192 Guibbory, Achsah. "Attitudes Towards Classical Mythology in Seventeenth-Century English Literature." *DAI* 31(1971):4161A(U.C. L.A.).

4:193 Guzzetti, Alfred F. "Dryden's Two Worlds: Restoration Society and the Literary Past." Diss. Harvard, 1968.

4:194 Hadzits, George D. *Lucretius and His Influence*. New York: Longmans, 1935.

4:195 Hagestad, William Thomson. "Restoration Patronage." *DA* 28(1967): 1050A(Wis.).

4:196 Hägin, Peter. *The Epic Hero and Decline of Epic Poetry*. (The Cooper Monographs 8.) Bern: Francke, 1964.

*4:197 Hagstrum, Jean H. *The Sister Arts: The Tradition of Literary Pictorialism and English Poetry from Dryden to Gray*. Chicago: University of Chicago Press, 1958. "Ideal Form in *All for Love*" reprinted in [20th Century Interpretations]:61-71. *See* W. K. Wimsatt, Jr., *PQ* 38:288-89; Bertrand H. Bronson, *MLN* 75:354-59; Johannes A. Gaertner, *JAAC* 19:102.

4:198 ———. "Verbal and Visual Caricature in the Age of Dryden, Swift, and Pope." [Culture and Society]:173-95. Verbal portraiture used as a satiric device.

4:199 Hale, Paul V. "'Enthusiasm' Rejected and Espoused in English Poetry and Criticism, 1660-1740." *DA* 24(1963):727(N.Y.U.).

4:200 Ham, Roswell G. "Otway's Duels with Churchill and Settle." *MLN* 41(1926):73-80.

4:201 Hamilton, G. Rostrevor. *English Verse Epigram*. (Writers and Their Work 188.) London: Longmans, 1965.

4:202 Hamilton, K. G. *John Dryden and the Poetry of Statement*. St. Lucia: University of Queensland Press, 1967. Reprinted East Lansing: Michigan State University Press, 1969. *See* Pierre Legouis, *EA* 21:308-09.

4:203 ———. *The Two Harmonies: Poetry and Prose in the Seventeenth Century*. Oxford: At the Clarendon Press, 1963.

4:204 Hammett, E. A. "A Note for the *NED*." *MLN* 54(1939):449. Gallicisms in Dryden.

4:205 Hammil, Carrie E. "The Celestial Journey and the Harmony of the Spheres in English Literature, 1300-1700." *DAI* 33(1972):2326A (Texas Christian).

4:206 Hardison, O. B., Jr. "The Decorum of *Lamia*." *MLQ* 19(1958):33-42. *See* Charles A. Langworthy, *RS* 2(1930):117-24.

4:207 Harman, Roland N. "Sir Walter Scott as Editor of John Dryden." Diss. Yale, 1938. *See* items 1:36, 2/1:11.

*4:208 Harris, Kathryn M. "John Dryden: Augustan Satirist." *DA* 29 (1968):1539A-40A(Emory).

4:209 Harris, Victor. *All Coherence Gone*. Chicago: University of Chicago Press, 1949. Background on the seventeenth-century controversy concerning the decay of nature.

4:210 Hart, Jeffrey. "John Dryden: The Politics of Style." *ModA* 8 (1964):399-408. Similarities between T. S. Eliot and Dryden; their poetic styles reflect political sensibilities.

*4:211 Harth, Phillip. *Contexts of Dryden's Thought*. Chicago: University of Chicago Press, 1968. Chaps. on *Religio Laici* and *The Hind and the Panther*. *See* Charles E. Ward, *SAQ* 67:707-08; Earl Miner, *PQ* 48:350-52; V. de Sola Pinto, *MLR* 65:147-48; Hoyt Trowbridge, *MP* 67:382-85; Pierre Legouis, *EA* 24:533-34.

4:212 ———. "Religion and Politics in Dryden's Poetry and Plays." *MP* 70(1973):236-42. Rev. art. *See* items 2/2:21, 8/2:8.

4:213 Haswell, Richard E. "The Heroic Couplet Before Dryden (1550-1675)." Diss. Illinois, 1931.

4:214 Hayman, John. "Raillery in Restoration Satire." *HLQ* 31(1968):
107–22.

4:215 Hazlitt, William. "On Dryden and Pope" [1818]. *Works*, eds. A.
R. Waller and Arnold Glover. 5:68–85. London: J. M. Dent; New
York: McClure, Phillips, 1902. Dryden and Pope were "masters of
the artificial style of poetry."

4:216 Hearnshaw, F. J. C. *English History in Contemporary Poetry:
Court and Parliament 1588–1688*. London: G. Bell for the Historical Association, 1913.

4:217 Heath-Stubbs, John. "Dryden and the Heroic Ideal." [King]:3–
23.

4:218 Hemphill, George. "Dryden's Heroic Line." *PMLA* 72(1957):863–
79. Reprinted in [Swedenberg]:519–40.

4:219 Henneman, John B. "Dryden After Two Centuries (1700–1900)."
SR 9(1901):57–72.

4:220 Highet, Gilbert. *The Classical Tradition: Greek and Roman Influences on Western Literature*. New York, London: Oxford University Press, 1949.

4:221 Hoefling, Sister Mary Chrysantha. *A Study of the Structure of
Meaning in the Sentences of the Satiric Verse "Characters" of
John Dryden*. Washington, D.C.: The Catholic University of Ameri-
ca, 1946. A tabular study.

4:222 Hoffman, Arthur W. "Dryden's Panegyrics and Lyrics." [Miner]:
120–55.

*4:223 ———. *John Dryden's Imagery*. Gainesville: University of Florida Press, 1962. Chap. 1 ("An Apprenticeship in Praise") reprinted in [King]:45–64; Chap. 6 ("Various John Dryden: 'All, All
of a Piece Throughout") reprinted in [Critical Essays]:165–80.
See William Frost, *PQ* 42:344–46; John Carey, *RES* 15:432–33; Bernard Schilling, *JEGP* 63:362–64; Pierre Legouis, *EA* 17:148–58;
John Aden, *SAQ* 62:439–40; V. de Sola Pinto, *MLR* 58:564–65.

4:224 ———. "Some Aspects of Dryden's Imagery." Diss. Yale, 1951.

4:225 Holland, Bernard. "John Dryden." *Dublin Review* 175(1924):29–47.

4:226 Hollander, John. *The Untuning of the Sky*. Princeton: Princeton
University Press, 1961. "The Sky Untuned" chap. excerpted as "The
Odes to Music" in [Critical Essays]:149–64. *See* Charles T. Harri-
son, *YR* 50:625–27; Rhodes Dunlap, *PQ* 41:552–53.

4:227 Horn, András. "Gedanken uber Rationalität und Illusion: Apro-
pos John Dryden." *Festschrift Rudolf Stamm zu seinem sechzigsten
Geburstag*, eds. Eduard Kolb and Jorg Hasler, pp. 189–201. Bern,
München: Francke, 1969.

4:228 Horsman, E. A. "Dryden's French Borrowings." *RES* 1(1950):346–
51. Dryden's use of French words.

4:229 Howarth, R. G. E. "Sitwell and Dryden." *Southerly* 12(1951):178.

4:230 Hoyles, John. *The Waning of the Renaissance 1640–1740: Studies
in the Thought and Poetry of Henry More, John Norris, and Isaac
Watts*. The Hague: Nijhoff, 1971.

*4:231 Hughes, Merritt Y. "Dryden as Statist." *PQ* 6(1927):334–50.
See R. S. Crane, *PQ* 7:174. *See also* items 4:43, 5/4:3, 8/1:229,
8/2:32.

4:232 Hughes, R. E. "John Dryden's Greatest Compromise." *TSLL* 2(1961):
458–63.

4:233 ———. "The Sense of the Ridiculous: Ridicule as a Rhetorical
Device in the Poetry of Dryden and Pope." *SDD-UW* 15(1955):613–15.

4:234   Hunt, Clay. "The Elizabethan Background of Neo-Classic Polite Verse." *ELH* 8(1941):273-304.

4:235 Huxley, Aldous. "Forgotten Satirists." *London Mercury* 1(1920): 565-73.

4:236   Illo, John. "Dryden, Sylvester, and the Correspondence of Melancholy Winter and Cold Age." *ELN* 1(1963):101-04.

*4:237   Jack, Ian. *Augustan Satire: Intention and Idiom in English Poetry 1660-1750*. Oxford: At the Clarendon Press, 1952. Chaps. on *Mac Flecknoe* (Mock-Heroic) and on *Absalom and Achitophel* (Witty Heroic Poem).

4:238   ———. "'The True Raillery'." *CSE* 4(1960):9-23. A general essay on "raillery," the combination of humor and satire, in Dryden and others.

4:239   Jackson, Wallace. "Satire: An Augustan Idea of Disorder." *Proceedings of the Modern Language Association Neoclassicism Conferences 1967-1968*, ed. Paul J. Korshin, pp. 13-26. New York: AMS Press, 1970. The satiric use of the theme of *discordia concors*.

4:240   Jaeger, Herman. *Dryden og hans tid*. Oslo: J. W. Cappelens, 1925.

4:241   James, D. G. *The Life of Reason: Hobbes, Locke, Bolingbroke*. London, New York: Longmans, Green, 1949.

4:242   Jefferson, D. W. "Aspects of Dryden's Imagery." *EIC* 4(1954):20-41. Reprinted in [King]:24-42. *See* item 4:506.

4:243   "John Dryden." *Citizen* 1(1896):291-93; ibid., 2(1896):17-19.

4:244   "John Dryden, Poet." *TLS* 16 February 1951, pp. 93-95. Rev. art. *See* item 2/2:22.

*4:245   Johnson, James William. "The Classics and John Bull, 1660-1714." [Culture and Society]:1-26. The influence of the classics on the literature and thought of the period.

4:246   ———. *The Formation of English Neo-Classical Thought*. Princeton: Princeton University Press, 1967.

4:247   ———. "The Meaning of 'Augustan'." *JHI* 19(1958):507-22.

4:248   Johnson, Lionel. "The Age of Dryden." *Post Liminium: Essays and Critical Papers*, ed. Thomas Whittemore, pp. 283-87. London: E. Mathews, 1911. Reprinted (Essay Index Reprint Series) Freeport, N.Y.: Books for Libraries Press, 1968. *See* item 4:177.

4:249   Johnson, Maurice. "A Literary Chestnut: Dryden's 'Cousin Swift'." *PMLA* 67(1952):1024-34.

*4:250   Johnson, Samuel. "John Dryden." *Lives of the English Poets*, ed. George Birkbeck Hill. 1:331-487. Oxford: At the Clarendon Press, 1905. Reprinted New York: Octagon Books, 1967.

4:251   Jones, Claude E. "'The Critical Review' and Some Major Poets." *NQ* 3(1956):114-15. Dryden's waning reputation.

4:252   Jones, H. W. "Some Further Pope-Dryden Indebtedness." *NQ* 198 (1953):199.

4:253   Jones, Richard Foster. *Ancients and Moderns: A Study of the Rise of the Scientific Movement in Seventeenth-Century England*. (Washington University Studies n.s. 6, Language and Literature.) St. Louis: Washington University Press, 1936. 2nd ed. 1961. Reprinted Berkeley, Los Angeles: University of California Press, 1965. *See* Moody E. Prior, *MP* 34:322-26. *See also* item 7:59.

4:254   ———. "The Background of *The Battle of the Books*" [1920]. [17th Century]:10-40.

4:255   Joost, Nicholas. "Poetry and Belief: Fideism from Dryden to Eliot." *Dublin Review* 226(1952):35-53.

4:256 Kantorowicz, Ernst. *The King's Two Bodies*. Princeton: Princeton University Press, 1957. An important analysis of the origin and symbolism of monarchical authority. *See* items 4:409, 4:565.

4:257 Kellett, E. E. "John Dryden." *Suggestions: Literary Essays*, pp. 185-204. Cambridge: At the University Press, 1923.

4:258 Kelly, Blanche M. *The Well of English*. New York, London: Harper, 1936.

4:259 Kelly, Edward H. "Petronius Arbiter and Neoclassical English Literature." *DAI* 31(1971):3508A(Rochester).

4:260 Kenyon, John. *The Popish Plot*. London: Heinemann, 1972. Provides a detailed chronology.

4:261 Ker, W. P. *Form and Style in Poetry*, ed. R. W. Chambers. London: Macmillan, 1928.

4:262 Kermode, Frank. "The Poet and His Public: Dryden, A Poets' Poet." *Listener* 57(1957):877-78.

4:263 Kernan, Alvin B. *The Plot of Satire*. New Haven, London: Yale University Press, 1965.

4:264 Kevin, Neil. "The Argument from Poetry." *IER* 50(1937):237-46. Dryden's conversion.

4:265 Kimmey, John L. "John Cleveland and the Satiric Couplet in the Restoration." *PQ* 37(1958):410-23.

4:266 King, Bruce. "Anti-Whig Satire in *The Duke of Guise*." *ELN* 2 (1965):190-93.

4:267 ———. "Dryden's Ark: The Influence of Filmer." *SEL* 7(1967): 403-14.

4:268 Kinsley, James. "Diction and Style in the Poetry of John Dryden." *ASLIB* 1(1950-51):17(Edinburgh).

*4:269 ———. "Dryden and the Art of Praise." *ES* 34(1953):57-64. Reprinted in [Swedenberg]:541-50. Defends Dryden against the charge of obsequiousness; his panegyrics were not only responses to important topical events, but they were also part of a desire to glorify heroic values.

4:270 ———, and Helen Kinsley, eds. *Dryden: The Critical Heritage*. (The Critical Heritage Series.) London: Routledge and Kegan Paul; New York: Barnes and Noble, 1971. Selections of comments on Dryden from 1663 to 1810.

4:271 Knight, Douglas. *Pope and the Heroic Tradition: A Critical Study of His "Iliad."* (Yale Studies in English 117.) New Haven: Yale University Press, 1951.

4:272 Knights, L. C. "The Restoration Period: Dryden and Halifax. The Lesson for Today." *Public Voices: Literature and Politics with Special Reference to the Seventeenth Century*, pp. 94-113. (The Clark Lectures for 1970-71.) London: Chatto and Windus, 1971.

4:273 Knox, Norman. *The Word "Irony" and Its Context, 1500-1755*. Durham: Duke University Press, 1961.

4:274 Korshin, Paul J. "Figural Change and the Survival of Tradition in the Later Seventeenth Century." *Studies in Change and Revolution: Aspects of English Intellectual History 1640-1800*, ed. Paul J. Korshin, pp. 99-128. Menston, Yorkshire: Scolar Press, 1972. The events of the Civil Wars affected the quality of imagery used by writers, but the habit of making Christological allusions persisted.

4:275 ———. *From Concord to Dissent: Major Themes in English Poetic Theory 1640-1700*. Menston, Yorkshire: Scolar Press, 1973. *See SEL* 14:458-59.

4:276 Kramer, L. J. "Formal Satire and Censorship in the Seventeenth
       Century." *Proceedings of the 8th Congress of the Australasian Uni-
       versities' Languages and Literature Association*, pp. 44–45. Can-
       berra: Australian National University, 1964.
4:277 Krutch, Joseph Wood. "Pope and our Contemporaries." [Clifford]:
       251–59. Dryden was more popular among students than was Pope in
       1949.
4:278 Kuchenbäcker, Karl. *Dryden as a Satirist.* Magdeburg: [n. pub.],
       1899.
4:279 Kupersmith, William R., Jr. "Neoclassical English Satire." *DAI*
       30(1970):3012A(Texas, Austin).
4:280 Latt, David J. "The Progress of Friendship: The *Topoi* for Soci-
       ety and the Ideal Experience in the Poetry and Prose of Seven-
       teenth-Century England." *DAI* 32(1972):4616A–17A(U.C.L.A.)
4:281 Leavis, F. R. "English Poetry in the Seventeenth Century."
       Scrutiny 4(1935):236–56. Comments on the change of taste affected
       by T. S. Eliot; on the occasion of the publication of *The Oxford
       Book of Seventeenth Century Verse*.
4:282 ———. "The Line of Wit." *Revaluation: Tradition and Develop-
       ment in English Poetry*, pp. 10–36. London: Chatto and Windus; New
       York: George W. Stewart, 1936. Reprinted in *Seventeenth-Century
       English Poetry: Modern Essays in Criticism*, ed. William R. Keast,
       pp. 31–49. New York: Oxford University Press, 1962. The line: Jon-
       son/Donne—Carew—Marvell—Dryden—Pope. *See* item 4:55.
4:283 Lee, Ronald James. "The Satires of John Oldham: A Study of
       Rhetorical Modes in Restoration Verse Satire." *DA* 28(1967):1080A
       (Stanford).
4:284 Legouis, Pierre. *André Marvell: poète, puritain, patriote 1621–
       1678.* Paris: Didier; London: Oxford University Press, 1928. Re-
       printed in an English language ed. as *Andrew Marvell: Poet, Puri-
       tan, Patriot*. Oxford: At the Clarendon Press, 1965.
4:285 ———. "Ouvrages récents sur Dryden." *EA* 17(1964):148–58. Rev.
       art. *See* items 2/1:11, 2/2:28, 3:193, 4:8, 4:223, 5/4:70.
4:286 ———. "A propos de Dryden." *Les Langues Modernes* 42(1948):A40-
       A-41. Rev. art. *See* items 5/3:1, 5/4:21.
4:287 ———. "La Religion dans L'Oeuvre de Dryden Avant 1682." *Revue
       Anglo-Américaine* 9(1932):383–92, 525–36.
4:288 ———. "Some Remarks on Seventeenth-Century Imagery: Defini-
       tions and Caveats." *Seventeenth-Century Imagery: Essays on Uses
       of Figurative Language from Donne to Farquhar*, ed. Earl Miner,
       pp. 187–97. (The 17th and 18th Centuries Studies Group, U.C.L.A.,
       Clark Memorial Library.) Berkeley, Los Angeles: University of
       California Press, 1971. A cautionary warning about the use of the
       terms "simile," "image," "metaphor," "myth," "symbol," "typology"
       and "emblem." *See* items 4:489, 4:491.
4:289 Levin, Mark J. "Literature and Numismatics in England, 1650–
       1750." *DAI* 35(1974):2230A–31A(Penn.).
*4:290 Levine, Jay Arnold. "The Status of the Verse Epistle Before
       Pope." *SP* 59(1962):658–84.
*4:291 Lewalski, Barbara Kiefer. *Donne's "Anniversaries" and the Po-
       etry of Praise: The Creation of a Symbolic Mode.* Princeton:
       Princeton University Press, 1973. Donne's influence on Dryden's
       elegies and panegyrics; an examination of poetic strategies used
       in the poetry of praise.

4:292 Lewis, C. S. "Shelley, Dryden, and Mr. Eliot." *Rehabilitations and Other Essays*, pp. 3-34. London: Oxford University Press, 1939. Reprinted in *English Romantic Poets*, ed. Meyer H. Abrams, pp. 247-67. New York: Oxford University Press, 1960. *See* item 4:136.

4:293 ———. *Studies in Medieval and Renaissance Literature*, comp. Walter Hooper. Cambridge: At the University Press, 1966.

4:294 Lieser, Paul. *Die englische Ode im Zeitalter des Klassizismus*. Bonn: Universität, 1932.

4:295 Link, Frederick M. "A Decade of Dryden Scholarship." *PLL* 8 (1972):427-43. Rev. art.

4:296 "Little Bayes." *Academy and Literature* 64(1903):34-36. *The Rehearsal* was originally intended as an attack on Davenant.

4:297 Little, David M., and George M. Kahrl, eds. *The Letters of David Garrick*. 3 vols. Assoc. ed. Phoebe deK. Wilson. Cambridge, Mass.: Belknap Press of Harvard University Press, 1963.

4:298 Loane, George G. "Notes on the Globe 'Dryden'." *NQ* 185(1943): 272-81. Rev. art. *See* item 2/2:5.

*4:299 Long, Ralph Bernard. "Dryden's Importance as Spokesman of the Tories." *Studies in English* (University of Texas) 21(1941):79-99. Dryden was not a major spokesman for the Tories in the controversies of 1677-84. *See* items 3:94, 3:142, 3:168, 3:183, 4:26, 5/5:4.

*4:300 Lowell, James Russell. "Dryden" [1870]. *The Complete Writings of James Russell Lowell: Among My Books*. 3:1-112. New York: AMS Press, 1966. A highly evaluative, subjective and perceptive survey of Dryden's life and work which sees him as the first of the moderns, in thought, style and the direction of his activity. *See* item 4:364.

4:301 Maccubbin, Robert P. "Unique Scribleriana Transferred, 1971-1973." *Scriblerian* 6(1973):46-48. The location of MSS. relevant to the study of Dryden and others.

4:302 Macdonald, Hugh. "The Law and Defamatory Biographies in the Seventeenth Century." *RES* 20(1944):177-98.

4:303 MacDonald, W. L. "John Dryden: 1631-1931." *Bookman* (New York) 72(1931):481-88.

4:304 Mace, Agnes K. "The Public Verse Epistle from Dryden to Burns." Diss. Catholic, 1954.

4:305 Mack, Maynard. "The Muse of Satire." *YR* 41(1951):80-92. Reprinted in [Boys]:219-31.

4:306 ———. "'Wit and Poetry and Pope': Some Observations on His Imagery." [Clifford]:20-40.

4:307 Maclean, Norman. "From Action to Image: Theories of the Lyric in the Eighteenth Century." *Critics and Criticism: Ancient and Modern*, ed. R. S. Crane, pp. 408-60. Chicago, London: University of Chicago Press, 1952. In developing the ode, Dryden used Cowley's example and Longinian principles of the sublime.

4:308 Maddison, Carol. *Apollo and the Nine: A History of the Ode*. Baltimore: Johns Hopkins Press, 1960. A detailed survey of classical, European and pre-Restoration uses of the ode.

4:309 Magnus, Lurie. "Dryden." *English Literature in Its Foreign Relations 1300-1800*, pp. 143-70. London: Kegan Paul; New York: E. P. Dutton, 1927.

4:310 Magoon, J. "Dryden and the Language of Poetry." *ASLIB* 10(1959-60):10(Wales, Swansea).

4:311 Maltby, Joseph. "The Effect of Irony on Tone and Structure in Some Poems of Dryden." *DA* 24(1963):2463-64(Wis.).

4:312   Marshall, Donald G. "The Development of Blank-Verse Poetry From Milton to Wordsworth." *DAI* 32(1971):1480A(Yale).

4:313   Masson, David I. "Dryden's Phonetic Rhetoric." *PLPLS* 11(1964): 1-5. Dryden was a transitional figure in the refinement of poetic "sound-patterning."

4:314   Maurer, A. E. Wallace. "Dryden and Pyrrhonism." *NQ* 4(1957):251-52.

4:315   ———. "Dryden's Knowledge of Historians, Ancient and Modern." *NQ* 6(1959):264-66.

4:316   ———. "Dryden's View of History." *SDD-UW* 15(1955):617-18.

4:317   Maxwell, J. C. "Charles Gildon and the Quarrel of the Ancients and Moderns." *RES* 1(1950):55-57. Praise for Dryden as a critic and poet.

4:318   Mayhead, Robin. *Understanding Literature*. Cambridge: Cambridge University Press, 1965. *See YWES* 46:27.

4:319   Mayo, Thomas. *Epicurus in England (1650-1725)*. Dallas: The Southwest Press, 1934.

4:320   Mazzeo, Joseph A. "Cromwell as Davidic King." *Reason and the Imagination*, ed. Joseph A. Mazzeo, pp. 29-55. New York: Columbia University Press, 1962. The figural significance of the Davidic King.

4:321   McCann, Garth A. "Dryden and Poetic Continuity: A Comparative Study." *SAQ* 72(1973):[311]-21.

4:322   McCoy, Dorothy Schuchman. *Tradition and Convention: A Study of Periphrasis in English Pastoral Poetry from 1557-1715*. (Studies in English Literature 5.) The Hague: Mouton, 1965. *See YWES* 46:182.

*4:323 McFadden, George. "Dryden and the Numbers of His Native Tongue." *DSPS* 5(1964):87-109. Dryden as an innovator in prosody.

4:324   ———. "Dryden, Boileau, and Longinian Imitation." *Proceedings of the IVth Congress of the International Comparative Literature Association*, ed. François Jost. 2:751-55. The Hague: Mouton, 1966. The influence of Boileau and Longinus on Dryden.

4:325   ———. "Political Satire in *The Rehearsal*." *YES* 4(1974):120-28. Henry Bennet, Earl of Arlington, not Dryden was the target of Buckingham's attack.

4:326   McFarland, Thomas. "Poetry and the Poem: The Structure of Poetic Content." *Literary Theory and Structure: Essays in Honor of William K. Wimsatt*, eds. Frank Brady, John Palmer and Martin Price, pp. 81-114. New Haven, London: Yale University Press, 1973.

4:327   Means, James A. "Three Notes on Pope." *NQ* 14(1967):410.

4:328   Meissner, Paul. *Die geistesgeschichtlichen Grundlagen des englischen Literaturbarocks*. München: M. Hueber, 1934. *See* R. S. Crane, *PQ* 14:152-54.

4:329   ———. "Die rationalistische Grundlage der englischen Kultur des 17. Jahrhunderts." *Anglia* 55(1931):321-67.

4:330   Milburn, D. Judson. "The Rhetoric of Wit in John Dryden's Poems: 'Upon the Death of the Lord Hastings' and 'Mac Flecknoe'." *The Age of Wit 1650-1750*, pp. 69-74. New York: Macmillan; London: Collier-Macmillan, 1966.

*4:331 Miles, Josephine. *The Continuity of Poetic Language: Studies in English Poetry from the 1540's to the 1940's*. (University of California Publications in English.) Berkeley, Los Angeles: University of California Press, 1951.

4:332   ——. "Dryden and the Classical Mode." *Eras & Modes in English Poetry*, pp. 33–47. Berkeley, Los Angeles: University of California Press, 1957.

4:333   ——. "Eras in English Poetry." *PMLA* 70(1955):853–75.

4:334   ——. *Renaissance, Eighteenth-Century, and Modern Language in English Poetry: A Tabular View*. Berkeley, Los Angeles: University of California Press, 1960. Modes in English literature are indicated by prosodic and rhetorical differences. *See* item 4:52.

4:335   Mill, Donald Charles, Jr. "Variations on Elegiac Themes: Dryden, Pope, Prior, Gray, Johnson." *DA* 22(1961):1159–60(Penn.).

4:336   Miller, Henry Knight. "The 'Whig Interpretation' of Literary History." *ECS* 6(1972):60–84. Distortions created by ahistorical critical approaches.

4:337   Miller, John. *Popery and Politics in England 1660-1688*. Cambridge: At the University Press, 1973.

4:338   Miller, Raymond D. "Secondary Accent in Modern English Verse (Chaucer to Dryden)." Diss. Johns Hopkins, 1904.

4:339   Miner, Earl. *The Cavalier Mode from Jonson to Cotton*. Princeton: Princeton University Press, 1971.

4:340   ——. "Distributing the Middle: Problems of 'Movement' in Narrative Poetry." *To Tell a Story: Narrative Theory and Practice*, introd. Robert Martin Adams, pp. 1–22. (Papers Read at a Clark Library Seminar February 14, 1972.) Los Angeles: Clark Memorial Library, University of California, 1973. A consideration of the different techniques used to establish narrative structure.

*4:341 ——. "Dryden and the Issue of Human Progress." *PQ* 40(1961): 120–29.

*4:342 ——. *Dryden's Poetry*. Bloomington, London: Indiana University Press, 1967. *See* Reuben A. Brower, *MLQ* 29:110–12; Patrick Cruttwell, *HudR* 21:197–207; Arthur W. Hoffman, *MP* 66:166–68; James William Johnson, *SCN* 26:40–41; Jay Arnold Levine, *Crit* 10: 244–49; Geoffrey Walton, *ELN* 6:134–36; *SEL* (Tokyo) 44:253–58; *TLS* 9 January 1969, p. 41; V. de Sola Pinto, *MLR* 64:399–401; Pierre Legouis, *EA* 20:311–12; Eugene Waith, *YR* 17:123–26; Ernest Tuveson, *PQ* 47:373–75.

4:343   ——. "From Narrative to 'Description' and 'Sense' in Eighteenth-Century Poetry." *SEL* 9(1969):471–87. Increasingly, sentiment is given greater importance than is plot in poetry.

*4:344 ——. "Forms and Motives of Narrative Poetry." [Miner]:234–66. Various narrative forms used by Dryden; a survey of his career.

4:345   ——. "In Satire's Falling City." *The Satirist's Art*, ed. H. James Jensen and Malvin R. Zirker, Jr., pp. 3–27. Bloomington: Indiana University Press, 1972.

*4:346 ——. "On Reading Dryden." [Miner]:1–26. A review of Dryden's reputation and a helpful introduction to his works.

4:347   ——, introd. *Poems on the Reign of William III (1690, 1696, 1699, 1702)*. (ARS 166.) Los Angeles: Clark Memorial Library, University of California, 1974.

*4:348 ——. *The Restoration Mode from Milton to Dryden*. Princeton: Princeton University Press, 1974. The "public" character of Dryden's works.

*4:349 ——. "Some Characteristics of Dryden's Use of Metaphor." *SEL* 2(1969):309–20. Reprinted in [Critical Essays]:115–24.

4:350 ———. "The Wild Man Through the Looking Glass." *The Wild Man Within: An Image in Western Thought from the Renaissance to Romanticism*, eds. Edward Dudley and Maximillan E. Novak, pp. 87-114. Pittsburgh: University of Pittsburgh Press, 1972.

4:351 Monk, Samuel Holt. "Dryden Studies: A Survey, 1920-1945." *ELH* 14(1947):46-63. Reprinted in [Swedenberg]:3-21.

4:352 ———. "Dryden the Craftsman." *SR* 54(1946):720-27.

4:353 Montgomery, Guy."Dryden and the Battle of the Books." *University of California Publications in English* 14(1943):57-72.

4:354 Moore, Charles A. "The Familar Verse Epistle from Dryden to Pope." *DAI* 31(1971):3513A(Oregon).

4:355 Moore, Judith K. "Early Eighteenth-Century Literature and the Financial Revolution." *DAI* 31(1971):6561A(Cornell). An economic-political analysis.

4:356 Morgan, Edwin. "Dryden's Drudging." *CamJ* 6(1953):414-29. Reprinted in [Critical Essays]:55-70.

4:357 Morley, Iris. *A Thousand Lives: An Account of the English Revolutionary Movement 1660-1685*. London: Andre Deutsch, 1954.

4:358 Morpurgo, J. E., ed. *Life Under the Stuarts*. London: Falcon, 1950.

4:359 Moulton, Charles Wèlls, ed. "John Dryden." *The Library of Literary Criticism of English and American Authors*. 2:462-507. Buffalo: Moulton, 1901. Critical commentary on Dryden from his contemporaries to the twentieth century.

4:360 Mundy, Percy Dryden. "Recent Work on Dryden." *NQ* 181(1941):131-32. Rev. art. *See* items 1:44, 1:45, 1:46, 3:144.

4:361 Murakami, Shikō. "Reverence for Human Nature: The Poetry of Dryden and Pope." *The Journal of the Faculty of Letters, Osaka University* 10(1963):i-vi, 1-84.

4:362 Murphy, Arthur. *New Essays*, ed. with introd. Arthur Sherbo. East Lansing: Michigan State University Press, 1963. A mid-eighteenth-century view of Dryden.

4:363 Murphy, Dennis. "Metaphor and Simile in Dryden's Non-Dramatic Poetry." Diss. Iowa, 1936.

4:364 Murray, Byron D. "Lowell's Criticism of Dryden and Pope." *DDARUI* 6(1953):434-41:

4:365 Myers, William. *Dryden*. London: Hutchinson, 1973. An introductory essay.

4:366 Neff, Emery. *A Revolution in European Poetry 1660-1900*. New York: Columbia University Press, 1940.

4:367 Nelson, Raymond S. "Eros Lost." *IEY* 22,iii(1972):42-47.

4:368 Nethercot, Arthur H. *Abraham Çowley: The Muse's Hannibal*. London: Oxford University Press, 1931. Reprinted New York: Russell and Russell, 1967.

4:369 Nevo, Ruth. *The Dial of Virtue: A Study of Poems on Affairs of State in the Seventeenth Century*. Princeton: Princeton University Press, 1963.

4:370 Nichols, James William. "Satiric Insinuation: A Study of the Tactics of English Indirect Satire." *DA* 24(1963):302(Wash.).

4:371 Nicoll, Allardyce. *Dryden and His Poetry*. (Poetry and Life Series 32.) London: George G. Harrap, 1923.

4:372 Novarr, David. "Swift's Relation with Dryden, and Gulliver's *Annus Mirabilis*." *ES* 47(1966):341-54.

4:373 Nussbaum, Frederick. *The Triumph of Science and Reason 1660-1685*. (The Rise of Modern Europe.) New York: Harper, 1953.

4:374 O'Brien, Robert David. "What about Dryden?" *America* 66(1941): 101-02.

4:375 Ogden, Henry V. S., and Margaret S. Ogden. *English Taste in Landscape in the Seventeenth Century*. Ann Arbor: University of Michigan Press, 1955.

4:376 Osborn, James M. "The First History of English Poetry." [Clifford]:230-50. Joseph Spence's *Anecdotes, Observations and Characters of Books and Men*

4:377 Parker, William Riley. *Milton: A Biography*. 2 vols. Oxford: At the Clarendon Press, 1968.

4:378 Parkin, Rebecca Price. "Some Rhetorical Aspects of Dryden's Biblical Allusions." *ECS* 2(1969):341-69.

4:379 Peltz, Catherine Walsh. "The Neo-Classic Lyric 1660-1725." *ELH* 11(1944):92-116.

4:380 Perlberg, Charley W. "The Public Verse Panegyrics of John Dryden." *DAI* 34(1973):1251A(No. Ill.).

4:381 Peterson, Richard G. "The Roman Image in English Literature from 1660 to 1700." *DA* 25(1964):2518(Minn.).

4:382 Pinkus, Philip. *Grub St. Stripped Bare*. Hamden, Conn.: Archon Books; London: Constable, 1968.

4:383 ———. "The New Satire of Augustan England." *UTQ* 38(1969):136-58.

4:384 ———. "Satire and St. George." *QQ* 70(1963):30-49.

4:385 Pinto, V. de Sola. "John Wilmot, Earl of Rochester, on the Right Veine of Satire." *Essays and Studies* 6(1953):56-70. Reprinted in [Keast]:474-89.

4:386 ———. *Restoration Carnival: Five Courtier Poets: Rochester, Dorset, Sedley, Etherege, and Sheffield*. London: Folio Society, 1954.

4:387 ———. "Rochester and Dryden." *RMS* 5(1961):29-48.

4:388 Piper, William Bowman. *The Heroic Couplet*. Baltimore. Case Western Reserve, 1969. *See* Paul Korshin, *PQ* 49:316-18.

4:389 "A Poet Hidden." *TLS* 14 September 1962, p. 688. Rev. art. *See* items 3:193, 5/4:70.

4:390 Pollard, Arthur. *Satire*. (The Critical Idiom 7.) London: Methuen, 1970.

4:391 Pollin, Burton R. "'The World Is Too Much with Us': Two More Sources—Dryden and Godwin." *WC* 1(1970):50-52.

4:392 Pollock, John. *The Popish Plot: A Study in the History of the Reign of Charles II*. London: Duckworth, 1903.

4:393 Press, John. *The Fire and the Fountain: An Essay on Poetry*. London, New York, Toronto: Oxford University Press, 1955.

4:394 Previté-Orton, C. W. "Political and Ecclesiastical Satire." [Cambridge History]:91-114.

4:395 ———. "The Satiric Age." *Political Satire in English Poetry*, pp. 92-136. Cambridge: At the University Press, 1910. Dryden was merely a hireling of the court.

*4:396 Price, Martin. "Dryden and Dialectic." *To the Palace of Wisdom: Studies in Order and Energy from Dryden to Blake*, pp. 28-78. Garden City, New York: Doubleday, 1964.

4:397 Prince, F. T. "Dryden Redivivus." *REL* 1,i(1960):71-79. A general survey of recent criticism.

4:398 ———. "The Study of Form and the Renewal of Poetry." *PBA* 50 (1964):45-61.

4:399   Q., O.D. "Dryden: Sources Wanted." *NQ* 196(1951):480. *See* ibid.,
177(1939):124-25 and response, ibid., 17(1970):262.

4:400   Quayle, Thomas. *Poetic Diction, A Study of Eighteenth Century
Verse*. London: Methuen, 1924.

4:401   Raine, Kathleen. "A Dryden Quotation." *TLS* 13 September 1957,
p. 547. From Blake's *The Gates of Paradise*.

4:402   Raleigh, Sir Walter Alexander. "John Dryden and Political Satire." *Some Authors*, pp. 156-73. Oxford: At the Clarendon Press,
1923.

4:403   Ramsey, Paul, Jr. *The Art of John Dryden*. Lexington: University of Kentucky Press, 1969. *See* Alan Roper, *PQ* 49:345-46; *YWES*
50:243.

4:404   ——. "The Image of Nature in John Dryden." *DA* 16(1956):2461
(Minn.).

4:405   ——. *The Lively and the Just: An Argument for Propriety*.
(University of Alabama Studies 15.) Montgomery: University of Alabama Press, 1962. *See PQ* 42:325.

4:406   "Ranger." "John Dryden." *Bookman* (London) 31(1906):68-70.

4:407   Rayan, Krishna. *Suggestion and Statement in Poetry*. London:
The Athlone Press, 1972.

4:408   Reed, Edward Bliss. *English Lyric Poetry from Its Origins to
the Present Time*. New Haven: Yale University Press, 1912. Reprinted New York: Haskell House, 1967.

*4:409   Reedy, Gerard, S. J. "Mystical Politics: The Imagery of
Charles II's Coronation." *Studies in Change and Revolution: Aspects of English Intellectual History 1640-1800*, ed. Paul J. Korshin, pp. 19-42. Menston, Yorkshire: Scolar Press, 1972. *See*
items 4:256, 4:565, 5/1:6.

4:410   ——. "Restoration Interpretation." *DAI* 34(1974):5201A(Penn.).
Methods of scriptural exegesis and the interpretation of King-
ship.

4:411   Reuss, Adam. "Das persönliche Geschlecht and unpersönlicher
Substantive bei John Milton und John Dryden." Diss. Kiel, 1913.

4:412   Reynolds, Myra. *The Learned Lady in England (1650-1760)*. Boston, New York: Houghton Mifflin, 1920. Dryden's relationships
with several women of letters are sketched.

4:413   ——. *The Treatment of Nature in English Poetry Between Pope
and Wordsworth*. Chicago: University of Chicago Press, 1896.

4:414   Rhys, Ernest. "Dryden and the Formalists." *Lyric Poetry*, pp.
241-46. (The Channels of English Literature.) London, Toronto:
J. M. Dent; New York: E. P. Dutton, 1913.

4:415   Richardson, Charles F. "Formal Rhyme." *A Study of English
Rhyme*, pp. 146-57. Hanover, N.H.: University Press, 1909.

4:416   Richter, Walter. *Der Hiatus im englischen Klassizismus (Milton,
Dryden, Pope)*. Schramberg: Gatzer and Hahn, 1934.

*4:417   Rivers, Isabel. "John Dryden: The Recreation of Monarchy."
*The Poetry of Conservatism, 1600-1745: A Study of Poets and Pub-
lic Affairs from Jonson to Pope*, pp. 127-74. Cambridge: Rivers
Press, 1973. Dryden's role as a public poet was complicated by
Stuart policies, which often sacrificed principle in favor of ex-
pediency.

4:418   ——. "The Poetry of Conservatism, 1600-1745: Jonson, Dryden,
and Pope." *DAI* 30(1970):4424A(Columbia).

4:419   Romagosa, Sister Edward, O. Carm. "A Compendium of the Opinions of John Dryden." *DA* 19(1959):3296(Tulane). A dictionary of Dryden's opinions.

4:420 Rommel, George W. "The Concept of France in England in the Restoration Period." *DA* 13(1953):1198-99(Northwestern).

4:421 Roper, Alan H. "Dryden and the Stuart Succession." Diss. Johns Hopkins, 1961.

*4:422 ———. *Dryden's Poetic Kingdoms*. London: Routledge and Kegan Paul; New York: Barnes and Noble, 1965. *See* Arthur C. Kirsch, *CE* 27:644; Pierre Legouis, *EA* 19:187-88; C. F. Williamson, *RES* 17: 205-07; *YWES* 46:217-18. *See* item 5/5:5.

4:423 Roscioni, Gian Carlo. "Sir Robert Howard's 'Sceptical Curiosity'." *MP* 65(1967):53-59.

4:424 Rose Marie, Sister. "John Dryden—Poet or Not?" *CathW* 139 (1934):283-89.

4:425 Roston, Murray. *Prophet and Poet: The Bible and the Growth of Romanticism*. Evanston: Northwestern University Press, 1965.

4:426 Roth, Frederic Hull, Jr. "'Heaven's Center, Nature's Lap': A Study of the English Country-Estate Poem of the Seventeenth Century." *DAI* 34(1974):5120A-21A(Virginia).

4:427 Rust, Isabel B. "Theory of the Ode Applied to the English Ode Before 1700." *DA* 7,i(1946):83-85(Mich.).

4:428 Ruthven, K. K. "The Decline of the Conceit." *The Conceit*, pp. 52-60. (The Critical Idiom.) London: Methuen; New York: Barnes and Noble, 1969.

4:429 Saintsbury, George. "The Age of Dryden." *A History of English Prosody From the Twelfth Century to the Present Day*. 2:359-444. London, New York: Macmillan, 1906. Reprinted New York: Russell and Russell, 1961. A general survey of prosodic theory and practice in Dryden's heroic plays, translations and poems, with comparisons to the works of his contemporaries.

4:430 ———. "The Heritage of Dryden and the World of 'The Spectator'." *The Peace of the Augustans*, pp. 1-42. London: G. Bell, 1916. Reprinted Oxford: World Classics, 1946.

4:431 ———. "The Prosody of the Seventeenth Century." [Cambridge History]:253-73.

4:432 Sánchez Escribano, Federico. "Lope de Vega Según una Alusión de John Dryden." *Hispano* 161(1962):101-02.

4:433 Schafer, William J. "The Sources of Augustan Satire: Polemic and Poetry." *DA* 28(1968):5027A-28A(Minn.).

4:434 Schap, Keith. "A Transformational Study of John Dryden's Metrical Practice." *DAI* 33(1973):5692A-93A(Ind.).

4:435 Schelling, Felix E. "Ben Jonson and the Classical School." *PMLA* 13(1898):221-49.

4:436 ———. *The English Lyric*. (The Types of English Literature.) Boston, New York: Houghton Mifflin, 1913.

4:437 Schilling, Bernard N. "The Man of Letters as Conservative: John Dryden." *SCN* 9(1951):1.

4:438 Schulte, E. *Profilo Storico Della Metrica Inglese*. Naples: Instituto Universitario Orientale, 1960.

4:439 Seaton, Ethel. *Literary Relations of England and Scandinavia in the Seventeenth Century*. Oxford: At the Clarendon Press, 1935.

4:440 Seidel, Michael A. "The Restoration Mob: Drones and Dregs." *SEL* 12(1972):429-43.

4:441 ———. "Satiric Theory and the Degeneration of State: The Tyrant and the Mob in Satiric Literature of the Restoration and Early Eighteenth Century." *DAI* 31(1971):3519A(U.C.L.A.).

*4:442   Seldon, Raman. "Roughness in Satire from Horace to Dryden."
     MLR 66(1971):264-72.
4:443   Sencourt, Robert/R. E. G. George (pseud.). *India in English
     Literature*. London: Simpkin, Marshall, Hamilton, Kent, 1923.
4:444   Shaheen, Abdel-Rahman A. "Satiric Characterization in John Dry-
     den's Later Works." *DAI* 33(1972):2905A-06A(Houston). The dramatic
     and nondramatic works should be seen as complementary in their
     use of satiric characterization and in their reflection of Dry-
     den's disillusionment with the contemporary scene.
*4:445   Sharpe, Robert L. *From Donne to Dryden: The Revolt Against
     Metaphysical Poetry*. Chapel Hill: University of North Carolina
     Press, 1940. Reprinted Hamden, Conn.: Archon Books, 1965. *See* Aus-
     tin Warren, *MLN* 56:312-13; James Sutherland, *RES* 19:84-85; René
     Wellek, *PQ* 20:90-92; Samuel Holt Monk, *SoR* 7:366-84. *See also*
     item 4:515.
*4:446   Sharrock, Roger. "Modes of Satire." [Rest. Theatre]:109-32.
4:447   Shawcross, John T., ed. "John Dryden 1631-1700" and "Milton
     and Neoclassical Literature." *The Critical Temper: A Survey of
     Modern Criticism on English and American Literature from the Be-
     ginnings to the Twentieth Century*, ed. Martin Tucker. 2:52-63.
     New York: Ungar, 1969. Excerpts from various commentators.
4:448   Sherburn, George, and Donald F. Bond. "The Restoration and
     Eighteenth Century (1660-1789)." *A Literary History of England*,
     ed. Albert C. Baugh, pp. 699-1108. 2nd ed. New York: Appleton-
     Century-Crofts, 1967. *See PQ* 47:344-45.
4:449   Shuster, George N. "John Dryden and the Restoration." *The En-
     glish Ode from Milton to Keats*, pp. 123-45. (Columbia University
     Studies in English and Comparative Literature 150.) New York: Co-
     lumbia University Press, 1940.
*4:450   Simon, Irène. "'Pride of Reason' in the Restoration and Ear-
     lier Eighteenth Century." *RLV* 25(1959):375-96, 453-73. Distrust
     of the imagination.
4:451   Sinclair, Giles M. "The Aesthetic Function of Rime in Dryden's
     Verse." *DA* 13(1953):801-02(Mich.).
4:452   Sloane, Eugene Hulse. *Robert Gould: Seventeenth Century Satir-
     ist*. Philadelphia: University of Pennsylvania, 1940.
4:453   Smith, Byron P. *Islam in English Literature*. Beirut: At the
     American Press, 1939.
4:454   Smith, Courtney Craig. "The Seventeenth-Century Drolleries."
     HLB 6(1952):40-51. An early version of the miscellany; Dryden's
     poems appear in *Westminster Drollery* (1671/72).
4:455   Smith, David Nichol. *John Dryden*. (Clark Lectures on English
     Literature, 1948-49.) Cambridge: At the University Press, 1950.
     Reprinted Hamden, Conn.: Archon, 1966. Chap. "Plays" excerpted in
     [20th Century Interpretations]:43-45. *See* B. G. MacCarthy, *Studies*
     39:347; *DUJ* 42:120-21; *NQ* 195:549-50; *TLS* 24 March 1951, p. 186;
     H. T. Swedenberg, Jr., *PQ* 30:268-69; Charles E. Ward, *MLN* 67:489-90.
4:456   Smith, Egerton. *Principles of English Metre*. Oxford: Oxford
     University Press, 1923.
4:457   Smith, John Harrington. "Some Sources of Dryden's Toryism,
     1682-1684." *HLQ* 20(1956-57):233-43.
4:458   Smith, Harold Wendell. "Nature, Correctness and Decorum." *Scru-
     tiny* 18(1952):287-314.
4:459   ———. "'Reason' and the Restoration Ethos." *Scrutiny* 18
     (1951-52):118-36, 175-88, 287-314. Discusses Restoration defini-
     tions of reason and the increasing division between the secular,

social and the religious, divine worlds. *See* correspondence, Marjorie Cox, ibid., 189; V. de Sola Pinto, ibid., 191.

4:460   Smith, J. L. "Some Aspects of the Verse-Epistle in English Literature before Pope." *ASLIB* 17(1966-67):18(Oxford).

4:461   Smith, Nowell. "Beamy." *TLS* 17 July 1930, p. 592. Dryden's use of the word.

4:462   Smith, R. Jack. "Drydeniana." *TLS* 27 December 1941, p. 655. Addenda to Macdonald.

4:463   Soule, George Alan, Jr. "Dryden and the Poetry of Public Action." Diss. Yale, 1960.

*4:464   Spencer, Jeffry B. "Dryden's Decorative Landscapes: Harmonizing the Classical and the Baroque." *Heroic Nature: Ideal Landscape in English Poetry from Marvell to Thomson*, pp. 139-89. Evanston: Northwestern Univeristy Press, 1973. The tradition of *ut pictura poesis*. *See* Paul J. Korshin, *ELN* 12:203-06.

4:465   ———. "Five Poetic Landscapes, 1650-1750: Heroic and Ideal Landscape in English Poetry from Marvell to Thomson." *DAI* 32 (1971):3271A(Northwestern).

4:466   Spencer, Theodore. "Antaeus or Poetic Language and the Actual World." *ELH* 10(1943):173-92.

4:467   Stallman, Robert W. "Dryden in Modern Poetry and Criticism." *SDD-UW* 7(1943):302-04. Defends Dryden by using the arguments and methodologies of the New Critics.

4:468   Stamm, Rudolf. "Englischer Literaturbarock?" *Die Kunstformen des Barockzeitalters*, ed. Rudolf Stamm, pp. 383-412. Berne: Francke, 1956. *See* Lowry Nelson, Jr., *PQ* 36:334-36.

4:469   Stauffer, Donald A. *English Biography before 1700*. Cambridge, Mass.: Harvard University Press, 1930. Reprinted New York: Russell and Russell, 1964.

4:470   Steger, Hugo. *David Rex et Propheta*. (Erlanger Beiträge zur Sprach- und Kunstwissenschaft 6.) Nürnberg: H. Carl, 1961.

4:471   Stevenson, Samuel W. *Romantic Tendencies in the Works of Dryden, Addison, Pope*. Diss. Johns Hopkins, 1932.

4:472   St. John, L. "Dryden's Political Tone." Diss. Alberta, 1972.

4:473   Strachan, L. R. M. "'Fry' in Dryden and Leigh Hunt." *NQ* (11th ser.) 2(1910):321-22.

4:474   Strahan, Speer. "A Wreath for John Dryden." *Commonweal* 14 (1931):400-01.

4:475   Straumann, Benno. *John Dryden: Order and Chaos*. Zürich: Juris, 1972.

4:476   Stuckey, Johanna Heather. "The Reputation and Influence of C. Petronius Arbiter Among English Men of Letters from 1600-1700." *DA* 27(1966):188A-89A(Yale).

4:477   Sutherland, James R. "Anne Greene and the Oxford Poets." *The Augustan Milieu: Essays Presented to Louis A. Landa*, eds. Henry Knight Miller, Eric Rothstein, and G. S. Rousseau, pp. 1-17. Oxford: At the Clarendon Press, 1970. Dryden reacted against the extravagances of earlier, "Metaphysical" poets.

4:478   ———. *English Literature of the Late Seventeenth Century*. (Oxford History of English Literature.) Oxford: At the Clarendon Press, 1969. *See* G. S. Rousseau, *ECS* 2:454-63; James M. Osborn, *PQ* 69:319-21.

4:479   ———. *English Satire*. (The Clark Lectures, 1956.) Cambridge: At the University Press, 1958.

*4:480   ———. "The Impact of Charles II on Restoration Literature." *Restoration and Eighteenth-Century Essays in Honor of Alan Dugald*

McKillop, ed. Carroll Camden, pp. 251-63. Chicago, London: University of Chicago Press for William Marsh Rice University, 1963.

4:481 ——. *John Dryden: The Poet as Orator*. (The twentieth W. P. Ker Memorial Lecture delivered in the University of Glasgow 21st February, 1962.) Glasgow: Jackson, 1963. *See TLS* 19 March 1964, p. 241.

4:482 ——. *A Preface to Eighteenth Century Poetry*. Oxford: At the Clarendon Press, 1948. *See* item 4:185.

4:483 Swayne, Mattie. "The Progress Piece in the Seventeenth Century." *Studies in English* (University of Texas) 16(1936):84-92.

*4:484 Swedenberg, H. T., Jr. "Dryden's Obsessive Concern with the Heroic." *Essays in English Literature of the Classical Period Presented to Douglad MacMillan*, eds. Daniel W. Patterson and Albrecht B. Strauss, pp. 12-26. (*SP* Extra Series 4.) Chapel Hill: University of North Carolina Press, 1967. Throughout his career and in all the various genres (excepting comedy) in which he worked, Dryden pursued heroic subjects and values. *See* items 4: 530-31, 6/2:81, 8/2:94.

4:485 Sypher, Wylie. *Four Stages of Renaissance Style: Transformations in Art and Literature 1400-1700*. Garden City, New York: Doubleday, 1955.

4:486 Taylor, Myron W. "Two Analogies for Poetry in the Seventeenth Century." *DA* 21(1961):3772(Washington Univ.). Painting and history.

*4:487 Thale, Mary. "Dryden's Unwritten Epic." *PLL* 5(1969):424-44. Dryden failed to write an epic because he was overawed by the Homeric and Virgilian precedents.

4:488 Thomson, J. A. K. *The Classical Influences on English Poetry*. London: George Allen and Unwin, 1948. A preliminary survey of Dryden's classicism.

*4:489 Thorpe, Peter. "'No Metaphor Swell'd High'": The Relative Unimportance of Imagery or Figurative Language in Augustan Poetry." *TSLL* 13(1972):593-612. Dryden, Pope and Johnson suppressed the use of imagery or evaded it entirely; an argument against current critical assumptions. *See* items 2:288, 4:559-60.

*4:490 ——. "The Nonstructure of Augustan Verse." *PLL* 5(1969):235-51. An argument against the new critical approach, which depersonalizes art and which attempts to examine structures of unity in works of seeming disorderliness. *See* items 4:60, 4:185.

*4:491 ——. "Some Fallacies in the Study of Augustan Poetry." *Criticism* 9(1967):326-36. A survey of errors committed by twentieth-century critics. *See YWES* 48:230-31. *See also* items 4:288, 4: 559.

4:492 Tillotson, Geoffrey. *Augustan Poetic Diction*. London: University of London, 1964.

4:493 ——. *Augustan Studies*. London: University of London (The Athlone Press), 1961.

4:494 ——. "Eighteenth-Century Poetic Diction." *Essays in Criticism and Research*, pp. 53-85. Cambridge: At the University Press, 1942. Reprinted Hamden, Conn.: Archon Books, 1967.

4:495 Tillyard, E. M. W. "Dryden." *The English Epic and Its Background*, pp. 465-81. Oxford: Oxford University Press, 1954. Reprinted New York: Barnes and Noble, 1966.

4:496 ——. *Poetry Direct and Oblique*. London: Chatto and Windus, 1934. Reprinted New York: Barnes and Noble, 1959.

4:497 Trickett, Rachel. "The Augustan Pantheon: Mythology and Personification in Eighteenth Century Poetry." *Essays and Studies* 6

(1953):71-86. The *ut pictura poesis* theme in literature and criticism.

4:498 ———. "Dryden." *The Honest Muse: A Study in Augustan Verse*, pp. 27-84. Oxford: At the Clarendon Press, 1967. Dryden was influential in the development of the figure of the honest persona and in its application to all genres.

4:499 Trnka, Bohumil. *On the Syntax of the English Verb from Caxton to Dryden*. (Travaux du Cercle linguistique de Prague 3.) Prague: Jednota československych matematiků a fysiků, 1930.

4:500 Tucker, Martin, ed. "John Dryden, 1631-1700." *Moulton's Library of Literary Criticism of English and American Authors*. 1:561-97. New York: Ungar, 1966. Excerpts from various sources on Dryden's life and works.

4:501 Tucker, T. G. *The Foreign Debt of English Literature*. London: G. Bell, 1907. Reprinted New York: Haskell House, 1966.

4:502 Turnell, G. M. "Dryden and the Religious Elements in the Classical Tradition." *EST* 70(1935):244-61. Dryden as an anti-Romantic.

4:503 Upham, Alfred Horatio. *The French Influence in English Literature: From the Accession of Elizabeth to the Restoration*. New York: Columbia University Press, 1908. Reprinted New York: Octagon Books, 1965.

4:504 Vallese, Tarquinio. *Politics and Poetry (Political Influence on English Poetry)*. Milano: Società anonima editrice Dante Alighieri, 1937.

4:505 Van Doren, Mark. "The Poetry of John Dryden." Diss. Columbia, 1920.

*4:506 ———. *The Poetry of John Dryden*. New York: Harcourt, Brace, 1920. Rev. ed., with introd. by Bonamy Dobrée. Cambridge: Minority Press, 1931. Reprinted New York: Rinehart, 1946. Reprinted as *John Dryden: A Study of His Poetry*. Bloomington: The University of Indiana Press, 1960. Chap. 6 ("The Lyric Poet") reprinted in [Keast]:425-53. *See* Stuart P. Sherman, *Nation* 111:619-20; George R. Noyes, *Weekly Review* 4:83-84; Joseph Wood Krutch, *Literary Review* 8 January 1921, p. 4; C. Van Doorn, *ES* 4:212-14; Elizabeth Nitchie, *SR* 31:376-77; T. S. Eliot, *TLS* 9 June 1921, pp. 361-62.

*4:507 Verrall, A. W. *Lectures on Dryden*, ed. Margaret de G. Verrall. Cambridge: At the University Press, 1914. Reprinted New York: Russell and Russell, 1963. *See* Reginald Hewitt, *Beiblatt* 25:239-42. *See also* item 4:257.

4:508 Vieth, David M. "Concept as Metaphor: Dryden's Attempted Stylistic Revolution." *Lang&S* 3:(1970):197-204.

4:509 ———. "Introductory Note [to special Fall issue on Restoration and Eighteenth Century Literature]." *PLL* 6(1966):291-92. Critical approaches used to study the period.

4:510 Walker, Hugh. "Classical Satire from Denham to Dryden." *English Satire and Satirists*, pp. 145-65. London, New York: J. M. Dent, 1925. Reprinted New York: Octagon Books, 1972.

*4:511 Wallace, John M. "Dryden and History: A Problem in Allegorical Reading." *ELH* 36(1969):265-90.

4:512 Wallerstein, Ruth C. "The Development of the Rhetoric and Metre of the Heroic Couplet, Especially in 1625-1645." *PMLA* 50 (1935):166-209.

*4:513 ———. *Studies in Seventeenth-Century Poetic*. Madison, Milwaukee: University of Wisconsin Press, 1950. Places Dryden into a seventeenth-century elegiac tradition.

4:514 Walton, Geoffrey. "Abraham Cowley and the Decline of Metaphysical Poetry." *Scrutiny* 6(1937):176-94.

4:515 ————. *Metaphysical to Augustan: Studies in Tone and Sensibility in the Seventeenth Century*. London: Bowes and Bowes, 1955.

4:516 Ward, A. W. "Dryden." [Cambridge History]:1-64.

4:517 ————. "Dryden's Verse [1880]." *Collected Papers* 4:64-79. Cambridge: At the University Press, 1921.

4:518 Warnke, Frank J. *Versions of Baroque: European Literature in the Seventeenth Century*. New Haven, London: Yale University Press, 1972.

4:519 Warren, Austin. *Alexander Pope as Critic and Humanist*. (Princeton Studies in English 1.) Princeton: Princeton University Press, 1929. Reprinted Gloucester, Mass.: Peter Smith, 1963.

*4:520 Wasserman, George R. *John Dryden*. (Twayne's English Authors Series.) New York: Twayne, 1964. A good introduction to Dryden's works.

4:521 Wasserman, Earl R. "The Return of the Enjambed Couplet." *ELH* 7 (1940):239-52. A historical survey of shifting attitudes about Dryden's prosody.

*4:522 Watson, George. "Dryden and the Jacobites." *TLS* 16 March 1973, pp. 301-02. A good summary of Dryden's situation after 1688.

4:523 ————. "Dryden and the Scientific Image." *Notes and Records of the Royal Society of London* 18(1963):25-35. The use of scientific analogies is evidence of the Royal Society's influence on Dryden. Includes a reproduction of a portrait by Kneller.

4:524 Watt, Ian. "Three Aspects of the Augustan Tradition: The Roman Analogy; The Georgian Background; The Ironic Voice." *Listener* 77 (1967):454-57, 489-91, 553-55. Two views of Augustus, tyrant and patron of the arts, and the use of irony.

4:525 Wedgwood, C. V. *Poetry and Politics under the Stuarts*. Cambridge: Cambridge University Press, 1960. *See* Maurice Ashley, *Listener* 63:415; *TLS* 1 April 1961, p. 209; J. C. Maxwell, *NQ* 7:437.

4:526 ————. *Seventeenth-Century English Literature*. London, New York, Toronto: Oxford University Press, 1950. 2nd ed. 1970.

4:527 Weinbrot, Howard D. "Robert Gould: Some Borrowings from Dryden." *ELN* 3(1965):36-40.

4:528 Welle, J. A. van der. *Dryden and Holland*. Groningen: Wolters, 1962. *See TLS* 23 January 1964, p. 69.

4:529 Wendell, Barrett. "The Age of Dryden." *The Temper of the Seventeenth Century in English Literature*, pp. 327-55. New York: Scribner, 1904. Reprinted (Essay Index Reprint Series) Freeport, N.Y.: Books for Libraries Press, 1967.

4:530 West, Michael D. "Dryden's Attitude Toward the Hero." Diss. Harvard, 1965.

*4:531 ————. "Shifting Concepts of Heroism in Dryden's Panegyrics." *PLL* 10(1974):378-93. *See* items 4:484, 6/2:81, 8/2:94.

4:532 Westerfrölke, Hermann. *Englische Kaffeehauser als Sammelpunkte der literarischen Welt im Zeitalter von Dryden und Addison*. (Janaer germanistische Forschungen 5.) Jena: Biedermann, 1924.

4:533 Weygant, Peter S. "Oldham's Versification and the Literary Style of the English Enlightenment." *EnlE* 3(1972):120-25. Dryden's strictures on Oldham's prosody.

4:534 White, Maurice D. "John Dryden's Poetry of Praise: The Question of Irony." *DAI* 32(1971):2071A(Ohio State). Seventeenth-century epideictic literature does not use irony.

4:535 Wild, B. Josef. *Dryden und die römische Kirche*. Leipzig: Universitätsverlag, 1925. *See PQ* 8:190.

*4:536 Wilding, Michael. "Dryden and Satire: *Mac Flecknoe*, *Absalom and Achitophel*, the *Medall*, and *Juvenal*." [Miner]:191-233. Examines Dryden's satiric procedures and their relation to seventeenth-century traditions of satire.

4:537 Wilkinson, John. "The Style of Dryden's Early Poetry and of *Absalom and Achitophel*." *DAI* 31(1971):4740A-41A(S.U.N.Y., Buffalo).

4:538 Williams, Charles. *Rochester*. London: A. Barker, 1935.

4:539 Williams, David W. "The Funeral Elegies of John Dryden." *DAI* 33(1973):5756A(Yale).

4:540 Williams, Kathleen. "Restoration Themes in the Major Satires of Swift." *RES* 16(1965):258-71.

4:541 Williams, Weldon M. "The Early Political Satire of the Restoration." *UW-AT* 5(1941):297-303.

4:542 Williamson, George. "Dryden and the Reaction." *The Donne Tradition: A Study in English Poetry from Donne to the Death of Cowley*, pp. 212-26. Cambridge, Mass.: Harvard University Press, 1930. Reprinted New York: Noonday, 1958.

4:543 ———. *The Proper Wit of Poetry*. Chicago: University of Chicago Press, 1961. In Restoration thought, wit is still part of the imagination.

4:544 ———. "The Restoration Revolt against Enthusiasm." *SP* 30 (1933):571-603. Reprinted in *Seventeenth Century Contexts*, pp. 202-39. London: Faber, 1960. Rev. ed. Chicago: University of Chicago, 1969.

4:545 ———. "The Rhetorical Pattern of Neo-Classical Wit." *MP* 33 (1935):55-81. Reprinted in *Seventeenth Century Contexts*, pp. 240-71. London: Faber, 1960. Rev. ed. Chicago: University of Chicago, 1969.

4:556 Winters, Yvor. *Forms of Discovery*. [Chicago]: Swallow, 1967. Considers Dryden a rather inept and dull poet.

4:557 Wolfe, Humbert. "The Golden Age of Satire." *Notes on English Verse Satire*, pp. 75-95. (Hogarth Lectures on Literature Series 10.) London: The Hogarth Press, 1929. Wants to maintain the distinction between satire, which is associated with prose, and verse.

4:548 Wölfel, Kurt. "Epische Welt und satirische Welt: Zur Technik des satirischen Erzählens." *WW* 10(1960):85-98.

4:549 Wood, Paul Spencer. "Native Elements in English Neo-Classicism." *MP* 24(1926):201-08. Reprinted in [Schilling]:392-401.

4:550 Woodhouse, A. S. P. "Romanticism and the History of Ideas." *English Studies Today: Papers Read at the International Conference of University Professors of English held in Magdalen College, Oxford, August 1950*, eds. C. L. Wrenn and Geoffrey Bollough, pp. 120-40. London: Oxford University Press, 1951.

4:551 Woods, Thomas Francis. "Dryden and the Prophetic Mode: An Examination of His Poetic Theory and Practice in Light of Seventeenth-Century Concepts of Prophecy." *DAI* 34(1974):7254A(Ohio State).

4:552 Woolf, Leonard. "Dryden." *Nation* (London) 33(1933):575.

4:553 Worcester, David. *The Art of Satire*. Cambridge, Mass.: Harvard University Press, 1940. Reprinted New York: Russell and Russell, 1960.

4:554 Wright, David. "Canons Ashby." *Moral Stories*. London: Derek Verschoyle, 1954. Reprinted in [Critical Essays]:181. Poem on Dryden.

4:555 Wyld, Henry C. *Studies in English Rhyme from Surrey to Pope*. London: Murry, 1923. Reprinted New York: Russell and Russell, 1965.

4:556 Yardley, E. "Dryden." *NQ* (9th ser.) 5(1900):353. Echoes in Gray, Tennyson, Milton, Johnson, Pope, Goldsmith.

4:557 Young, Donald L. "The Reputation of John Dryden, 1895-1956." *DA* 21(1960):908-09(Boston Univ.).

4:558 Young, George. *An English Prosody on Inductive Lines*. Cambridge: At the University Press, 1928.

4:559 Youngren, William H. "Generality in Augustan Satire." *In Defense of Reading*, eds. Reuben A. Brower and Richard Poirier, pp. 206-34. New York: E. P. Dutton, 1962. Calls for a revaluation of critical attitudes in the treatment of Augustan poetry. *See* items 4:489, 4:491.

*4:560 ———. "Generality, Science and Poetic Language in the Restoration." *ELH* 35(1968):158-87. *See* Scott Elledge, *PMLA* 62:147-82; Robert D. Hume, *PQ* 48:329-30. *See also* items 4:489, 4:491.

4:561 Zeuthen, Ralph M. *John Dryden, Poet and Dramatist*. Minneapolis: Privately printed, 1936.

4:562 Zimmerman. Franklin B. *Henry Purcell, 1659-1695: His Life and Times*. London: Macmillan; New York: St. Martin's, 1967. *See* J. A. Westrup, *Purcell* (The Master Musicians Series), London: J. M. Dent; New York: Farrar, Strauss and Giroux, 1965.

4:563 ———. "Sound and Sense in Purcell's 'Single Songs'." *Words to Music: Papers on English Seventeenth-Century Song, Read at a Clark Library Seminar, December 11, 1965*, introd. Walter H. Rubsamen, pp. 43-90. Los Angeles: Clark Memorial Library, University of California, 1967. *See* items 5/12:6, 5/12:16.

4:564 Zwicker, Steven N. "Dryden and the Sacred History of the English People: A Study of Typological Imagery in Dryden's Political Poetry: 1660-1688." *DAI* 33(1972):737A(Brown).

*4:565 ———. *Dryden's Political Poetry: The Typology of King and Nation*. Providence: Brown University Press, 1972. *See* Paul J. Korshin, *PQ* 52:495-96; *MLR* 68:893-94; Eric Rothstein, *JEGP* 72:563-65; Ted-Larry Pebworth, *SCN* 31:3; William Frost, *SEL* 13:552-55. *See also* items 4:274, 4:409.

5. Nondramatic Poems

5/1. *ASTRAEA REDUX*

5/1:1 Leed, Jacob. "A Difficult Passage in *Astraea Redux*." *ES* 47 (1966):127-30. Lines 159-68.

5/1:2 Maupin, Larry M. "Dryden's *Astraea Redux*, 163-168." *Expl* 31 (1973):Item 64.

*5/1:3 Maurer, A. E. Wallace. "The Structure of Dryden's *Astraea Redux*." *PLL* 2(1966):13-20. The poem has the structure of the classical oration.

*5/1:4 Swedenberg, H. J., Jr. "England's Joy: *Astraea Redux* in Its Setting." *SP* 50(1953):30-44. Historical background and an explication of the important symbols.

5/1:5 Wasserman, George R. "The Domestic Metaphor in 'Astraea Redux'."
ELN 3(1965):106-111. England is a bride, marrying the newly re-
turned Charles II.

5/1:6 Zwicker, Steven N. "The King and Christ: Figural Imagery in
Dryden's Restoration Panegyrics." PQ 50(1971):582-98. See item
4:409.

See also items 2/2:13, 4:145, 4:223, 4:247, 4:380, 4:525, 4:564-65,
8/2:8-9.

5/2. TO MY HONOURED FRIEND DR. CHARLETON

*5/2:1 Golden, Samuel A. "Dryden's Praise of Dr. Charleton." Herma-
thena 103(1966):59-65. See item 5/2:4.

5/2:2 ———. "Dryden's 'To My Honored Friend, Dr. Charleton,' 37-44."
Expl 24(1966):Item 53.

5/2:3 Lynn, W. T. "Dryden and the Propagation of Light." NQ (9th ser.)
12(1903):504.

*5/2:4 Wasserman, Earl R. "Dryden's Epistle to Charleton." JEGP 55
(1956):201-12. Reprinted in The Subtler Language, pp. 15-33. Baltimore: Johns Hopkins Press, 1959. Also in [Critical Essays]:71-
85. A political reading. See Arnold Stein, YR 49:122-24; Hoyt
Trowbridge, MP 57:127-33. See also item 5/2:1.

See also items 2/2:13, 3:342, 4:78, 4:122, 4:184, 4:211, 4:422.

5/3. ANNUS MIRABILIS

*5/3:1 Hooker, Edward N. "The Purpose of Dryden's Annus Mirabilis."
HLQ 10(1946):49-67. Reprinted in [Swedenberg]:281-99 and in
[Boys]:120-39.

*5/3:2 Kinsley, James. "The 'Three Glorious Victories' in Annus Mi-
rabilis." RES 7(1956):30-37.

5/3:3 McKeon, Michael. "Meanings of Dryden's Annus Mirabilis." DAI
33(1972):2942A-43A(Columbia). A historical and formal analysis.

5/3:4 Miner, Earl. "Dryden's Annus Mirabilis, 653-656." Expl 24
(1966):Item 75.

*5/3:5 ———. "The 'Poetic Picture, Painted Poetry' of The Last In-
structions to a Painter." MP 63(1966):288-94. Reprinted in Andrew Marvell: A Collection of Critical Essays, ed. George deFor-
est Lord, pp. 165-74. Englewood Cliffs, N.J.: Prentice Hall, 1968.

5/3:6 Olivero, F[ederico]. "Virgil in Seventeenth and Eighteenth Century English Literature." Poetry Review 21(1930):171-92.

5/3:7 Pughe, F. "Kleine Bemerkungen." EST 22(1896):455. Annus Mirabilis 66,iv.

5/3:8 Rosenberg, Bruce A. "Annus Mirabilis Distilled." PMLA 79
(1964):254-58. Alchemical and astrological metaphors unify the
poem.

See also items 2/2:13, 2/2:37, 3:162, 4:36, 4:55, 4:105, 4:115, 4:122,
4:197, 4:202, 4:223, 4:280, 4:323, 4:327, 4:342, 4:344, 4:348, 4:
350, 4:369, 4:372, 4:380, 4:422-23, 4:451, 4:455, 4:486, 4:495,
4:506-07, 4:525, 4:528, 4:531, 4:551, 6/2:65, 8/2:8-9.

5/4. ABSALOM AND ACHITOPHEL, I AND II

5/4:1 Archer, Stanley. "Benaiah in Absalom and Achitophel II." ELN 3
(1966):183-85. Identified as Colonel Edward Sackville, the hero
of Tangier.

5/4:2 Arnoldt, Johannes. "Das Charakterbild des Earl of Shaftesbury in der politischen Satire der Restaurationszeit unter Berucksichtigung des historischen Hintergrundes." Diss. Marburg, 1951.

*5/4:3 Ball, Albert. "Charles II: Dryden's Christian Hero." *MP* 59 (1961):25-35. David overcomes his imperfections and becomes the infallable voice of divine authority.

5/4:4 Baumgartner, A. M. "Dryden's Caleb and Agag." *RES* 13(1962):394-97. *See* items 2/2:18, 5/4:22, 5/4:53.

5/4:5 Bevan, Allan R. "Poetry and Politics in Restoration England." *DR* 39(1959):314-25.

5/4:6 Blondel, Jacques. "The Englishness of Dryden's Satire in *Absalom and Achitophel.*" *Travaux du Centre d'Etudes Anglaises et Américaines*. Vol. 1. Aix-en-Provence: Faculté des Lettres et Sciences Humaines, 1962.

*5/4:7 Brodwin, Leonora L. "Miltonic Allusion in *Absalom and Achitophel*: Its Function in the Political Satire." *JEGP* 68(1969):24-44.

5/4:8 Brown, Wallace C. "Dramatic Tension in Neoclassic Satire." *CE* 6(1945):263-69. Also discusses Pope, Johnson and Churchill.

*5/4:9 Budick, Sanford, "Dryden's Circle of Divine Power." *Poetry of Civilization: Mythopoeic Displacement in the Verse of Milton, Dryden, Pope, and Johnson*, pp. 81-110. New Haven, London: Yale University Press, 1974. Satiric procedures used by Dryden in the fulfillment of his role as a spokesman for legitimized power.

5/4:10 Cable, William G. "*Absalom and Achitophel* as Epic Satire." *Studies in Honor of John Wilcox*, eds. A. Dayle Wallace and Woodburn O. Ross, pp. 51-60. Detroit: Wayne University Press, 1958. Johnson incorrectly faulted the structure of the poem; he failed to realize that the narration itself gave a unity to the poem.

5/4:11 Chambers, A. B. "*Absalom and Achitophel*: Christ and Satan." *MLN* 74(1959):592-96.

5/4:12 Chapple, J. A. V. *Dryden's Earl of Shaftesbury: An Inaugural Lecture*. Hull: University of Hull, 1973.

5/4:13 Clayes, Stanley A. "Richard Duke's Satires on the Popish Plot." *DA* 11(1951):1034-35(Penn.).

5/4:14 Conlon, Michael J. "Politics and Providence: John Dryden's *Absalom and Achitophel.*" Diss. Florida, 1969.

5/4:15 Cook, Richard I. "Dryden's *Absalom and Achitophel* and Swift's Political Tracts, 1710-1714." *HLQ* 24(1961):345-48.

5/4:16 Crawford, John W. "*Absalom and Achitophel* and Milton's *Paradise Lost.*" *UDR* 7,ii(1971):29-37.

5/4:17 Crider, J. R. "Dryden's 'Absalom and Achitophel,' 169-172." *Expl* 23(1965):Item 63.

5/4:18 Cunningham, Hugh T. "The Political and Literary Backgrounds of Dryden's *Absalom and Achitophel.*" Diss. Yale, 1940.

5/4:19 ———. "Sons of Belial." *TLS* 10 June 1939, p. 342.

5/4:20 Cunningham, William F., Jr. "Charles Churchill and His Native Tongue." *DSPS* 5(1964):110-32. The use of satiric portraits.

*5/4:21 Davies, Godfrey. "The Conclusion of Dryden's *Absalom and Achitophel.*" *HLQ* 10(1946):69-82. Reprinted in [Swedenberg]:210-24.

5/4:22 de Beer, E. S. "*Absalom and Achitophel*: Literary and Historical Notes." *RES* 27(1941):298-309. Establishes the identity of the persons and events alluded to in the poem. *See* correspondence, James Kinsley, ibid., 6:291-97; E. S. de Beer, ibid., 7:410-14; James Kinsley, ibid., 414-15.

5/4:23 Dickson, Arthur. "Dryden's *Absalom and Achitophel*, 192-197." *Expl* 5(1946):Item 2. *See* Henry Pettit, ibid., Item 61; Curt A.

Zimansky, ibid., Item 34; Arthur Dickson, ibid., 6(1947):Item 17.

5/4:24 Dyson, A. E., and Julian Lovelock. "Beyond the Polemics: A Dialogue on the Opening of *Absalom and Achitophel*." *Critical Survey* 5(1971):133–45.

5/4:25 Emslie, McD. "Dryden's Couplets: Wit and Conversation." *EIC* 11(1961):264–73. *See* item 5/4:67.

5/4:26 Freedman, Morris. "Dryden's Miniature Epic." *JEGP* 57(1958): 211–19. Demonstrates the relationship between the poem and Milton's epics.

5/4:27 ———. "Satan and Shaftesbury." *PMLA* 74(1959):544–47.

5/4:28 French, A. L. "Dryden, Marvell and Political Poetry." *SEL* 8 (1968):397–413. Attacks the idea that the poem has unity.

5/4:29 Graham, W. *Absalom and Achitophel (John Dryden)*. (Notes on English Literature Series.) Oxford: Blackwell, 1964.

5/4:30 Greany, Helen T. "On the Opening Lines of *Absalom and Achitophel*." *SNL* 2(1964):29–31.

*5/4:31 Guilhamet, Leon M. "Dryden's Debasement of Scripture in *Absalom and Achitophel*." *SEL* 9(1969):395–413. The praise of David-Charles violates the sense of the Biblical story and comes close to being blasphemous.

5/4:32 Hammond, H. "'One Immortal Song'." *RES* 5(1954):60–62. Annotates lines 196–97. *See* item 5/4:54.

5/4:33 Jones, Harold Whitmore, ed. *Anti-Achitophel (1682): Three Verse Replies to "Absalom and Achitophel" by John Dryden. "Absalom Senior" by Elkanah Settle, "Poetical Reflections," by Anonymous, "Azaria and Hushai" by Samuel Pordage*. Gainesville, Florida: Scholars' Facsimilies and Reprints, 1961.

*5/4:34 Jones, Richard F. "The Originality of *Absalom and Achitophel*." *MLN* 46(1931):211–18. Reprinted in [Swedenberg]:201–09 and in [Boys]:140–48. The popularity of the 2 Samuel-English history parallel. *See* items 5/4:46, 5/4:71.

5/4:35 Jump, J. D. "Thomas Philipott and John Dryden. And John Keats!" *NQ* 196(1951):535–36. Lines 156–58.

5/4:36 Kaye, F. B. "La Rochefoucauld and the Character of Zimri." *MLN* 39(1924):251.

5/4:37 Kiehl, James M. "Dryden's Zimri and Chaucer's Pardoner: A Comparative Study of Verse Portraiture." *Thoth* 6(1965):3–12.

5/4:38 King, Bruce. "*Absalom and Achitophel*: A Revaluation." [King]: 65–83.

5/4:39 ———. "*Absalom and Achitophel*: Machiavelli and the False Messiah." *EA* 16(1963):251–54.

5/4:40 ———. "Absalom and Dryden's Earlier Praise of Monmouth." *ES* 46(1965):332–33.

5/4:41 ———. "Dryden's *Absalom and Achitophel*, 150–166." *Expl* 21 (1962):Item 28.

5/4:42 ———. "Wordplay in *Absalom and Achitophel*: An Aspect of Style." *Lang&S* 2(1969):330–38. The use of puns.

5/4:43 Kinneavy, Gerald B. "Judgment in Extremes: A Study of Dryden's *Absalom and Achitophel*." *UDR* 3,i(1966):15–30.

5/4:44 LeComte, Edward S. "'Amnon's Murther'." *NQ* 10(1963):418.

*5/4:45 Levine, George R. "Dryden's 'Inarticulate Poesy': Music and the Davidic King in *Absalom and Achitophel*." *ECS* 1(1968):291–312.

5/4:46 Lewalski, Barbara Kiefer. "*David's Troubles Remembered*: An Analogue to *Absalom and Achitophel*." *NQ* 11(1964):340–43.

*5/4:47 ———. "The Scope and Function of Biblical Allusion in *Absalom and Achitophel*." *ELN* 3(1965):29-35. The biblical allusions unify the poem and give it an epic dimension. *See* item 4:565.

5/4:48 Leyburn, Ellen Douglas. *Satiric Allegory: Mirror of Man.* (Yale Studies in English 130.) New Haven: Yale University Press, 1956. *See* Benjamin Boyce, *PQ* 36:327-28. Chap. on *Mac Flecknoe*. *Absalom and Achitophel* is an "allegory controlled by plot;" *Mac Flecknoe* is an "allegory of mock heroes."

*5/4:49 Lord, George deF. "*Absalom and Achitophel* and Dryden's Political Cosmos." [Miner]:156-90. Dryden used the theme of restoration as his central myth.

5/4:50 Macklem, Michael. "'Dashed and Brew'd with Lies': The Popish Plot and the Country Party." *The Augustan Milieu: Essays Presented to Louis A. Landa*, eds. Henry Knight Miller, Eric Rothstein and G. S. Rousseau, pp. 32-58. Oxford: At the Clarendon Press, 1970.

5/4:51 Maresca, Thomas E. "Dryden." *Epic to Novel*, pp. 3-75. Columbus: Ohio State University Press, 1974. Epic material in *Absalom and Achitophel* and *Mac Flecknoe*.

5/4:52 Maurer, A. E. Wallace. "Dryden's *Absalom and Achitophel*, 745-746." *Expl* 17(1959):Item 56; ibid., 20(1961):Item 6.

5/4:53 ———. "Dryden's Balaam Well Hung?" *RES* 10(1959):398-401. Balaam identified as the Earl of Huntingdon.

5/4:54 ———. "The Immortalizing of Dryden's 'One immortal song'." *NQ* 5(1958):341-43. *See* item 5/4:32.

5/4:55 ———. "Who Prompted Dryden to Write *Absalom and Achitophel*?" *PQ* 60(1961):130-38. Possibly, Edward Seymour.

5/4:56 McManaway, James G. "Notes on 'A Key . . . to . . . Absalom and Achitophel'." *NQ* 184(1943):365-66.

5/4:57 Moore, John Robert. "Milton Among the Augustans: the Infernal Council." *SP* 48(1951):15-25.

5/4:58 Ogilvie, R. M. "Two Notes on Dryden's *Absalom and Achitophel*." *NQ* 17(1970):415-16. *See* correspondence, Margaret P. Boddy, ibid., 18(1971):463-64.

5/4:59 Parsons, James H. "A Study of the Political Ideas in John Dryden's *Absalom and Achitophel*." *DAI* 33(1972):322A(Texas, Austin). Dryden relied on Hobbesian ideas to defend Charles II.

*5/4:60 Paulson, Ronald. "From Panurge to Achitophel." *The Fictions of Satire*, pp. 75-128. Baltimore: Johns Hopkins Press, 1967. Dryden placed the facts of the Popish Plot into the fiction of his satire and thereby further developed the evolving Tory myth of monarchical power threatened by degenerative forces.

*5/4:61 Peterson, R. G. "Larger Manners and Events: Sallust and Virgil in *Absalom and Achitophel*." *PMLA* 82(1967):236-44. A study of the poem from the point of view of its classical rather than its biblical allusions.

5/4:62 Poyet, Albert. "Un écho d'*Absalom and Achitophel* dans le prologue d'Otway à *Venice Preserved*." *Caliban* 6(1969):27-28.

5/4:63 Prince, F. T. "Dryden's Political Satires." *Listener* 64(1960):148-49. *See PQ* 40:387.

5/4:64 Prince, Gilbert Parker, Jr. "Poetry and Propaganda in Defoe's Three Major Verse Satires During the Reign of William III." *DAI* 33(1972):2340A(Calif., Santa Barbara). *Absalom and Achitophel's* influence on Defoe's *A New Discovery*.

5/4:65 Purser, K. L. "The Exclusion Bill Controversy in Imaginative Literature, 1678-1682." *ASLIB* 3(1952-53):9(King's College).

5/4:66   Rawson, C. J. "*Beppo* and *Absalom and Achitophel*: A Parallel."
NQ 11(1964):25.

*5/4:67   Ricks, Christopher. "Dryden's Absalom." *EIC* 11(1961):273-89.
Dryden condemns Absalom for succumbing to the temptation. *See*
item 5/4:24.

5/4:68   Saslow, Edward L. "Dryden and Achitophel: The Social Context,
Historical Background, and Political Perspective of Dryden's Writings Pertinent to the Exclusion Crisis." Diss. Calif., Berkeley,
1972.

*5/4:69   ——. "Shaftesbury Cursed: Dryden's Revison of the *Achito-
phel* Lines [180-91]." *SB* 28(1974):276-83. Combines a bibliographical analysis with a close reading to suggest the genesis of the
final text of the passage. *See* item 2/2:32.

*5/4:70   Schilling, Bernard. *Dryden and the Conservative Myth: A Read-
ing of "Absalom and Achitophel."* New Haven: Yale University Press,
1961. *See* John M. Aden, *CE* 23:512; Ronald Paulson, *JEGP* 61:643-48;
Macdonald Emslie, *CritQ* 4:190-92; Aubrey Williams, *YR* 51:615-20;
Pierre Legouis, *EA* 17:148-58; Samuel Holt Monk, *MP* 61:246-52; Curt
A. Zimansky, *Crit* 6:182-84; Earl Miner, *PQ* 41:583-84. *See also*
item 4:422.

5/4:71   Schless, Howard H. "Dryden's *Absalom and Achitophel* and *A Dialogue between Nathan and Absolome*." *PQ* 60(1961):139-43. An additional example of a pre-Dryden poetic version of the Absalom
story.

5/4:72   Sutherland, W. O. S., Jr. *The Art of the Satirist: Essays on
the Satire of Augustan England*. Austin: University of Texas Press,
1965.

5/4:73   Thomas, W. K. "Dryden's *Absalom and Achitophel*, 581." *Expl* 27
(1969):Item 66.

5/4:74   ——. "The Matrix of *Absalom and Achitophel*." *PQ* 49(1970):
92-99. The argument and structure of the poem are linked to the
pamphlet warfare surrounding the Exclusion Crisis.

5/4:75   ——. "The Structure of *Absalom and Achitophel*." *RUO* 39
(1969):288-97.

5/4:76   Tillotson, Geoffrey. "*Absalom and Achitophel*." *Listener* 27
(1942):51-52.

*5/4:77   Wallerstein, Ruth. "To Madness Near Allied: Shaftesbury and
His Place in the Design and Thought of *Absalom and Achitophel*."
HLQ 6(1943):445-71. A defense of the poem's structural complete-
ness; its design is based on the aesthetics of "character" and on
contemporary ideas about melancholy and madness. *See* Hoyt Trowbridge, *PQ* 23:164.

5/4:78   Wellington, James E. "Conflicting Concepts of Man in Dryden's
Absalom and Achitophel." *SNL* 4(1966):2-11.

5/4:79   Wolf, J. Q. "A Note on Dryden's Zimri." *MLN* 47(1932):97-99.
I Kings xvi. 9-20.

See also items 2/1:6, 2/2:23, 2/2:27, 2/2:32, 2/2:34, 2/2:38, 2/2:43,
3:60, 3:66, 3:172, 3:183, 3:188, 4:16, 4:36, 4:39, 4:47, 4:55, 4:
57, 4:59, 4:65, 4:77, 4:105, 4:155-56, 4:158, 4:163, 4:167-68, 4:
177, 4:197-98, 4:202, 4:206, 4:208, 4:214, 4:219, 4:221, 4:223,
4:237-38, 4:243, 4:265, 4:267, 4:272, 4:275, 4:279-80, 4:299, 4:
302, 4:305, 4:311, 4:342, 4:344, 4:348-49, 4:355, 4:369, 4:371,
4:378, 4:388, 4:396, 4:398, 4:403, 4:417, 4:422, 4:425, 4:444, 4:
446, 4:448, 4:451, 4:455, 4:479, 4:490, 4:493, 4:506-07, 4:511,
4:520, 4:525, 4:536-37, 4:546, 4:551, 4:564-65, 5/6:24, 7:82, 8/1:
156.

5/5. THE MEDALL

5/5:1 Edwards, Thomas R. "Satire and Political Doubt: Dryden's *The Medal*." *Imagination and Power: A Study of Poetry on Public Themes*, pp. 86-102. New York: Oxford University Press, 1971. *The Medall* demonstrates Dryden's conflicted responses to political life: his commitment to political values and his cynicism about politics.

5/5:2 Eidmans, Kathleen M. D. "Dryden's 'Medal,' a Text and a Study." *ASLIB* 1(1950-51):17(london, Birkbeck).

5/5:3 Golden, Samuel A. "A Numismatic View of Dryden's *The Medal*." *NQ* 9(1962):383-84. *See* item 4:422.

5/5:4 Joost, Nicholas. "Dryden's *Medall* and the Baroque in Politics and the Arts." *ModA* 3(1959):148-55. L'Estrange was a more effective propagandist than was Dryden. *See* item 4:299.

5/5:5 Legouis, Pierre. "Dryden's Scipio and Hannibal." *TLS* 15 July 1965, p. 602. *See* item 4:422.

*5/5:6 Maurer, A. E. Wallace. "The Design of Dryden's *The Medall*." *PLL* 2(1966):293-304. Dryden engraves his own medal with satirical emblems; his advice to himself as the medalist creates the design of the poem.

5/5:7 Reverand, Cedric D. "Patterns of Imagery and Metaphor in Dryden's *The Medall*." *YES* 2(1972):103-14.

5/5:8 Roper, Alan H. "Dryden's *Medal* and the Divine Analogy." *ELH* 29(1962):396-417. Dryden uses metaphoric language to reinforce the interrelatedness of the political and ethical worlds.

*5/5:9 Sutherland, W. O. S., Jr. "Dryden's Use of Popular Imagery in *The Medal*." *Studies in English* (University of Texas) 35(1956):123-34.

5/5:10 Wasserman, Earl R. "The Meaning of 'Poland' in *The Medal*." *MLN* 73(1958):165-67. The Whigs and Shaftesbury are linked to examples of elected monarchies among the Germanic groups.

See also items 2/1:6, 2/2:23, 2/2:27, 2/2:32, 3:183, 4:42, 4:46, 4:57, 4:65, 4:168, 4:198, 4:202, 4:208, 4:265, 4:272, 4:275, 4:279, 4:299, 4:302, 4:311, 4:369, 4:371, 4:388, 4:422, 4:434, 4:440, 4:446, 4:508, 4:520, 4:536, 4:551, 4:564-65, 5/4:9, 5/4:27, 5/4:65.

5/6. MAC FLECKNOE

*5/6:1 Alssid, Michael W. "Shadwell's *MacFlecknoe*." *SEL* 7(1967):387-402. Finds political as well as literary satire in the poem.

5/6:2 Amis, George T. "Style and Sense in Three Augustan Satires: *Mac Flecknoe*, Book I of *The Dunciad Variorum*, *The Vanity of Human Wishes*." *DA* 29(1968):558A(Yale). A tabular study.

5/6:3 Archer, Stanley. "Dryden's 'MacFlecknoe,' 47-48." *Expl* 26 (1967):Item 37.

5/6:4 Babington, Percy L. "Dryden Not the Author of 'MacFlecknoe'." *MLR* 13(1918):25-34. Claims that John Oldham is the true author. *See* items 5/6:5, 5/6:40.

5/6:5 Belden, H. M. "The Authorship of *MacFlecknoe*." *MLN* 33(1918): 449-56. *See* correction, ibid., 35(1920):58. *See also* items 5/6:4, 5/6:40.

5/6:6 Broich, Ulrich. "Drydens *Mac Flecknoe* und seine frühen Nachahunmgen." *Studien zum Komischen Epos*, pp. 239-42. Tübingen: Niemeyer, 1968.

5/6:7 Brooks, Harold. "When Did Dryden Write *MacFlecknoe*?—Some Additional Notes." *RES* 11(1935):74-78. Reprinted in [Swedenberg]: 165-69. In 1678. *See* item 5/6:40.

5/6:8 Castrop, Helmut. "Dryden and Flecknoe: A Link." *RES* 23(1972):
455-58. Dryden's reasons for attacking Richard Flecknoe.

5/6:9 Clark, John R. "Dryden's 'MacFlecknoe,' 48." *Expl* 29(1971):
Item 56. Excremental references.

5/6:10 Crider, J. R. "The Anti-Poet in *Mac Flecknoe*." *BSE* 9(1970):11-
18.

*5/6:11 Dearing, Vinton A. "Dryden's *Mac Flecknoe*: The Case for Au-
thorial Revision." *SB* 7(1955):85-102. Establishing a copy text.
See item 5/6:16.

5/6:12 Dearmin, Michael G. "Thomas Shadwell: Playwright." *DA* 28(1967):
623A(Wis.). A defense of Shadwell.

5/6:13 Diffenbaugh, Guy L. *The Rise and Development of the Mock Heroic Poem in England from 1660 to 1714: Dryden's "MacFlecknoe."* Urbana: University of Illinois Press, 1926.

5/6:14 Donnelly, Jerome J. "Movement and Meaning in Dryden's *Mac-
Flecknoe*." *TSLL* 12(1971):569-82. Images of movement used as a satiric device.

5/6:15 Evans, G. Blakemore. "Dryden's *Mac Flecknoe* and Dekker's *Sat-
iromastix*." *MLN* 76(1961):598-600.

*5/6:16 ———. "The Text of Dryden's *Mac Flecknoe*." *HLB* 7(1953):32-54.
A preliminary discussion in the establishment of a copy text. *See*
item 5/6:11.

5/6:17 French, David P. "Dryden's *Mac Flecknoe*, 48." *Expl* 21(1963):
Item 39.

5/6:18 Gamble, Giles Y. "Dryden's *Mac Flecknoe*, 25-28 and 38-42."
Expl 26(1968):Item 45.

5/6:19 Goodman, Paul. *The Structure of Literature*. Chicago: University of Chicago Press, 1954.

*5/6:20 Jack, Ian. "Mock-Heroic: *MacFlecknoe*." *Augustan Satire: Intention and Idiom in English Poetry, 1660-1750*, pp. 43-52. Oxford:
At the Clarendon Press, 1952. Reprinted in [Keast]:464-89. The poem is a lampoon.

5/6:21 King, Bruce. "The Conclusion of *MacFlecknoe* and Cowley." *ANQ*
7(1969):86-87.

5/6:22 Koomjohn, Charlotte A. "*MacFlecknoe*: Dryden's Satire in Theory and Practice." *DAI* 32(1971):1478A(Rochester). A reading of the
poem in conjunction with the *Discourse of Satire*.

*5/6:23 Korn, A. L. "*Mac Flecknoe* and Cowley's *Davideis*." *HLQ* 14
(1951):99-127. Reprinted in [Swedenberg]:170-200. *Mac Flecknoe*
attacks the excesses of Cowley's epic and thus is a mock-epic.

5/6:24 Kunz, Don R. "Shadwell and His Critics: The Misuse of Dryden's *Mac Flecknoe*." *RECTR* 12,i(1973):14-27. Accuses critics of
Shadwell of beginning their studies with Dryden's portrait in
mind.

5/6:25 Kurak, Alex. "Imitation, Burlesque Poetry, and Parody: A
Study of Some Augustan Critical Distinctions." *DA* 24(1963):2014-
15(Minn.).

5/6:26 Lawlor, Nancy Katherine. "His Flecknotique Majesty: A Study
of Richard Flecknoe and His Critics." *DAI* 35(1974):406A(Rutgers).

*5/6:27 Maresca, Thomas E. "Language and Body in Augustan Poetic."
ELH 37(1970):374-88. Satiric connections between language and
bodily functions.

5/6:28 McFadden, George. "Elkanah Settle and the Genesis of *MacFlecknoe*." *PQ* 43(1964):55-72.

5/6:29 McKeithan, Daniel Morely. "The Occasion of *MacFlecknoe*." *PMLA*

47(1932):766-71. In response to the dedication of *The History of Timon of Athens* (1678).

5/6:30 Miner, Earl. "Dryden's *MacFlecknoe*." *NQ* 3(1956):335-37. Borrowings and analogues. *See* replies, Richard Merton, ibid., 505; William J. Cameron, ibid., 4(1957):39; Pierre Legouis, ibid., 5 (1968):180.

5/6:31 Monk, Samuel Holt. "Shadwell 'Flail of Sense': 'Macflecknoe' Line 89." *NQ* 7(1960):67-68.

5/6:32 Mullin, Joseph E. "The Occasion, Form, Structure, and Design of John Dryden's *MacFlecknoe*: A Varronian Satire." *DA* 28(1968): 3645A(Ohio State). Dates the poem in late 1677 or early 1678.

5/6:33 Novak, Maximillian E. "Dryden's 'Ape of the French Eloquence' and Richard Flecknoe." *BNYPL* 72(1968):499-506. Dating the motivation for the attack on Flecknoe as early as 1661. *See* item 5/6: 36.

5/6:34 O'Connor, Gerald William. "Four Approaches to Satire: The Archetypal, the Historical, the Rhetorical, and the Anthropological." *DA* 29(1969):2222A-23A(B.U. Grad. School). Frye, Rosenheim, Kernan, Elliott; uses all four approaches to explicate *Mac Flecknoe*.

5/6:35 Pearsall, Ronald. "The Case for Shadwell." *The Month* 30(1963): 364-67.

5/6:36 Smith, John Harrington. "Dryden and Flecknoe: A Conjecture." *PQ* 33(1954):338-41. The motivation for Dryden's attack. *See* item 5/6:33.

5/6:37 Smith, R. Jack. "The Date of *MacFlecknoe*." *RES* 18(1942):322-23. Argues that the poem was available in manuscript before 4 October 1682.

*5/6:38 Tanner, J. E. "The Messianic Image in *Mac Flecknoe*." *MLN* 76(1961):220-23. *See* items 4:565, 5/6:23, 6/2:59.

5/6:39 Taylor, Aline M. "Dryden's 'Enchanted Isle' and Shadwell's 'Dominion'." *Essays in English Literature of the Classical Period Presented to Dougald MacMillan*, eds. Daniel W. Patterson and Albrecht B. Strauss, pp. 39-53. (*SP* Extra Series 4.) Chapel Hill: University of North Carolina Press, 1967. Identifies an allusion to Shadwell's operatic version of *The Tempest*.

5/6:40 Thorn-Drury, George. "Dryden's *Mac Flecknoe*. A Vindication." *MLR* 13(1918):276-81. Reprinted in [Swedenberg]:157-64. Defends Dryden's authorship. *See* items 5/6:4, 5/6:5.

5/6:41 Towers, Tom H. "The Lineage of Shadwell: An Approach to *MacFlecknoe*." *SEL* 3(1963):323-34. Points of commonality between Shadwell and the other dramatists with whom he is associated in the poem.

5/6:42 Vroonland, James A. "The Dryden-Shadwell Controversy: A Preface to *MacFlecknoe*." *DAI* 33(1972):2399A(Kan. State). Dates the poem in 1678.

5/6:43 Weinbrot, Howard D. "On the Discrimination of Augustan Satires." *Proceedings of the Modern Language Association Neoclassicism Conferences 1967-1968*, ed. Paul J. Korshin, pp. 5-12. New York: AMS Press, 1970. While *Mac Flecknoe* signals a victory, *The Dunciad* marks a defeat for the satirist.

5/6:44 West, Michael. "Some Neglected Continental Analogues for Dryden's *MacFlecknoe*." *SEL* 13(1973)437-50. Continental sources and analogues for the poem.

5/6:45 Whitlock, Baird W. "Elijah and Elisha in Dryden's *Mac Fleck-noe*." *MLN* 70(1955):19-20.
5/6:46 Wilding, Michael. "Allusion and Innuendo in *MacFlecknoe*." *EIC* 19(1969):355-70.
5/6:47 Willson, Robert F., Jr. "The Fecal Vision in *Mac Flecknoe*." *SNL* 8(1970):1-4.

See also items 2/1:6, 2/2:23, 2/2:32, 2/2:39, 2/2:43-44, 2/2:47, 3: 188, 4:28, 4:46, 4:55, 4:67, 4:79, 4:95, 4:101, 4:136, 4:168, 4: 202, 4:208, 4:221, 4:237, 4:243, 4:245, 4:265, 4:275, 4:279, 4: 311, 4:330, 4:342, 4:344, 4:348-49, 4:369, 4:371, 4:434, 4:448, 4:479, 4:506, 4:520, 4:525, 4:536, 4:546, 4:551, 4:564-65, 5/4: 48, 5/4:51, 5/4:60, 5/10:4, 7:82, 7:231, 7:283.

5/7. *RELIGIO LAICI*

5/7:1 Benson, Donald R. "Who 'Bred' *Religio Laici*?" *JEGP* 65(1966): 238-51. Dryden relied on Stillingfleet and Baxter in writing the poem.
5/7:2 Brown, David D. "Dryden's 'Religio Laici' and the 'Judicious and Learned Friend'." *MLR* 56(1961):66-69. John Tillotson.
*5/7:3 Budick, Sanford. *Dryden and the Abyss of Light: A Study of "Religio Laici" and "The Hind and the Panther."* New Haven: Yale University Press, 1970. *See* Phillip Harth, *PQ* 50:424-26; *TLS* 21 May 1971, p. 588; Victor M. Hamm, *JEGP* 70:670-74; William Myers, *MLR* 66:866-67; Gerard Reedy, S. J., *Thought* 46:613-15.
5/7:4 ———. "Dryden's *Religio Laici*: A Study in Context and Mean-ing." *DA* 27(1967):4216A(Yale).
5/7:5 ———. "New Light on Dryden's *Religio Laici*." *NQ* 16(1969):375-79.
*5/7:6 Chiasson, Elias J. "Dryden's Apparent Scepticism in *Religio Laici*." *HTR* 54(1961):207-21. Reprinted in [Swedenberg]:245-60 and in [King]:84-98. A rejection of the idea that Dryden was a scep-tic in the tradition of fideism. *See* Maurice J. Quinlan, *PQ* 41: 581-82. *See also* items 3:57, 4:43, 4:211, 5/7:9.
5/7:7 Corder, Jim W. "Rhetoric and Meaning in *Religio Laici*," *PMLA* 82(1967):245-49. An analysis of the formal rhetorical structures in the poem, with a focus on the section repudiating the Deists.
5/7:8 Field, P. J. C. "Dryden and Rochester." *NQ* 17(1970):259-60. Dryden's image of the sun as a reproof of *Satire against Reason and Mankind*.
*5/7:9 Fujimura, Thomas H. "Dryden's *Religio Laici*: An Anglican Po-em." *PMLA* 76(1961):205-17. Denies that the poem is essentially Catholic in spirit. *See* Maurice J. Quinlan, *PQ* 41:581-82. *See also* items 3:57, 4:211, 5/7:6, 5/7:12.
5/7:10 Golladay, Gertrude L. "The Rhetorical Poetic Tradition in Dryden's Two Verse Essays." Diss. Texas Christian, 1968.
5/7:11 Gosse, Edmund. "Dryden's 'Religio Laici'." *Athenaeum* 3720(11 February 1899):179. *See* reply, George Neilson, ibid., 3722(25 Feb-ruary 1899):241.
*5/7:12 Ham, Victor M. "Dryden's *Religio Laici* and Roman Catholic Apologetics." *PMLA* 80(1965):190-98. *See* items 4:43, 5/7:9.
5/7:13 Hooker, Edward N. "Dryden and the Atoms of Epicurus." *ELH* 24(1957):177-90. Reprinted in [Swedenberg]:232-44 and in [Criti-cal Essays]:125-35. The poem is concerned with politics not with religion.

5/7:14 Lynn, W. T. "Dryden and Greek." *NQ* (8th ser.) 7(1895):386.
See correspondence, ibid., 451-52; ibid., 8(1896):14, 97.

5/7:15 McGann, Jerome. "The Argument of Dryden's *Religio Laici*."
Thoth 3(1962):78-89.

5/7:16 McHenry, Robert W., Jr. "Anglican Rationalism, Right Reason,
and John Dryden." *DAI* 33(1973):5132A(Mich.).

5/7:17 ———. "Dryden's *Religio Laici*: An Augustan Drama of Ideas."
EnlE 4(1973):60-64. Sees the poem as powerfully emotional and a
personal work addressed to a friend.

5/7:18 Murakami, Shikō. "Kokkakyo ka Kyukyo ka—*Religio Laici* no
baai." *EigoS* 115(1969):10-12. Considers whether the poem is Anglican or Catholic.

5/7:19 Perkinson, Richard H. "A Note on Dryden's *Religio Laici*." *PQ*
28(1949):517-18.

5/7:20 Pollard, Arthur. "Five Poets on Religion: 1. Dryden, Pope,
and Young." *Church Quarterly Review* 160(1959):352-62.

5/7:21 Reedy, Gerard, S. J. "Noumenal and Phenomenal Evidence in England, 1622-1682." *EnlE* 2(1971):137-48. Father Simon had taken a
phenomenal approach in his study of the Bible, and Dryden had
countered with a noumenal approach which placed less stress on
rational exegesis.

5/7:22 "Religio Laici." *Spectator* 97(1906):673-74.

5/7:23 Rippy, Francis Mayhew. "Imagery, John Dryden, and 'The Poetry
of Statement'." *BSTCF* 1,ii(1960-61):13-20. Attacks the view, held
by Van Doren (4:506) and Eliot (4:135), that no neoclassic poetry
is prosaic.

5/7:24 Sampson, Herbert Grant. "The Anglican Tradition in Eighteenth-
Century Verse." *DA* 25(1965):6602(Mich. State).

5/7:25 Sykes, Norman. *From Sheldon to Secker: Aspects of English
Church History, 1660-1768.* Cambridge: At the University Press,
1959. The poem is deistic. *See* item 4:211.

5/7:26 Ward, Charles E. "*Religio Laici* and Father Simon's *History*."
MLN 61(1946):407-12. Reprinted in [Swedenberg]:225-31. Identifies
Dickinson.

*5/7:27 Welcher, Jeanne K. "The Opening of *Religio Laici* and its Virgilian Associations." *SEL* 8(1968):391-96.

5/7:28 Woodhouse, A. S. P. "Religion and Poetry, 1660-1780." *The Poet and His Faith: Religion and Poetry in England from Spenser to
Eliot and Auden*, pp. 123-159. (Frank L. Weil Institute for Studies in Religion and the Humanities.) Chicago, London: University
of Chicago Press, 1965. A general essay on neoclassic religious
poetry.

See also items 1:69, 2/2:32, 3:57, 3:161, 4:29-30, 4:39, 4:43, 4:47-
48, 4:65, 4:95, 4:115, 4:122, 4:127, 4:158, 4:167, 4:202, 4:208,
4:211, 4:223, 4:245, 4:255, 4:299, 4:303, 4:344, 4:378, 4:396, 4:
410, 4:448, 4:450, 4:455, 4:506-07, 4:520, 5/4:9, 7:82, 7:164.

5/8. *MISCELLANIES*

*5/8:1 Boys, Richard C. "Some Problems of Dryden's Miscellany." *ELH*
7(1940):130-143. The "miscellany" is not a new genre. *See* item
5/8:1.

*5/8:2 Havens, Raymond D. "Changing Taste in the Eighteenth Century:
A Study of Dryden's and Dodsley's Miscellanies." *PMLA* 44(1929):
501-36.

5/8:3 Lange, Victor. *Die Lyrik und ihre Publikum im England des 18. Jahrhunderts. Eine geschmacksgeschichtliche Untersuchung über die englischen Anthologien von 1670-1780.* Weimar: H. Böhlaus Nachf, 1935.

5/8:4 Roberts, William. "Saint-Amant, Orinda, and Dryden's Miscellany." *ELN* 1(1963):191-96.

5/8:5 Wasserman, Earl R. "Pre-Restoration Poetry in Dryden's Miscellany." *MLN* 52(1937):545-55. *See* items 5/8:1-2.

See also items 1:12, 1:16, 1:66, 2/1:3, 2/2:21, 2/2:32, 2/2:44, 4:454, 4:506, 6/2:10.

5/9. *TO THE MEMORY OF MR. OLDHAM*

5/9:1 Bache, William B. "Dryden and Oldham: Hail and Farewell." *CLAJ* 12(1969):237-43. Finds an ironic and thus qualifying element in Dryden's praise of Oldham.

5/9:2 Brown, Wallace Cable. "The 'Heresy' of the Didactic." *University of Kansas City Review* 11(1945):178-84. Argues that poems which are didactic can also be suggestive.

5/9:3 Clark, John R. "'To the Memory of Mr. Oldham': Dryden's Disquieting Lines." *CP* 3,i(1970):43-49. Contradictions and paradoxes threaten the surface restraint of the poem; sees a painful confrontation in the speaker's consideration of Oldham's death.

5/9:4 King, Bruce. "'Lycidas' and 'Oldham'." *EA* 19(1966):60-63. Borrowings.

5/9:5 Mell, Donald Charles, Jr. "Variations on Elegiac Themes: Dryden, Pope, Prior, Gray, Johnson." *DA* 22(1961):1159-60(Penn.).

5/9:6 Moskovit, Leonard. "An Echo of Gellius in Dryden's 'Oldham'." *NQ* 19(1972):26-27.

5/9:7 Parkin, Rebecca Price. "The Journey Down the Great Scale Reflected in Two Neoclassical Elegies." *EnlE* 1(1970):197-204. *Oldham* is compared with Johnson's "On the Death of Dr. Robert Levet."

5/9:8 Peterson, R. G. "The Unavailing Gift: Dryden's Roman Farewell to Mr. Oldham." *MP* 66(1969):232-36.

5/9:9 Tillotson, Geoffrey. "Pope's 'Epistle to Marley': An Introduction and Analysis." [Clifford]:58-77. Pope's poem and *Oldham*.

See also items 2/2:32, 4:79, 4:127, 4:172, 4:223, 4:342, 4:348, 4:442, 4:506, 4:533, 4:539.

5/10. *TO THE PIOUS MEMORY OF ANNE KILLIGREW*

5/10:1 Heath-Stubbs, John. "Baroque Ceremony: A Study of Dryden's 'Ode to the Memory of Mistress Anne Killigrew' (1686)." *CSE* 3 (1959):76-84.

5/10:2 Hoffman, Arthur W. "Note on a Dryden Ode." *TLS* 19 June 1959, p. 369. Annotating "Epicetus's lamp." *See* correspondence, Pierre Legouis, ibid., 3 July, p. 399.

5/10:3 Hope, A. D. "Anne Killigrew, or the Art of Modulating." *SoR* 1(1963):4-14. Reprinted in *The Cave and the Spring: Essays on Poetry*, pp. 129-43. Adelaide: Rigby, 1965. Also in [King]:99-113. *See* item 5/10:9.

5/10:4 Mary Eleanor, Mother. "*Anne Killigrew* and *Mac Flecknoe*." *PQ* 43(1964):47-54. Parallels in imagery.

5/10:5 Richards, I. A. "The Interactions of Words." *The Language of Poetry*, ed. Allen Tate, pp. 65-87. Princeton: Princeton University Press, 1942. Reprinted New York: Russell and Russell, 1960.

5/10:6 Shawcross, John T. "Some Literary Uses of Numerology." *HSL* 1,
i(1969):50-62. Focuses on "Killigrew" and Milton's "Lycidas."

5/10:7 Shuchter, J. D. "Fitzgerald's 'Piety Nor Wit'." *NQ* 16(1969):
213.

5/10:8 Tillyard, E. M. W. "Dryden: *Ode on Anne Killigrew*, 1686."
*Five Poems 1470-1870: An Elementary Essay on the Background of
English Literature*, pp. 49-65. London: Chatto and Windus, 1948.
Retitled *Poetry and its Background: Illustrated by Five Poems*.
London: Chatto and Windus, 1955. Reprinted in [Critical essays]:
136-48.

5/10:9 Vieth, David M. "Irony in Dryden's Ode to Anne Killigrew." *SP*
63(1965):91-100.

*5/10:10 Wallerstein, Ruth. "On the Death of Mrs. Killigrew: The Per-
fecting of a Genre." *SP* 44(1947):519-28. Reprinted in [Keast]:454-
63 and in [Swedenberg]:576-85. Establishes a literary background
for the ode by tracing a line of development from Donne through
Cowley to Dryden.

See also items 2/2:21, 4:6, 4:36, 4:46, 4:172, 4:202, 4:223, 4:291,
4:342, 4:348, 4:375, 4:405, 4:449, 4:465, 4:483, 4:506, 4:511, 4:
513, 4:524, 4:539.

5/11. *THE HIND AND THE PANTHER*

5/11:1 Anselment, Raymond A. "Martin Marprelate: A New Source for
Dryden's Fable of the Martin and the Swallows." *RES* 17(1966):256-
67.

5/11:2 Armistead, Jack M. "A Study of Structure and Poetics in Dryden's *The Hind and the Panther*." *DAI* 34(1973):718A(Duke). The poem is unified in its fusion of elements from natural history,
folklore and literary traditions.

5/11:3 Budick, Sanford. "Dryden's 'Mysterious Writ' Deciphered." *TLS*
3 April 1969, p. 371. *See* correspondence, Earl Miner, ibid., 1
May 1969, p. 466; Sanford Budick, ibid., 22 May 1969, p. 559;
Earl Miner, ibid., 3 July 1969, p. 730. The story of St. Chad,
Bishop of Lichfield, and his doe is a source for the allegory of
the hind.

5/11:4 Burnett, A. D. "An Early Verse Reply to Dryden's *The Hind and
the Panther*." *NQ* 15(1968):378-80. By William Darrell.

5/11:5 Burton, Thomas R. "The Animal Lore and Fable Tradition in
John Dryden's *The Hind and the Panther*." *DA* 29(1968)225A-26A
(Wash.).

5/11:6 C., B. L. R. "Literary Parallel." *NQ* (8th ser.) 9(1896):65.
"Elegy upon . . . General Deane."

5/11:7 Davis, Ira B. "Religious Controversy: John Dryden's 'The Hind
and the Panther'." *CLAJ* 4(1961):207-14.

5/11:8 Dillard, Nancy Frey. "The English Fabular Tradition: Chaucer,
Spenser, Dryden." *DAI* 34(1974):7186A(Tenn.).

5/11:9 Duggan, Margaret M. "Aspects of Dryden's *The Hind and the
Panther*." Diss. Columbia, 1972.

5/11:10 ———. "Mythic Components in Dryden's *Hind and Panther*." *CL*
26(1974):110-23. Dryden's use of Ovidian myth.

5/11:11 Ellis, Harry James/Brother Felician Patrick. "A Critical Analysis of John Dryden's *The Hind and the Panther*." *DA* 22(1961):
563-64(Penn.).

5/11:12 Foster, Edward E. "Dryden and the Poetry of Conversion: A
Reading of *The Hind and the Panther*." *DA* 26(1965):3301-02(Roch-

ester). The poem is a religious controversialist version of "Poems on Affairs of State."

*5/11:13 Fujimura, Thomas H. "The Personal Drama of Dryden's *The Hind and the Panther*." *PMLA* 87(1972):406-16.

5/11:14 Galvin, Brother Ronan. "*The Hind and the Panther*: A Varronian Satire." *DAI* 32(1971):2054A-55A(Fordham).

*5/11:15 Hamm, Victor M. "Dryden's 'The Hind and the Panther' and Roman Catholic Apologetics." *PMLA* 83(1968):400-15. White, Rushworth, Cressy, Sergeant, Worsley, Woodhead. *See* items 4:43, 5/7:3, 5/7:9, 5/7:12, 5/11:25.

5/11:16 Hooker, Helene Maxwell. "Charles Montagu's Reply to *The Hind and the Panther*." *ELH* 8(1941):51-73.

5/11:17 Kern, John D. "An Unpublished Manuscript by Charles Montague, Lord Halifax (1661-1715)." *JEGP* 32(1933):66-69. *See* item 5/11:16.

5/11:18 Kinsley, James. "Dryden's Bestiary." *RES* 4(1953):331-36. A defense of Dryden's handling of the beast fable.

5/11:19 Lakas, Robert Raymond, S. J. "*The Hind and the Panther*: Dryden's Use of the Three Styles." Diss. Yale, 1957.

5/11:20 Manley, Francis. "Ambivalent Allusions in Dryden's Fable of the Swallows." *MLN* 71(1956):485-87.

5/11:21 Martz, William J. "Dryden's Religious Thought: A Study of *The Hind and the Panther* and Its Background." Diss. Yale, 1957.

5/11:22 Means, James A. "May's Lucan and *The Hind and the Panther*." *NQ* 17(1970):416-17.

5/11:23 Miller, Clarence H. "The Styles of *The Hind and the Panther*." *JEGP* 61(1962):511-27.

5/11:24 Miner, Earl. "Allusions in *The Hind and the Panther*." *NQ* 11 (1964):237. Queries.

5/11:25 ———. "Dryden and 'The Magnified Piece of Duncomb'." *HLQ* 28 (1964):93-98. Dryden rebuked Stillingfleet for claiming a Protestant authorship for a treatise on humility.

5/11:26 ———. "The Significance of Plot in *The Hind and the Panther*." *BNYPL* 69(1965):446-58.

5/11:27 ———. "The Wolf's Progress in *The Hind and the Panther*." *BNYPL* 67(1963):512-16. The heresy of Presbyterian voluntarism.

5/11:28 Myers, William. "Politics in *The Hind and the Panther*." *EIC* 19(1969):19-34.

5/11:29 Nakano, Nancy Yoshiko. "The Authority of Narrative: Technique and Argument in Milton, Bunyan, Dryden, and John Reynolds." *DAI* 34(1974):7199A(U.C.L.A.). The plot and the narrator's seeming disinterestedness unify the poem.

5/11:30 Parkin, Rebecca P. "Heroic and Anti-Heroic Elements in *The Hind and the Panther*." *SEL* 12(1972):459-66. The tension between heroic and antiheroic elements gives structural unity to the poem.

5/11:31 Probyn, Clive T. "The Source for Swift's *Fable of the Bitches*." *NQ* 15(1968):206.

5/11:32 R., H. "Johnson on a Metaphor of Dryden's." *NQ* 185(1943):256. 1:57-58.

5/11:33 Russ, Jon R. ["Dryden's 'milk-white hind'."] *RES* 15(1964): 303-04. Annotates the first line of the poem using Edward Topsell's *Historie of Four-Footed Beastes* (1607).

5/11:34 Shawcross, John T. "An Unnoticed Reaction to Dryden's 'The Hind and the Panther'." *ELN* 11(1973):110-12. Robert Jenkin's "An Historical Examination of the Authority of General Councils."

5/11:35   Shea, John Stephen. "Studies in the Verse Fable from La Fontaine to Gay." *DA* 28(1968):5029A(Minn.).

5/11:36   Swearingen, James. "Time and the Character of the Wolf in
The Hind and the Panther." *CP* 6,ii(1973):45-52.

5/11:37   Wasserman, George. "Dryden's *The Hind and the Panther*, III,
1-21." *Expl* 26(1966):Item 71.

5/11:38   ———. "A Note on Dryden's Panther [III, 639-43]." *NQ* 13
(1966):380-82.

5/11:39   Weidhorn, Manfred. "Dreams in Seventeenth-Century English
Literature." *DA* 26(1965):1638(Columbia). The feigned divine dream
in *The Hind and the Panther*.

See also items 1:69, 2/1:4, 2/2:21, 3:24, 3:55, 3:161, 3:166, 4:16,
4:29-30, 4:43, 4:47-48, 4:65, 4:90, 4:115, 4:158, 4:202, 4:208,
4:211-12, 4:255, 4:287, 4:303, 4:311, 4:342, 4:344, 4:348, 4:
371, 4:378, 4:396-97, 4:444, 4:448, 4:450, 4:455, 4:506-07, 4:
520, 4:525, 4:535, 4:551, 5/4:9, 5/7:3, 5/7:10, 5/7:16, 5/7:20,
5/7:25, 7:82.

5/12. ST. CECILIA'S DAY POEMS: *A SONG FOR*

ST. CECILIA'S DAY; ALEXANDER'S FEAST

*5/12:1   Brenneche, Ernest, Jr. "Dryden's Odes and Draghi's Music."
PMLA 49(1934):1-34. Reprinted in [Swedenberg]:425-65. Includes
the musical score.

5/12:2   Bronson, Bertrand H. "Some Aspects of Music and Literature
in the Eighteenth Century. [Clark Library]:127-60. Handel's setting of *Alexander's Feast*.

5/12:3   Butler, Christopher. *Number Symbolism*. London: Routledge and
Kegan Paul, 1970.

5/12:4   D., S. N. "Dryden's Ode on St. Lucy's Day." *Month* 158(1931):
540-44. *See* item 5/14:14.

5/12:5   Davies, H. Neville, "Dryden and Vossius: A Reconsideration."
JWCI 29(1966):282-95. Disputes Dean T. Mace's argument that Dryden used Isaac Vossius's *De poematum cantu* in developing a theory
of *rhythmus* which would give the poet domination over the com-
poser. *See* item 5/12:16. *See also* correspondence, Dean T. Mace,
ibid., 29(1966):296-310.

5/12:6   ———. "The Structure of Shadwell's *A Song for St. Cecilia's
Day, 1690*." *Silent Poetry: Essays in Numerological Analysis*, ed.
Alastair Fowler, pp. 201-233. London: Routledge and Kegan Paul,
1970. *See* item 5/12:8.

5/12:7   Demmery, Morton. "The Hybrid Critic." *Music and Letters* 37
(1957):128-40. Considers whether *Alexander's Feast* is weakened or
strengthened by Handel's music. *See* items 5/12:16, 4:563.

5/12:8   Eddy, William Alfred. "Dryden Quotes Ben Jonson." *MLN* 46(1931):
40-41.

5/12:9   Fowler, Alastair, and Douglas Brooks. "The Structure of Dryden's *Song for St Cecilia's Day, 1687*." *EIC* 17(1967):434-47. Reprinted in *Silent Poetry: Essays in Numerological Analysis*, ed.
Alastair Fowler, pp. 185-200. London: Routledge and Kegan Paul,
1970. Explicates the numerological and musical structures of the
song.

5/12:10   Harder, Franz. "Eine deutsche Anregung zu Dryden's 'Alexander's Feast'?" *EST* 61(1927):177-82.

5/12:11 Heath-Stubbs, John. *The Ode*. London: Oxford University Press, 1969.

*5/12:12 Jensen, H. James. "Comparing the Arts in the Age of Baroque." *ECS* 6(1973):334-47. Baroque theory saw art in affective terms, with an emphasis on the arousal of specific emotions in the audience of spectators. Dryden's "Song for St Cecilia's Day" is compared with examples of European baroque art, pictorial and musical.

5/12:13 Kinsley, James. "Dryden and the *Encomium Musicae*." *RES* 4 (1953):263-67. *Alexander's Feast* as part of a Renaissance tradition.

*5/12:14 Levine, Jay Arnold. "Dryden's 'Song for Saint Cecilia's Day, 1687'." *PQ* 44(1965):38-50. A detailed rhetorical analysis, focusing on prosody and imagery, together with a discussion of other poems written to celebrate St. Cecilia's Day.

5/12:15 L[oane], G. G. "Dryden's 'Alexander's Feast'." *NQ* (12th ser.) 7(1920):87-88. Discussed together with Jeremy Collier's *Essay on Music*.

5/12:16 Maccubbin, Robert P. "A Critical Study of Odes for St. Cecilia's Day, 1683-1697." *DAI* 30(1969):1142A-43A(Illinois).

5/12:17 Mace, Dean T. "Musical Humanism, the Doctrine of Rhythmus, and the Saint Cecilia Odes of Dryden." *JWCI* 27(1964):251-92. Dryden's odes should be seen in light of the century-long debate among Florentine theoreticians about the meaningfulness of music. *See* item 5/12:5.

5/12:18 McIntosh, William A. "The Harmonic Muse: Musical Currents in Literature 1450-1750." *DAI* 35(1974):3692A-93A(Virginia).

5/12:19 Moore, John Robert. "*Alexander's Feast*: A Possible Chronology of Development." *PQ* 37(1958):495-98. The genesis of the poem.

5/12:20 Myers, Robert Manson. *Handel, Dryden, and Milton. Being a Series of Observations on the Poems of Dryden and Milton, as Alter'd and Adapted by Various Hands, and Set to Music by Mr. Handel to which are added, Authentic Texts of Several of Mr. Handel's "Oratorio's."* London: Bowes and Bowes, 1956. *See TLS* 16 November 1956, p. 676.

5/12:21 ———. "Neo-Classical Criticism of the Ode for Music." *PMLA* 62(1947):399-421.

5/12:22 Pettit, Henry. "'The Pleasing Paths of Sense': The Subject Matter of Augustan Literature." *Literature and Science*, pp. 169-74. (International Federation for Modern Languages and Literatures: Proceedings of the Sixth Triennial Congress, Oxford, 1954.) Oxford: Blackwell, 1955. Sensation is "the key to human knowledge."

5/12:23 Phillips, James E. "Poetry and Music in the Seventeenth Century." [Clark Library]:1-21. Dryden and musical humanism.

5/12:24 Proffitt, Bessie. "Political Satire in Dryden's *Alexander's Feast*." *TSLL* 11(1970):1307-16. An attack on William III.

5/12:25 S. "Timotheus in Dryden's St. Cecilia's Ode (1697)." *NQ* 157 (1929):64. *See* correspondence, L. R. M. Strachan, ibid., 103.

5/12:26 Seronsy, Cecil C. "Chapman and Dryden." *NQ* 5(1956):64.

5/12:27 Steadman, John M. "Timotheus in Dryden, E. K., and Gafori." *TLS* 16 December 1960, p. 819.

5/12:28 Swaminathan, S. R. "Virgil, Dryden and Yeats." *NQ* 19(1972): 328-30.

5/12:29 Wasserman, Earl. "Pope's 'Ode for Musick'." *ELH* 28(1961): 163-86.

A Song for St. Cecilia's Day: *See also* items 2/2:21, 4:14, 4:36, 4: 142, 4:202, 4:219, 4:226, 4:297, 4:341, 4:403, 4:449, 4:455, 4: 506, 4:562, 5/12:9, 5/12:16.

Alexander's Feast: *See also* items 2/2:34, 2/2:36, 2/2:40, 4:172, 5/12: 28.

5/13. PROLOGUES AND EPILOGUES

5/13:1   Arnold, Claude. "Reflections of Political Issues in the Plays, Prologues, and Epilogues of John Dryden." Diss. Case Western, 1958.

5/13:2   Ausprich, Harry. "A Rhetorical Analysis of the Restoration Prologue and Epilogue." *DA* 25(1964):1400(Mich. State).

5/13:3   Avery, Emmett L. "Rhetorical Patterns in Restoration Prologues and Epilogues." *Essays in American and English Literature Presented to Bruce Robert McElderry, Jr.*, ed. Max F. Schulz with William D. Templeman and Charles R. Metzger, pp. 221-37. Athens, Ohio: Ohio University Press, 1967.

5/13:4   Castrop, Helmut. "Die Satire in Drydens Prologen und Epilogen." *Archiv* 208(1971):267-85.

5/13:5   Danchin, Pierre. "Le public des théâtres londoniens à l'époque de las Restauration d'après les prologues et les èpilogues." *Dramaturgie et Société: Rapports entre l'oeuvre théâtrale*, ed. Jean Jacquot, assisted by Elie Konigson and Marcel Oddon. 2:847-88. (Colloques internationaux du centre national de la recherche scientifique: Sciences humaines.) Paris: Editions du centre national de las recherche scientifique, 1968.

5/13:6   de Beer, E. S. "Dryden: Date of a Prologue, 'Gallants, a Bashful Poet'." *NQ* 179(1940):440-41.

5/13:7   Fletcher, C. R. L. "A Dryden Allusion." *TLS* 9 February 1933, p. 92. *See* correspondence, Hibernicus, ibid., 16 February 1933, p. 108; L. R. M. Strachan, ibid., 16 February 1933, p. 108; Edwin Nungezer, ibid., 2 November 1933, p. 751. Prologue to *Secret Love*.

5/13:8   Frost, William. "Dryden's Prologue and Epilogue to *All for Love*." *Expl* 10(1951):Querry 1.

5/13:9   Gardner, William B. "Dryden and the Authorship of the Epilogue to Crowne's *Calisto*." *Studies in English* (University of Texas) 27(1948):234-38. Argues for Crowne's authorship.

5/13:10   Ghosh, J. C. "Prologue and Epilogue to Lee's 'Constantine the Great'." *TLS* 14 March 1929, p. 207.

5/13:11   Gousseff, James W. "The Staging of Prologues in Tudor and Stuart Plays." *DA* 23(1963):3548(Northwestern).

5/13:12   Ham, Roswell G. "Dryden's Epilogue to *The Rival Ladies*, 1664." *RES* 13(1937):76-80.

5/13:13   ———. "Some Uncollected Verse of John Dryden." *London Mercury* 21(1930):421-26.

5/13:14   ———. "Uncollected Verse by John Dryden." *TLS* 27 December 1928, p. 1025. The Prologue and Epilogue to Lee's *Mithridates*, an Epilogue "Spoke before His Majesty at Oxford," and the Prologue and Epilogue to "The History of Bacon in Virginia" are attributed to Dryden. *See* item 5/13:13 for additional information. *See also* items 5/13:15-16.

5/13:15   Hiscock, W. G. "A Dryden Epilogue." *TLS* 5 March 1931, p. 178. *See* item 5/13:14.

5/13:16 ——. "Oxford History." *TLS* 13 October 1932, p. 734. Oxford Epilogue.

5/13:17 Lawrence, W. J. "Oxford Restoration Prologues." *TLS* 16 January 1930, p. 43.

5/13:18 Maxwell, J. C. "Dryden." *TLS* 25 September 1970, p. 1095.

5/13:19 McCutcheon, R. P. "Dryden's Prologue to the *Prophetess*." *MLN* 39(1924):123-24.

5/13:20 Meyerstein, E. H. W. "'Fame Like a Wayward Girl'." *TLS* 22 March 1923, p. 200. Keats and the Epilogue to *The Conquest of Granada*.

5/13:21 Morton, R. E. "The Prologue and Epilogue in Restoration Literature." *ASLIB* 4(1953-54):9(Oxford, Waldham).

5/13:22 Osenburg, F. C. "The Prologue to Dryden's *Wild Gallant* Reexamined." *ELN* 7(1969):35-39. Astrological references. *See* item 2/5:9.

5/13:23 Ringler, Richard N. "Two Dryden Notes." *ELN* 1(1964):256-61. The Archimedian Sphere from Claudius and "mechanique arts" from John Wilkins.

5/13:24 Rosecke, Jngo. "Drydens Prologe und Epiloge." Diss. Hamburg, 1938.

5/13:25 Smith, John Harrington. "Dryden's Prologue and Epilogue to *Mithridates*, Revived." *PMLA* 68(1953):251-67. Establishes and annotates the text.

5/13:26 Stroup, Thomas B. "The Authorship of the Prologue to Lee's 'Constantine the Great'." *NQ* 1(1954):387-88. *See* item 5/13:13.

*5/13:27 Sutherland, James. "Prologues, Epilogues and Audience in the Restoration Theatre." *Of Books and Humankind: Essays and Poems Presented to Bonamy Dobrée*, ed. John Butt, pp. 37-54. London: Routledge and Kegan Paul, 1964.

5/13:28 Thorp, Willard. "A New Manuscript Version of Dryden's Epilogue to *Sir Fopling Flutter*." *RES* 9(1933):198-99. *See* item 3:188.

*5/13:29 Vieth, David M. "The Art of the Prologue and Epilogue: A New Approach Based on Dryden's Practice." *Genre* 5(1972):271-92. The prologue and the epilogue create a dynamic interrelationship among several constituent elements: imagery, tone, the play itself, the poet, the audience, the speaker, contemporary circumstances.

5/13:30 W., H. "Red Playbills." *NQ* (9th ser.) 12(1903):248. Prologue to *Arviragus and Philicia*.

5/13:31 Wiley, Autrey Nell. "The English Vogue of Prologues and Epilogues." *MLN* 47(1932):255-57.

5/13:32 ——, ed. *Rare Prologues and Epilogues 1642-1700*. London: George Allen and Unwin, 1940.

5/13:33 Williams, Sheila. "The Pope-Burning Processions of 1679, 1680 and 1681." *JWCI* 21(1958):104-18. "Prologue" to Southerne's *The Loyal Brother* (1682).

5/13:34 Zwicker, Steven N. "Dryden's Borrowing from Ben Jonson's 'Panegyre'." *NQ* 15(1968):105-06. "Prologue" to John Banks' *Unhappy Favorite*.

See also items 2/1:3-5, 2/1:7, 2/2:10, 2/2:13, 2/2:21, 2/2:27, 2/2:31-32, 2/2:41-42, 3:25, 3:76, 3:81, 3:172, 4:105, 4:218, 4:223, 4:362, 4:506, 7:276, 8/1:196, 8/1:209, 8/8:9.

5/14. OTHER NONDRAMATIC POEMS

5/14:1 Aden, John M. "Shakespeare in Dryden's First Published Poem?" *NQ* 2(1955):22-23. *Hastings.*

5/14:2 Beckingham, C. F. "Selvaggi and Dryden." *NQ* 167(1934):169. A suggested borrowing in Dryden's poem on Milton.

5/14:3 Benson, Donald R. "Platonism and Neoclassic Metaphor: Dryden's *Eleonora* and Donne's *Anniversaries*." *SP* 68(1971):340-56. Establishes a definition of Plantonism from Dryden's criticism.

5/14:4 Cameron, W. J. "An Overlooked Dryden Printing." *NQ* 198(1953): 344. A 1697 text of "A letter to Sir George Etheridge."

5/14:5 Cope, Jackson I. "Science, Christ, and Cromwell in Dryden's *Heroic Stanzas*." *MLN* 71(1956):483-85.

5/14:6 Crinò, Anna Maria. "Dryden MS." *TLS* 22 September 1966, p. 879. A new MS of "Heroique Stanzas." *See EM* 17(1966):311-20 for a fuller discussion and a photo-reproduction of the text.

5/14:7 "Hibernicus." "Dryden's Epigram on Milton." *NQ* 173(1937):149-50.

5/14:8 Hoffman, Arthur W. "Dryden's *To Mr. Congreve*." *MLN* 75(1960): 553-56. The architectural metaphor.

5/14:9 Johnson, James William. "Dryden's 'Epistle to Robert Howard'." *BSTCF* 2,i(1961):20-24. A structural analysis of the poem, with a view to its revitalization of a hackneyed genre, the complimentary epistle. *See* item 5/14:24.

5/14:10 Judkins, David. "Studies in Seventeenth Century Political Poetry of the English Civil War." *DAI* 31(1970):2387A(Mich. State). *Heroic Stanzas.*

*5/14:11 Levine, Jay Arnold. "John Dryden's Epistle to John Driden." *JEGP* 63(1964):450-74. Reprinted in [King]:114-42. A placement of the poem into its historical context and an analysis of the imagery, argument, and strategies of the poem.

*5/14:12 Miner, Earl. "Dryden's *Eikon Basilike*: To Sir Godfrey Kneller." *Seventeenth-Century Imagery: Essays on Uses of Figurative Language from Donne to Farquhar*, ed. Earl Miner, pp. 151-67. (The 17th and 18th Centuries Studies Group, U.C.L.A., Clark Memorial Library.) Berkeley, Los Angeles: University of California Press, 1971.

5/14:13 ———. "Dryden's Ode on Mrs. Anastasia Stafford." *HLQ* 30 (1967):103-11. Dates the poem in December 1687 and conjectures what the conclusion might have been.

5/14:14 Newdigate, B. H. "An Overlooked Ode by John Dryden." *London Mercury* 22(1930):438-42. *On the Marriage of . . . Anastasia Stafford to . . . George Holman.*

5/14:15 Parker, Karl T. *Oliver Cromwell in der schönen Literatur Englands: Eine literarische Studie.* Freiburg: Speyer and Kärner, 1920.

5/14:16 Parsons, Edward S. "A Note upon Dryden's Heroic Stanzas on the Death of Cromwell." *MLN* 19(1904):47-49. Annotates 1. 15 ("His palms, tho' . . .").

5/14:17 Poland, Harry B. "Dryden on Milton's Portrait." *NQ* (10th ser.) 11(1909):246.

5/14:18 Rye, Walter. "Epitaph by Dryden." *NQ* (8th ser.) 9(1896):328. *See* reply, Edward H. Marshall, ibid., 377.

5/14:19 Sargeaunt, John. "Disdaunted." *NQ* (10th ser.) 20(1908):328. The inscription on the monument of Sir Palmes Fairborne in Westminster Abbey. *See* replies, John Sargeaunt, ibid., 10(1908):352; R. Vaughan Gower, ibid., 10(1908):377.

5/14:20   Swedenberg, H. T., Jr. "More Tears for Lord Hastings." *HLQ* 16(1952):43-51.

5/14:21   Sweney, John R. "The Dedication of Thomas Southerne's *The Wives Excuse* 1692." *Library* (5th ser.) 25(1970):154-55. "To Mr. Southern."

5/14:22   ———. "Dryden's 'Lines to Mrs. Creed'." *PQ* 51(1972):489-90.

5/14:23   T[horn]-D[rury], G. "Dryden's Verses 'To the Lady Castlemain, upon Her Incouraging His First Play'." *RES* 6(1930):193-94.

5/14:24   Vieth, David M. "Irony in Dryden's Verses to Sir Robert Howard." *EIC* 22(1972):239-43. *See* item 5/14:9.

5/14:25   Wilson, Gayle Edward. "Genre and Rhetoric in Dryden's 'Upon the Death of the Lord Hastings'." *SSJ* 35(1970):256-66.

6. Translations

6/1. GENERAL STUDIES

6/1:1   Amos, Flora Ross. "From Cowley to Pope." *Early Theories of Translation*, pp. 135-78. (Studies in English and Comparative Literature.) New York: Columbia University Press, 1920.

6/1:2   Brooks, Harold F. "The 'Imitation' in English Poetry, Especially in Formal Satire, Before the Age of Pope." *RES* 25(1949):124-40.

6/1:3   Brower, Reuben. *Mirror on Mirror: Translation, Imitation, Parody*. (Harvard Studies in Comparative Literature.) Cambridge, Mass.: Harvard University Press, 1975.

6/1:4   Callan, Norman. "Pope and the Classics." *Writers and their Background: Alexander Pope*, ed. Peter Dixon, pp. 230-49. Athens, Ohio: Ohio University Press, 1972. Dryden and Pope are compared as translators and classicists. *See* item 6/2:28.

6/1:5   Chester, Allan Griffith. *Thomas May: Man of Letters 1595-1650*. Philadelphia: [n. pub.], 1932.

*6/1:6   Culioli, Antoine. "Dryden, Traducteur et Adaptateur de Chaucer et de Boccace." Diss. Sorbonne, 1960.

6/1:7   Frost, William. "Dryden and the Art of Translation." Diss. Yale, 1946.

*6/1:8   ———. *Dryden and the Art of Translation*. (Yale Studies in English 128.) New Haven: Yale University Press; London: Oxford University Press, 1955. Reprinted Hamden, Conn.: Archon Books, 1969. *See* John Sherwood, *CL* 8:255; Joseph McG. Bottkol, *PQ* 35:290-91; *TLS* 28 October 1955, p. 634; James Kinsley, *RES* 7:316-18; Vinton A. Dearing, *JEGP* 55:650-51; Reuben A. Brower, *MLN* 71:46-48.

6/1:9   ———. "More About Dryden as Classicist." *NQ* 19(1972):23-26. *See* item 2/2:22.

6/1:10   Gifford, Henry. *Comparative Literature: Concepts of Literature*. London: Routledge and Kegan Paul, 1969.

6/1:11   Hoban, Thomas M. "The Contexts and Structure of Dryden's *Fables Ancient and Modern*." *DAI* 32(1972):3953A-54A(Neb.). The unity of the *Fables*.

*6/1:12   Jünemann, Wolfgang. *Drydens Fabeln und ihre Quellen*. Hamburg: de Gruyter, 1932. *See* H. Jantzen, *Beiblatt* 44:205-09.

6/1:13   Knox, R. A. *On English Translation*. Oxford: At the Clarendon Press, 1957.

6/1:14 Moskovit, Leonard A. "Pope and the Tradition of the Neoclassical Imitation." *SEL* 8(1968):445-62.

6/1:15 Nitchie, Elizabeth. "Dryden and Pope." *Vergil and the English
Poets*, pp. 148-78. New York: Columbia University Press, 1919. Reprinted New York: AMS Press, 1966.

6/1:16 Nulle, Stebelton H. "Julian and the Men of Letters." *CJ* 54
(1958-59):257-66.

6/1:17 Pinto, V. de Sola. "Dryden and Thomas Shipman." *NQ* 192(1947):
389. Dedication to the *Fables*.

6/1:18 Restaino, Katherine M. "The Troubled Streams of Translation:
A Study of Translation in the Eighteenth Century." *DA* 27(1967):
2507A-08A(Fordham).

6/1:19 Rzesnitzek, F. *Das Verhältnis der Fables von John Dryden zu
den entsprechenden mittelenglischen Vorlagen.* Zurich, 1903.

*6/1:20 Sloman, Judith. "An Interpretation of Dryden's *Fables*." *ECS*
4(1971):199-211. The arrangement of the translations in the
Fables exemplifies the conflict Dryden saw between classical,
heroic ideals and Christian ideals of humility and harmoniousness.

6/1:21 ———. "The Structure of Dryden's *Fables*." *DA* 29(1968):1906A
(Minn.).

6/1:22 Weinbrot, Howard D. *The Formal Strain: Studies in Augustan
Imitation and Satire.* Chicago, London: University of Chicago
Press, 1969.

6/1:23 Wright, Herbert G. "Some Sidelights on the Reputation and Influence of Dryden's 'Fables'." *RES* 21(1945):23-37.

See also items 2/1:3, 2/2:7, 2/2:13, 2/2:21, 2/2:32, 2/3:1, 4:26, 4:
39, 4:49, 4:56, 4:142, 4:202, 4:218, 4:245, 4:339, 4:362, 4:371,
4:429, 4:444, 4:446, 4:448, 4:455, 4:464-65, 4:495, 4:506, 4:536,
4:546, 5/12:28, 7:15, 7:54, 7:109, 7:135, 7:290, 7:293, 7:333,
8/9:75.

6/2. CLASSICAL TRANSLATIONS

6/2:1 Adams, Betty S. "Dryden's Translation of Vergil and Its Eighteenth-Century Successors." *DAI* 32(1971):417A(Mich. State). Dryden's influence on Benson, Trapp, Pitt, Warton, Beresford and
Sotheby.

6/2:2 Adams, Robert Martin. *Proteus, His Lies, His Truth: Discussions of Literary Translation.* New York: Norton, 1973. In his
translation of Juvenal, Dryden inflates the verse and reduces
particulars to generalities.

*6/2:3 Austin, Norman. "Translation as Baptism: Dryden's Lucretius."
Arion 7(1968):576-602. Demonstrates the ways in which Dryden
transformed Lucretius into an anti-hedonist.

6/2:4 Baier, Lee "An Early Instance of 'Daydreams'." *NQ* 17(1970):409.

6/2:5 Beller, Manfred. *Philemon and Baucis in der europäischen Literatur.* Heidelberg: Winter, 1967.

6/2:6 Bernard, M. L. "Dryden's *Aeneid*: The Theory and the Poem."
ASLIB 20(1969-70):16(Cambridge).

6/2:7 Bisson, L. A. "Valéry and Virgil." *MLR* 53(1958):501-11. Different theories of translation.

6/2:8 Bliss, Carey S. *Some Aspects of Seventeenth Century English
Printing with Special Reference to Joseph Moxon*, introd. Ward
Ritchie. (William Andrews Clark Memorial Library Seminar.) Los
Angeles: University of California Press, 1965. Tonson's edition
of Dryden's *Virgil* (1697).

6/2:9 Boddy, Margaret P. "Contemporary Allusions in Lauderdale's *Aeneid*." *NQ* 9(1962):386-88.

6/2:10 ———. "The Manuscripts and Printed Editions of the Translation of Virgil Made by Richard Maitland, Fourth Earl of Lauderdale, and the Connexion with Dryden." *NQ* 12(1965):144-50.

6/2:11 ———. "The 1692 *Fourth Book of Virgil*." *RES* 15(1964):364-80. Compares the translations of Dryden, Ogilby, Mulgrave, Sedley, Addison and Lauderdale.

6/2:12 ———. "The Translations of Virgil into English Verse from Douglas Through Dryden: A Study in the Development of Poetic Expression." Diss. Minnesota, 1935.

*6/2:13 Bottkol, Joseph McG. "Dryden's Latin Scholarship." *MP* 40 (1943):241-54. Reprinted in [Swedenberg]:397-424. By examining the texts used by Dryden, Bottkol demonstrates that he was not a weak Latinist. *See* item 6/2:38.

6/2:14 Broderson, G. L. "Seventeenth Century Translations of Juvenal." *Phoenix* 7(1953):57-76.

6/2:15 Brooks, Harold F. "Dryden's Juvenal and the Harveys." *PQ* 48 (1969):12-19. Dates the beginning of Dryden's Juvenal project in 1687.

6/2:16 Brower, Reuben A. "Visual and Verbal Translations of Myth: Neptune in Virgil, Rubens, Dryden." *Daedalus* 101,i(1972):155-82.

6/2:17 Burrows, L. R. "Juvenal in Translation." *Australasian Universities Language and Literature Association: Proceedings and Papers of the Twelfth Congress Held at the University of Western Australia, 5-11 February 1969*, ed. A. P. Treweek, pp. 193-201. Sydney: AULIA, 1970.

6/2:18 Carnochan, W. B. "Some Suppressed Verses in Dryden's Translation of Juvenal VI." *TLS* 21 January 1972, pp. 73-74. Includes the Huntington Library copy of what may be Jacob Tonson's handwritten transcription of the "seamier sections" of the translation. *See* correspondence, Kenneth Monkman, ibid., 28 January, p. 99; Paul J. Korshin, ibid., 17 March, pp. 307-08; R. A. Leeson, ibid., 24 March p. 337. *See also* item 2/1:3.

6/2:19 Chalker, John. "Theory and Practice: Dryden's Translation of the 'Georgics' and Addison's 'Essay'." *The English Georgic: A Study in the Development of a Form*, pp. 17-33. (Ideas and Forms in English Literature.) Baltimore: Johns Hopkins Press, 1969. Dryden exploits the mock-heroic elements of Virgil's poem.

6/2:20 Chester, Allan Griffith. "Dryden and Thomas May." *TLS* 19 July 1934, p. 511. Indebtedness to May and Ogilby.

6/2:21 Coldwell, David F. C., ed. *Selections from Gavin Douglas*. With an Introd., Notes and Glossary. Oxford: At the Clarendon Press, 1964. Dryden's translation of the *Aeneid* is negatively compared with that of Douglas.

6/2:22 Deane, C. V. "Virgil and his Translators: Dryden and Warton." *Aspects of Eighteenth Century Nature Poetry*, pp. 33-47. Oxford: Blackwell, 1935.

6/2:23 Durling, Dwight L. *Georgic Tradition in English Poetry*. (Columbia University Studies in English and Comparative Literature 121.) New York: Columbia University Press, 1935. Dryden's translation of Virgil stimulated English use of the Georgic tradition.

6/2:24 Eade, Christopher. "Some English Iliads: Chapman to Dryden." *Arion* 6(1967):336-45. Dryden's comments on Hobbes's translation, together with some excerpts from Dryden's translation.

6/2:25 Eames, Marian. "John Ogilby and his Aesop." *BNYPL* 65(1961):73–78.

6/2:26 Elkin, P. K. "Dryden's Translation of Juvenal's Sixth Satire." *Australasian Universities Language and Literature Association: Proceedings and Papers of the Twelfth Congress Held at the University of Western Australia, 5–11 February 1969*, ed. A. P. Treweek, pp. 202–10. Sydney: AULLA, 1970.

6/2:27 Fitzgerald, Robert. "Dryden's *Aeneid*." *Arion* 2,iii(1963):17–31.

*6/2:28 Frost, William. "Dryden and the Classics: With a Look at His *Aeneis*." [Miner]:267–96. A good review of all the troublesome questions relating to Dryden's translations.

6/2:29 ———. "Dryden's Versions of Ovid." *Expression, Communication and Experience in Literature and Language* (Proceedings of the Twelfth Congress of the International Federation for Modern Languages Held at Cambridge University, 20 to 26 August 1972), ed. Ronald G. Popperwell, pp. 289–90. London: Modern Humanities Research Association, 1973.

6/2:30 ———. "English Persius: The Golden Age." *ECS* 2(1968):77–101.

6/2:31 Gallagher, Mary. "Dryden's Translation of Lucretius." *HLQ* 28 (1964):19–29. Reasons for Dryden's success in his translation of Lucretius.

6/2:32 Galloway, William Francis. "English Adaptations of Roman Satire, 1660–1800." Diss. Michigan, 1937.

6/2:33 Gerevini, Silvano. *Dryden e Teocrito: Barocco e neoclassicismo nella Restaurazione inglese*. Milano: Mursia, 1966. Dryden's translation compared with that of Creech. *See Dryden e Teocrito*. Pavia: Fusi, 1958.

6/2:34 Gordon, George. "Virgil in English Poetry." *PBA* 17(1931):39–53. Reprinted in *The Discipline of Letters*, pp. 19–34. Oxford: At the Clarendon Press, 1946.

6/2:35 Hardin, Richard F. "Ovid in Seventeenth-Century England." *CL* 24(1972):44–62.

6/2:36 Harrison, T. W. "Dryden's *Aeneid*." [King]:143–67.

6/2:37 Hauser, David R. "The Neo-Classical Ovid: Ovid in English Literature, 1660–1750." Diss. Johns Hopkins, 1957.

*6/2:38 Hooker, Helene Maxwell. "Dryden's *Georgics* and English Predecessors." *HLQ* 9(1945–46):273–310. An important examination of Dryden's indebtedness to his English predecessors, May, Lauderdale, Addison, Sedley, in his translation of Virgil. *See* Joseph McG. Bottkol, *PQ* 26:118–19. *See also* item 6/2:13.

6/2:39 Hopkins, D. W. "An Echo of La Fontaine in Dryden's 'Baucis and Philemon'." *NQ* 20(1973):178–79.

6/2:40 ———. "Two Hitherto Unrecorded Sources for Dryden's Ovid Translations." *NQ* 21(1974):419–21.

6/2:41 Hughes, R. E. "Dryden and Juvenal's Grandmother." *NQ* 1(1954):521. Juvenal's third satire, 11.192–93.

6/2:42 Johnson, Donald R. "Plowshares, Politics and Poetry: The Georgic Tradition from Dryden to Thomson." *DAI* 33(1973):6314A (Wis.).

6/2:43 Johnson, Maurice. "Dryden's Note on Depilation." *NQ* 196(1951):471–72. Dryden's Note numbered 7 and a phrase from Note 8 to his translation of the 4th Satire of Persius. *See* item 2/2:22.

6/2:44 Johnston, Arthur. "'The Purple Year' in Pope and Gray." *RES* 14(1963):389–93. Dryden's translation of Virgil's "*purpureum ver*" in the 9th Eclogue.

6/2:45   Kelsall, M. M. "What God, What Mortal? The *Aeneid* and English Mock-Heroic." *Arion* 8(1969):359-79.

6/2:46   King, Anne R. "Translation from the Classics during the Restoration with Special Reference to Dryden's *Aeneis*." Diss. Cornell, 1950.

6/2:47   Kupersmith, William. "Juvenal as Sublime Satirist." *PMLA* 87 (1972):508-11. *See* W. B. Carnochan, *PMLA* 85:260-67.

6/2:48   Little, Evelyn S. "Homer and Theocritus in English Translation: A Critical Bibliography Designed as a Guide for Librarians in the Choice of Editions for the General Reader." *DA* 3,ii(1941): 60-61(Mich.).

*6/2:49   Løsnes, Arvid. "Dryden's *Æneis* and the Delphin *Virgil*." *The Hidden Sense and Other Essays*, pp. 113-57. (Norwegian Studies in English 9.) Oslo: Universitets-forlaget, 1963. Dryden used the *interpretatio* of the Delphin *Virgil* (1682, 2nd ed.) to help him in his translation.

6/2:50   Macpherson, Charles. *Über die Virgil-Übersetzung des John Dryden*. Berlin: Mayer, 1910. *See* S. B. Liljegren, *EST* 52:278-83.

6/2:51   Martin, R. H. "A Note on Dryden's *Aeneid* [I,459-63]." *PQ* 30 (1951):89-91.

6/2:52   Mason, H. A. "Dryden's 'Georgics' and Pope's 'Essay on Criticism'." *NQ* 21(1974):252.

6/2:53   ———. "Introducing Homer's *Iliad*." *CQ* 4(1968):15-37.

6/2:54   ———. "Introducing the *Iliad* (II): Pope and Dryden as Mediators." *CQ* 4(1969):150-68.

6/2:55   ———. "'Short Excursions' in Dryden and Pope." *NQ* 16(1969): 341.

6/2:56   Maxwell, J. C. "Dryden's Paraphrase of Horace and 'The Staple of News'." *NQ* 197(1952):389.

6/2:57   ———. "Pope's Statius and Dryden's Ovid." *NQ* 11(1964):56.

6/2:58   Means, J. A. "An Echo of Dryden in Pope." *NQ* 16(1969):187.

6/2:59   Miner, Earl. "Dryden's Messianic Eclogue." *RES* 11(1960):299-301. The translation of the 4th Eclogue was to celebrate the birth of Princess Anne's first child.

*6/2:60   O'Connor, Mark. "John Dryden, Gavin Douglas and Virgil." *Restoration Literature: Critical Approaches*, ed Harold Love, pp. 247-75. London: Methuen, 1972. A demand that Dryden's translation be seen in terms of contemporary practice and aesthetics and that, accordingly, it be revaluated. *See* item 6/2:63.

6/2:61   O'Sullivan, Maurice J., Jr. "Dryden and Juvenal: A Study in Interpretation." *DAI* 31(1971):3515A-16A(Case Western Reserve).

6/2:62   Papajewski, Helmut. "Die literarische Wertung Ovids am Ausgang des 17. und zu Beginn des 18. Jahrhunderts." *Anglia* 78 (1960):422-48.

*6/2:63   Proudfoot, L. *Dryden's "Aeneid" and Its Seventeenth Century Predecessors*. Manchester: University Press, 1960. A thorough examination of the seventeenth-century tradition of Virgilian translation, but marred by an evident dislike of Dryden's translation. *See* Robert Fagles, *PQ* 40:387-88; *TLS* 25 November 1961, p. 760; Ernest Sirluck, *SCN* 19,iii(1961):40-41. *See also* item 3:20.

6/2:64   ———. "Dryden's *Aeneis* and Its Seventeenth Century English Sources." *ASLIB* 6(1955-56):10(Manchester).

6/2:65   Ram, Tulsi. *The Neo-Classical Epic (1650-1720)*. Delhi: National, 1971. Dryden chose to translate Virgil instead of Homer because the events of the *Aeneid* were more directly relevant to his own times. *See* John Buxton, *RES* 25:86-87.

6/2:66   Rawson, C. J. "'Ida's Shady Brow': Parallels to Blake." *NQ* 12 (1965):183.

6/2:67   Real, Hermann Josef. *Untersuchungen zur Lukrez-Übersetzung von Thomas Creech*. (Linguistica et Litteraria 9.) Berlin, Zürich: Max Gehlen, 1970. Translation of Lucretius.

6/2:68   Røstvig, Maren-Sofie. *The Happy Man: Studies in the Metamorphoses of a Classical Ideal 1600-1700*. (Oslo Studies in English 2.) Oslo: Akademisk Forlag; Oxford: Basil Blackwell, 1954. The place of Dryden's translations of Virgil in the *beatus ille*-tradition.

6/2:69   Russell, Robert E. "Dryden's Juvenal and Persius." *DA* 28 (1967):209A(Calif., Davis).

*6/2:70   Selden, Raman. "Juvenal and Restoration Modes of Translation." *MLR* 68(1973):481-93. Shadwell's and Dryden's translations of Juvenal's tenth Satire are compared.

6/2:71   Seronsy, Cecil C. "Dryden and Belinda's Toilet." *NQ* 198(1953): 28. Juvenal's sixth Satire.

6/2:72   Shea, Peter K. "Juvenal's Tenth Satire Englished: The Art of Translation, 1617-1802." *DAI* 35(1974):3769A(N.C.).

6/2:73   Sherbo, Arthur. *A Computer Concordance of John Dryden's Translation of Virgil's Poetry*. 2 vols. East Lansing: Michigan State University, 1969.

6/2:74   ———. *Frequency Lists of John Dryden's Translations of Virgil's Poetry*. East Lansing: Michigan State University, Computer Center, 1971.

6/2:75   ———. "Virgil, Dryden, Gay, and Matters Trivial." *PMLA* 85 (1970):1063-71. Gay's borrowings from Dryden's translation of Virgil.

6/2:76   Smith, Constance I. "An Echo of Dryden in Pope." *NQ* 12(1965): 451. *See* correspondence, [editor], ibid., 14(1967):146; Constance I. Smith, ibid., 15(1968):431.

6/2:77   Sühnel, Rudolf. "Vergil in England." *Festschrift fur Walter Hübner*, eds. Dieter Riesner and Helmut Gneuss, pp. 122-38. Berlin: Schmidt, 1964.

6/2:78   Swedenberg, H. T., Jr., ed. *George Stepney's Translation of the Eighth Satire of Juvenal*. Berkeley: Clark Memorial Library, University of California Press, 1948.

6/2:79   Wain, John. "Ovid in English." *Preliminary Essays*, pp. 36-77. London: Macmillan; New York: St. Martin's, 1957.

6/2:80   Ward, Charles E. "The Publication and Profits of Dryden's *Virgil*." *PMLA* 53(1938):807-12.

*6/2:81   West, Michael. "Dryden's Ambivalence as a Translator of Heroic Themes." *HLQ* 36(1973):347-66. Evidence of Dryden's ambivalence toward heroic values is found in a comparison between his translation and Virgil's *Aeneid*; in his translations of Homer, Ovid and Boccaccio, Dryden is openly antagonistic towards those values.

6/2:82   Wilkinson, L. P. "Virgil, Dryden, and Tennyson." *TLS* 9 October 1969, p. 1159.

See also items 1:81, 2/1:5, 2/2:21, 2/2:32, 2/3:2-3, 2/3:5, 3:13, 3:20, 3:21, 3:43, 3:112, 3:197, 4:57-58, 4:60, 4:79, 4:192, 4:246, 4:271, 4:322, 5/7:27, 7:49, 8/8:6.

6/3. TRANSLATIONS OF HYMNS

6/3:1   *Benedictine Hours for Sundays and All Feasts of First and Second Class Rank.* York: [Ampleforth Abbey], 1934. *See* items 2/3:4,
6/3:4.

6/3:2   Brunner, Frieda. *John Dryden's Hymnen.* Freiburg: Karl Henn,
1931.

6/3:3   ————. "Dryden's Hymn Translations." *TLS* 3 July 1930, p. 554.

6/3:4   "Dryden a Hymnodist?" *TLS* 12 April 1934, p. 258. *See* items 2/3:
4, 6/3:1.

6/3:5   Shewring, W. H. "Dryden and the Primer of 1706." *DownR* 56(1938):
303-10. Rev. art. *See* item 2/3:4.

6/3:6   ————. "The Office Hymns of John Dryden." *Ampleforth Journal*
39(1933):18-27.

See also items 2/3:4, 4:90.

6/4. ITALIAN TRANSLATIONS

6/4:1   Galigani, Giuseppi. *Il Boccaccio nella Cultura Inglesa a Anglo-
Americana.* Firenze: Olschki, 1974.

6/4:2   Hinnant, Charles H. "Dryden and Hogarth's *Sigismunda.*" *ECS* 6
(1973):462-74.

6/4:3   Low, D. M. "An Error in Dryden." *TLS* 30 April 1925, p. 300.
Theodore and Honoria.

6/4:4   Scenna, Desiderato. *Spigolature critichi: Minuzie carducciane.
Dryden e Boccaccio.* Chieti, 1911.

6/4:5   Sloman, Judith. "Dryden's Originality in *Sigismonda and Guis-
cardo.*" *SEL* 12(1972):445-57. Sigismonda is compared with Dryden's
female characters in the heroic drama.

6/4:6   Wieruszowski, Kurt E. *Untersuchungen über John Drydens Boc-
caccio-Paraphrasen.* Bonn: Foppen, 1904.

6/4:7   Wright, Herbert G. *Boccaccio in England from Chaucer to Tennyson.* London: University of London, Athlone, 1957. Dryden's
choice of tales from Boccaccio reflects his own advancing age and
the temper of the times; considers Dryden's influence on later
translators of Boccaccio.

See also items 4:86, 4:105.

6/5. FRENCH TRANSLATIONS

*6/5:1   Archer, Stanley. "On Dryden's *History of the League* (1684)."
PLL 4(1968):103-06. Dryden modified Maimbourg's history to make
it more violently antagonistic to the League. *See* item 6/5:3.

6/5:2   Burns, G. "St. Francis Xavier and England: John Dryden's
Translation of His Life." *Tablet*(London) 200(6 December 1952):454.

6/5:3   Cameron, L. W. "The Cold Prose Fits of John Dryden." *RLC* 30
(1956):371-79. After comparing Dryden's translation with Maimbourg's *Historie de la Ligue,* Cameron concludes that Dryden is
faithful to the tone of the original and, at the same time, is
aware of the linguistic boundaries of English. *See* item 6/5:1.

*6/5:4   Roper, Alan. "A Critic's Apology for Editing Dryden's *The
History of the League.*" *The Editor as Critic and The Critic as
Editor* (*Papers Read at a Clark Library Seminar November 13, 1971*),
introd. Murray Krieger, pp. 41-72. Los Angeles: Clark Memorial

Library, University of California, 1973. A witty explanation of
why he would edit the *History* and an explanation of its importance in the study of Dryden's thought.

6/5:5 ———. "Dryden's *The History of the League* and the Early Editions of Maimbourg's *Histoire de la Ligue*." *PBSA* 66(1972):245-
75.

6/5:6 Turner, Margaret. "A Note on the Standard of English Translations from the French, 1685-1720." *NQ* 1(1954):516-21.

6/5:7 Wimsatt, W. K., Jr. "Samuel Johnson and Dryden's *Du Fresnoy*."
SP 48(1951):26-39.

See also 2/3:7-9.

6/6. ENGLISH TRANSLATIONS

6/6:1 Alderson, William L., and Arnold C. Henderson. "Dryden's *Fables*." *Chaucer and Augustan Scholarship*, pp. 53-68. (English
Studies 35.) Berkeley, Los Angeles: University of California
Press, 1970. Makes note of the Middle English texts printed at
the end of the *Fables*; Dryden used more than one edition of Chaucer in the preparation of his translation.

6/6:2 Atwater, N. B. "Dryden's Translation of Chaucer." *ASLIB* 19
(1968-69):16(Exeter).

6/6:3 Bird, Roger A. "Dryden's Medieval Translations." *DAI* 30(1970):
4396A(Minn.).

*6/6:4 Dobbins, Austin C. "Dryden's 'Character of a Good Parson':
Background and Interpretation." *SP* 53(1956):51-59. In accord with
the seventeenth-century view of Chaucer, Dryden makes the Parson
into an example of a non-juring clergyman, committed to the support of the established monarchy.

6/6:5 ———. "The Employment of Chaucer by Dryden and Pope." *UNCR-RP*
491(1950):124-26. A defense of Dryden's translation.

6/6:6 Dorman, Peter J. "Chaucer's Reputation in the Restoration and
Eighteenth Century." *DAI* 32(1972):5734A(N.Y.U.). *See* item 7:46.

6/6:7 Hinnant, Charles H. "Dryden's Gallic Rooster." *SP* 65(1968):
647-56. The cock and Louis XIV.

6/6:8 Kinsley, James "Dryden's 'Character of a Good Parson' and Bishop Ken." *RES* 3(1952):155-58.

6/6:9 Levy, Robert A. "Dryden's Translation of Chaucer: A Study of
the Means of Re-Creating Literary Models." *DAI* 34(1974):5108A-09A
(Tenn.). Argues that Dryden's translations should be studied without reference to Chaucer, since Dryden so radically alters the
characters and statements of the originals.

6/6:10 Middleton, Anne. "The Modern Art of Fortifying: *Palamon and
Arcite* as Epicurean Epic." *ChauR* 3(1968):124-43. Dryden's unsuc-
cessful transformation of the romance into an epic, with an ac-
companying shift in moral focus, is in opposition to Chaucer's design.

*6/6:11 Miner, Earl. "Chaucer in Dryden's *Fables*." *Studies in Criticism and Aesthetics, 1660-1800: Essays in Honor of Samuel Holt
Monk*, eds. Howard Anderson and John S. Shea, pp. 58-72. Minneapolis: Minnesota University Press, 1967. The quality of Dryden's
changes of the Chaucerian originals is explained in terms of the
historia, *fabula* and *argumentum* of classical narrative.

6/6:12 Mudrick, Marvin. "Chaucer as Librettist." *PQ* 38(1959):21-29.

6/6:13 Spector, Robert D. "Dryden's *Palamon and Arcite*." *Expl* 11
   (1952):Item 7.
6/6:14 ———. "Dryden's Translation of Chaucer: A Problem in Neo-
   Classical Diction." *NQ* 2(1956):23-26.
6/6:15 Tupper, Frederick, Jr. "Dryden and Speght's Chaucer." *MLN* 12
   (1897):347-53. Dryden's use of Speght's edition.
6/6:16 Williams, W. H. "'Loves Extreamest Line'." *MLR* 6(1911):386.
   Palamon and Arcite.
6/6:17 ———. "'Palamon and Arcite' and 'The Knightes Tale'." *MLR* 9
   (1914):161-72, 309-23.

See also items 2/3:6, 4:396.

7. Critical Writings and Prose

7:1 Achitert, Walter S. "A History of English Studies to 1883 Based
   on the Research of William Riley Parker." *DAI* 33(1972):2313A
   (N.Y.U.).
7:2 Adam, Donald G. "John Dryden: A Study of His Prose Achievement."
   DA 24(1963):2025-26(Rochester).
*7:3 Aden, John, comp. *The Critical Opinions of John Dryden: A Dic-
   tionary*. Nashville: Vanderbilt University Press, 1963. *See* Donald
   F. Bond, *MP* 62:72-75; C. J. Rawson, *NQ* 10:439-40; *TLS* 23 January
   1964, p. 69; *SP* 43:355-56.
*7:4 ———. "Dryden and Boileau: The Question of Critical Influence."
   SP 50(1953):491-509. Concludes that Dryden was not significantly
   influenced by Boileau. *See* item 7:43.
*7:5 ———. "Dryden and the Imagination: The First Phase." *PMLA* 74
   (1959):28-40. Establishes Dryden's definitions of important critical terms, from 1664 to 1672. *See* item 7:137.
*7:6 ———. "Dryden and Saint Evremond." *CL* 6(1954):232-39.
*7:7 ———. "Dryden, Corneille, and the *Essay of Dramatic Poesy*."
   RES 6(1955):147-56. Corneille was not an important influence on
   Dryden.
*7:8 ———. "'Nisi Artifex': Dryden and the Poet as Critic." *SAB* 35
   (1970):3-10.
*7:9 ———. "The Question of Influence in Dryden's Use of the Major
   French Critics." *UNCR-RP* 492(1951):121-22.
7:10 Adolph, Robert. *The Rise of Modern Prose Style*. Cambridge, Mass.,
   London: M.I.T., 1968. Disagrees with Croll over the importance of
   the New Science in the development of Restoration prose style.
7:11 Alden, Raymond M. "The Doctrine of Verisimilitude in French and
   English Criticism of the Seventeenth Century." *Matzke Memorial
   Volume*, pp. 38-48. Stanford: Stanford University, 1911.
7:12 Anala, Philip Z. "John Dryden's Place in the Development of
   Seventeenth-Century English Prose." Diss. St. Louis, 1971.
7:13 Anderson, Augustus E. "Theory of Fancy and Imagination in English Thought from Hobbes to Coleridge." *DA* 13(1953):226(Vanderbilt).
7:14 Archer, Stanley. "The Persons in *An Essay of Dramatic Poesy*."
   PLL 2(1966):305-14. *See* items 7:142, 7:225.
7:15 "Art of Translation." *QR* 182(1895):324-53.

7:16   Atkins, J. W. H. *English Literary Criticism: 17th and 18th Centuries*. London: Methuen; New York: Barnes and Noble, 1951. *See* James R. Sutherland, *RES* 4:184-85; W. K. Wimsatt, Jr., *JAAC* 11: 421-22; R. S. Crane, *UTQ* 22:376-91; T. A. Birrell, *ES* 35:25-27; E. N. Hooker, *PQ* 31:244. *See also* item 7:51.

7:17   Auerbach, Erich. *Mimesis*. Trans. William R. Trask. Princeton: Princeton University Press, 1953.

7:18   Aurner, Robert Ray. "The History of Certain Aspects of the Structure of the English Sentence." *PQ* 2(1923):187-208.

7:19   Baizer, Asher. "The Theory of Imitation in English Neoclassical Criticism." *DA* 20(1960):194(N.Y.U.). Differences in critical theory about the meaning of "imitation" and of "nature."

7:20   Bate, Walter Jackson. *From Classic to Romantic: Premises in Eighteenth-Century England*. Cambridge, Mass.: Harvard University Press, 1946. Reprinted New York: Harper and Row, 1961.

7:21   Bately, Janet M. "Dryden and Branded Words." *NQ* 12(1965):134-39.

7:22   ———. "Dryden's Revisions in the *Essay of Dramatic Poesy*: The Preposition at the End of the Sentence and the Expression of the Relative." *RES* 15(1964):268-82. *See* items 2/4:21, 7:274.

7:23   Baxter, F. C. "Criticism and Appreciation of the Elizabethan Drama: Dryden to Swinburne." Diss. Cambridge, Trinity, [n.d.].

7:24   Bennett, Joan. "An Aspect of the Evolution of Seventeenth-Century Prose." *RES* 17(1941):281-97. The development of an empirically based prose style.

7:25   Benson, Donald R. "The Artistic Image and Dryden's Conception of Reason." *SEL* 11(1971):427-35.

7:26   Bentley, Gerald Eades. *Shakespeare and Jonson: Their Reputations in the Seventeenth Century Compared*. 2 vols. Chicago: University of Chicago Press, 1945. Reprinted in one vol. 1965.

*7:27   Björk, Lennart A. "The 'Inconsistencies' of Dryden's Criticism of Shakespeare." *Anglia* 91(1973):219-40. Considers whether or not Dryden's criticism is systematic.

*7:28   Blair, Joel. "Dryden on the Writing of Fanciful Poetry." *Criticism* 12(1970):89-104. Strictures on the misuse of fancy in poetry.

7:29   Bohn, William E. "The Development of John Dryden's Critical Theory." Diss. Michigan, 1906.

*7:30   ———. "The Development of John Dryden's Literary Criticism." *PMLA* 22(1907):56-139. Finds a five-period development in Dryden's criticism. *See* items 7:135, 7:316.

*7:31   Bond, Donald F. "'Distrust' of Imagination in English Neo-Classicism." *PQ* 14(1935):54-69. Reprinted in [Schilling]:281-301.

7:32   ———. "The Neo-classical Psychology of the Imagination." *ELH* 4(1937):245-64.

7:33   Bowers, R. H. "Dryden's Influence on Cuthbert Constable." *NQ* 4 (1957):13-14.

7:34   Boyd, John D., S. J. *The Function of Mimesis and Its Decline*. Cambridge, Mass.: Harvard University Press, 1968.

7:35   Bradley, J. F., and J. Q. Adams. *The Jonson Allusion-Book: A Collection of Allusions to Ben Jonson from 1597 to 1700*. New Haven: Yale University Press, 1922.

7:36   Bredvold, Louis I. "The Tendency Toward Platonism in Neo-Classical Esthetics." *ELH* 1(1934):91-119. Reprinted in [Schilling]:302-32.

7:37 Brown, Calvin S. "John Dryden as Comparatist." *CLS* 10(1973):112-24.

7:38 Brown, David D. "John Tillotson's Revisions and Dryden's 'Talent for English Prose'." *RES* 12(1961):24-39. Dryden's indebtedness to Tillotson as a model for his prose style. *See* items 7:274, 8/4:12.

7:39 Bullitt, John, and Walter Jackson Bate. "Distinctions between Fancy and Imagination in Eighteenth-Century English Criticism." *MLN* 60(1945):8-15.

7:40 Cameron, Lester W. "A Study of Dryden's Prose Style." *SDD-UW* 2 (1938):292-94.

7:41 Carver, George. *Alms for Oblivion: Books, Men and Biography.* Milwaukee: Bruce, 1946. The Dryden Plutarch.

7:42 Christensen, Francis. "John Wilkins and the Royal Society's Reform of Prose Style." *MLQ* 7(1946):179-87, 279-90.

7:43 Clark, A. F. B. *Boileau and the French Classical Critics in England (1660-1830).* Paris: Champion, 1925. Reprinted New York: Russell and Russell, 1965. *See* items 7:4, 7:140.

7:44 Cole, Elmer J., Jr. "The Consistency of John Dryden's Literary Criticism in Theory and Practice." *DAI* 31(1971):5356A(N.M.).

7:45 Congleton, J. E. *Theories of Pastoral Poetry in England 1684-1798.* Gainesville, Florida: University of Florida Press, 1952.

7:46 Connelly, William J. "Perspectives in Chaucer Criticism: 1400-1700." *DAI* 33(1972):721A(Okla.). *See* item 6/6:6.

7:47 Cooke, Arthur L. "Did Dryden Hear the Guns?" *NQ* 196(1951):204-05. *Of Dramatic Poesy.* No, he heard thunder.

7:48 Cowl, R. P. *The Theory of Poetry in England: Its Development in Doctrines and Ideas from the Sixteenth to the Nineteenth Century.* London: Macmillan, 1914.

7:49 Craig, Hardin. "Dryden's Lucian." *Classical Philology* 16(1921):141-63. Provides a history of seventeenth-century translations of Lucian; Dryden's defense of Lucian against attacks of heathenism.

7:50 Crane, R. S. "English Neoclassical Criticism: An Outline Sketch." *The Dictionary of World Literature,* ed. Joseph T. Shipley, pp. 116-27. New York: Philosophical Library, 1943. Reprinted in *Critics and Criticism: Ancient and Modern,* ed. R. S. Crane, pp. 372-88. Chicago, London: University of Chicago Press, 1952. The importance of Dryden and Rymer in the development of literary criticism as an important branch of learning.

7:51 ——. "On Writing the History of English Criticism, 1650-1800." *UTQ* 22(1953):376-91. Rev. art. *See* items 7:16, 7:256.

7:52 "Critics who have Influenced Taste: John Dryden and James Sutherland." *Times*(London) 11 April 1963, p. 15.

7:53 Culler, A. Dwight. "Edward Bysshe and the Poet's Handbook." *PMLA* 63(1948):858-85.

7:54 Current, Randall D. "The Curious Art: A Study of Literary Criticism in Verse in the Seventeenth Century." *DAI* 33(1972):304A (U.C.L.A.).

7:55 Daiches, David. *Critical Approaches to Literature.* Englewood Cliffs, N.J.: Prentice-Hall, 1956. An introductory survey. *See* Emerson R. Marks, *PQ* 35:321.

7:56 Daniels, Walter M. *St. Evremond en Angleterre.* Versailles: L. Luce, 1907.

7:57 Davie, Donald A. "*Dramatic Poetry*: Dryden's Conversation-Piece." *CamJ* 5(1951-52):553-61.

7:58   de Beer, E. S. "Mr. Montague Summers and Dryden's *Essay of Dramatic Poesy*." *RES* 8(1932):453-56. Rev. art. *See* correspondence, Montague Summers, ibid., 9(1933):202-03; E. S. de Beer, ibid., 203. *See also* item 2/5:12.

7:59   Diede, Otto. "John Dryden" and "Drydens Zeitgenossen." *Der Streit der Alten und Modernen in der englischen Literaturgeschichte des XVI. und XVII. Jahrhunderts*, pp. 78-95, 95-107. Greifswald: Adler, 1912. *See* item 4:253.

7:60   Dike, Edwin B. "Our Obsolete Vocabulary: Some Historical Views." *PQ* 13(1934):48-55.

7:61   Dillon, George L. "The Art How to Know Men: A Study of Rationalist Psychology and Neo-Classical Dramatic Theory." *DAI* 31(1970): 727A(Berkeley).

7:62   Dobrée, Bonamy. "Dryden's Prose." [King]:171-88.

7:63   Doederlein, Sue W. "A Compendium of Wit: The Psychological Vocabulary of John Dryden's Literary Criticism." *DAI* 31(1971):3542A (Northwestern).

7:64   Dowlin, Cornell March. "Plot as an Essential in Poetry." *RES* 17 (1941):166-83. Dryden was indebted to Hobbes for his ideas about narrative.

7:65   ———. *Sir William Davenant's "Gondibert," Its Preface, and Hobbes's Answer: A Study in English Neo-Classicism*. Philadelphia: [University of Pennsylvania], 1934.

*7:66   Doyle, Anne. "Dryden's Authorship of *Notes and Observations on The Empress of Morocco* (1674)." *SEL* 6(1966):421-45. On the basis of a stylistic analysis, Dryden is established as the author of the "Preface," the "Postscript," the major portion of the notes on the second act and the "Errata" in the "Epistle."

7:67   ———. "*The Empress of Morocco*: A Critical Edition of the Play and the Controversy Surrounding It." *DA* 24(1963):296(Ill.).

7:68   Eade, J. C. "Johnson and Dryden's Answer to Rymer." *NQ* 17(1970): 302.

7:69   Eberwein, Robert T. "The Imagination and Didactic Theory in Eighteenth-Century English Criticism." *DAI* 30(1969):1132A-33A (Wayne State).

7:70   Eidson, John O. "Dryden's Criticism of Shakespeare." *SP* 33 (1936):273-80.

7:71   Elkin, P. K. "The Defence of Satire from Dryden to Johnson." *ASLIB* 17(1966-67):18(Oxford).

7:72   ———. "In Defence of Hippocentaurs." *AUMLA* 5(1956):18-25. The difference between history and poetry. *See* item 7:135.

7:73   Elledge, Scott. "Cowley's Ode *Of Wit* and Longinus on the Sublime: A Study of One Definition of the Word *Wit*." *MLQ* 9(1948): 185-98.

7:74   Elliott, Robert C. *The Power of Satire: Magic, Ritual, Art*. Princeton: Princeton University Press, 1960. Dryden's comments on Roman verse satire in *Discourse of Satire*.

7:75   Ellis, Amanda M. *John Dryden and Prose Fiction*. (Colorado College Publication, General Series 168.) Colorado Springs: Colorado College, 1930. Dryden's criticism of prose fiction.

7:76   ———. "Horace's Influence on Dryden." *PQ* 4(1925):39-60.

7:77   Emerson, Oliver Farrar. "Dryden and the English Academy." *MLR* 20(1925):189-90.

7:78   ———. "John Dryden and a British Academy." *PBA* 10(1921):45-58. Reprinted in [Swedenberg]:263-80.

7:79   Empson, William. "Wit in the Essay on Criticism." *HudR* 2(1950):
       559-77. Reputation of Dryden's definition of "wit" in Pope's time.
       See item 7:125.

7:80   Evans, G. Blakemore. "Addison's Early Knowledge of Milton."
       JEGP 49(1950):204-07. Dryden's influence on Addison's criticism
       of Milton.

7:81   Falle, George G. "Dryden: Professional Man of Letters." *UTQ* 26
       (1957):443-55.

7:82   Faulkner, Susan N. "The Concept of Decorum in Dryden's Works."
       DAI 34(1974):7229A(C.U.N.Y.).

7:83   Fink, Jack E. "St. Evremond in the French and English Critical
       Traditions." *DA* 14(1954):971-72(Stanford).

7:84   Flasdieck, Hermann M. *Der Gedanke einer englischen Sprach-
       akademie in Vergangenheit und Gegenwart.* (Jenaer germanistische
       Forschungen 11.) Jena: Frommannschen, 1928.

7:85   Folkierski, Wladyslaw. "Ut Pictura Poesis: ou l'étrange fortune
       du *De Arte Graphica* de Du Fresnoy en Angleterre." *RLC* 27(1953):
       385-402.

7:86   Forrest, James E. "Dryden, Hobbes, Thomas Godwin and the Nimble
       Spaniel." *NQ* 9(1962):381-82. *See* replies, George Watson, ibid.,
       10(1963):230-31; H. Neville Davies, ibid., 349-50.

*7:87 Fowler, John. "Dryden and Literary Good Breeding." *Restoration
       Literature: Critical Approaches*, ed. Harold Love, pp. 225-46. Lon-
       don: Methuen, 1972. Applies the Horatian-Jonsonian idea that the
       good poet must be a good man to Dryden's concern with heroic poet-
       ry.

7:88   Freedman, Morris. "Milton and Dryden on Rhyme." *HLQ* 24(1960-61):
       337-44. The Howard-Dryden debate on rhyme is seen as the motiva-
       tion for Milton's defense of blank verse in the preface to *Para-
       dise Lost*. *See* item 7:160.

7:89   ———. "Milton and Dryden on Tragedy." *English Writers of the
       Eighteenth Century*, ed. John H. Middendorf, pp. 158-71. New York,
       London: Columbia University Press, 1971. Dryden and Milton are
       compared as critics.

7:90   Freehafer, John. "Shakespeare, the Ancients, and Hales of Eton."
       SQ 23(1972):63-68. Dryden's comments about the criticism of John
       Hales of Eton.

7:91   Freeman, Edmund. "A Proposal for an English Academy in 1660."
       MLR 19(1924):291-300.

7:92   Fried, Gisela. "Das Charakterbild Shakespeares im 17. und 18.
       Jahrhundert." *Jahrbuch der Deutschen Shakespeare-Gesellschaft
       West*, ed. Hermann Heuer, pp. 161-83. Heidelberg: Quelle and Meyer,
       1965.

7:93   Friedland, Louis S. "The Dramatic Unities in England." *JEGP* 10
       (1911):56-89, 280-99, 453-67. Sees Dryden as an opportunist and
       as inconsistent.

7:94   Frost, William. "Dryden and 'Satire'." *SEL* 11(1971):401-16. *Dis-
       course of Satire*.

*7:95 ———. "Dryden's Theory and Practice of Satire." [King]:189-
       205.

*7:96 Frye, Prosser H. "Dryden and the Critical Canons of the Eigh-
       teenth Century." *UNS* 7(1907):1-39. Reprinted in *Literary Reviews
       and Criticisms*, pp. 130-89. London: Putnam, 1908. Reprinted New
       York: Gordian, 1968.

7:97   Gallaway, Francis. *Reason, Rule, and Revolt in English Classicism.* New York: Scribner, 1940. Reprinted New York: Octagon Books,
1965. Emphasizes the importance of the Graeco-Roman influence in
the development of English classicism.

7:98   Gatto, Louis C. "An Annotated Bibliography of Critical Thought
concerning Dryden's *Essay of Dramatic Poesy.*" *RECTR* 5,i(1966):18-
29.

7:99   Geist, Edward V., Jr. "Temple, Dryden and Saint-Evremond: A
Study in Libertine Aesthetic and Moral Values." *DAI* 32(1972):
4563A(Va.).

7:100   Giovannini, G. "The Theory of Tragedy as History in Renaissance and Neo-classical Criticism." Diss. Michigan, 1940.

7:101   Golden, Samuel A. "An Early Defense of Farce." *Studies in Hon-
or of John Wilcox*, eds. A. Doyle Wallace and Woodburn O. Ross,
pp. 61-70. Detroit: Wayne State University Press, 1958. Dryden's
objections to farce.

7:102   Good, John W. "Studies in the Milton Tradition." *University
of Illinois Studies in Language and Literature* 1(1915):93-402.
Dryden's praise of Milton and the controversy of blank versus
rhymed verse.

7:103   Gosse, Edmund. "Dryden's 'Art of Painting'." *Athenaeum* 4059
(12 August 1905):208-09. *See* correspondence, Henry B. Wheatley,
ibid., 4060 (19 August 1905):242; Edmund Gosse, ibid., 4062 (2
September 1905):305.

7:104   Grace, Joan C. "Tragic Theory in the Critical Works of Thomas
Rymer, John Dennis, and John Dryden." *DAI* 30(1970):4410A-11A(Columbia).

7:105   Green, Clarence C. *The Neo-Classical Theory of Tragedy in England During the Eighteenth Century.* (Harvard Studies in English
11.) Cambridge, Mass.: Harvard University Press, 1934. Reprinted
New York: Blom, 1966. Corrects Dryden.

*7:106   Guibbory, Achsah. "Dryden's Views of History." *PQ* 52(1973):
187-204.

7:107   Guite, Harold. "An Eighteenth-Century View of Roman Satire."
The Varied Pattern: Studies in the Eighteenth Century, eds. Peter
Hughes and David Williams, pp. 113-20. (Publications of the Mc-
Master University Association for 18th-Century Studies 1.) Toron-
to: Hakkert, 1971. *Discourse of Satire.*

7:108   Gwynn, Stephen. "Dryden and the Prose Writers of the Restoration." *The Masters of English Literature*, pp. 137-55. London:
Macmillan, 1904.

7:109   Hadley, Paul E. "Principles of English Literary Translation."
Diss. U.S.C., 1955.

7:110   Halewood, William H. "'The Reach of Art' in Augustan Poetic
Theory." *Studies in Criticism and Aesthetics, 1660-1800. Essays
in Honor of Samuel Holt Monk*, eds. Howard Anderson and John S.
Shea, pp. 193-212. Minneapolis: University of Minnesota Press,
1967. Ideas of genius in Renaissance and Augustan theories of
painting and poetry. *See* item 4:197.

7:111   Ham, Roswell G. "Dryden's Dedication for *The Music of the
Prophetesse*, 1691." *PMLA* 50(1935):1065-75. *See TLS* 8 October 1931,
p. 778.

7:112   Hamelius, Paul. *Die Kritik in der englischen Litteratur des 17.
und 18. Jahrhunderts.* Bruxelles: Office de Publicité, 1897. *See*
item 7:29.

*7:113 Hamilton, K. G. "Dryden and Seventeenth-Century Prose Style."
   [Miner]:297-324. Rather than evaluating Dryden's prose style in
   terms of later developments, his work is placed in a seventeenth-
   century context.
7:114 Hansen, David A. "Addison on Ornament and Poetic Style." *Studies in Criticism and Aesthetics, 1660-1800. Essays in Honor of
   Samuel Holt Monk*, eds. Howard Anderson and John S. Shea, pp. 94-
   127. Minneapolis: University of Minnesota Press, 1967.
7:115 Hanzo, Thomas A. *Latitude and Restoration Criticism.* (*Anglistica* 12.) Copenhagen: Rosenkilde and Bagger, 1961. Dryden's emphasis on moderation and toleration in critical theory reflects the
   influence of Latitudinarian thought.
*7:116 Hathaway, Baxter. "John Dryden and the Function of Tragedy."
   PMLA 58(1943):665-73. Concerning the function of tragedy, Dryden
   was at the cross-roads between neo-Stoic thought with its emphasis upon purgation and the developing sentimental theory with its
   emphasis upon empathy. *See* Edward N. Hooker, *PQ* 23:162-63.
7:117 Havens, Raymond D. "The Early Reputation of *Paradise Lost*."
   EST 40(1909):187-99.
7:118 ———. *The Influence of Milton on English Poetry*. Cambridge,
   Mass.: Harvard Univeristy Press, 1922. Reprinted New York: Russell and Russell, 1961.
7:119 Heigl, Franz. *Die dramatischen Einheiten bei Dryden*. Munich:
   Hueber, 1912.
7:120 Herrick, Marvin T. "The Place of Rhetoric in Poetic Theory."
   QJS 34(1948):1-22.
7:121 ———. *The Poetics of Aristotle in England*. (Cornell Studies
   in English 17.) New Haven: Yale University Press; London: Oxford
   University Press, 1930.
7:122 Höltgen, Karl J. "John Drydens 'nimble spaniel': Zur Schnel-
   ligkeit der 'inventio' und 'imaginatio'." *Lebende Antike: Sympo-
   sium für Rudolf Sühnel*, eds. Horst Meller and Hans-Joachim Zim-
   mermann, pp. 233-49. Berlin: Schmidt, 1967.
7:123 Hooker, Edward N., ed. *The Critical Works of John Dennis.*
   Baltimore: Johns Hopkins Press, 1939-1943.
7:124 ———. "Dryden's Allusion to the Poet of Excessive Wit." *NQ*
   168(1935):421. *Parallel betwixt Painting and Poetry.*
7:125 ———. "Pope on Wit: The *Essay on Criticism*." *HudR* 2(1950):
   559-77. Reprinted in [17th Century]:225-46. The influence of Dryden's definition of "wit." *See* item 7:79.
7:126 Hopkins, D. W. "Dryden and Sandys's Ovid: A Note." *NQ* 21(1974):
   104. *Of Dramatic Poesy.*
7:127 Houston, Percy H. "The Inconsistency of John Dryden." *SR* 22
   (1914):469-82. Examines Dryden's lack of adherence to the rules,
   which Houston attributes to a lack of personal conviction and to
   the character of Charles II's court.
7:128 Howard, William Guild. "*Ut pictura poesis*." *PMLA* 24(1909):40-
   123.
7:129 Howell, Elmo H. "The Role of the Critic in the Restoration and
   Early Eighteenth Century." *DA* 20(1959):1363-64(Fla.).
7:130 Hughes, Leo. "Attitudes of Some Restoration Dramatists toward
   Farce." *PQ* 19(1940):268-87.
7:131 ———. *A Century of English Farce*. Princeton: Princeton University Press, 1956.

7:132   ———. "The Early Career of Farce in the Theatrical Vocabulary."
   Studies in English (University of Texas) 20(1940):82-95.
7:133   Hughes, Richard E. "'Wit': The Genealogy of a Theory." *CLAJ* 5
   (1962):142-44.
7:134   Hume, Robert D. "Dryden's Criticism." *DAI* 30(1969):2485A(Penn.).
*7:135   ———. *Dryden's Criticism*. Ithaca, London: Cornell University
   Press, 1970. *See* Frank L. Huntley, *MP* 71:89-90; Lennart A. Björk,
   RES 25:87-90; Phillip Harth, *PQ* 50:427-28; Emerson R. Marks, *JAAC*
   30:264-65; Earl Miner, *MLQ* 32:439-40; Oliver F. Sigworth, *ECS* 6:
   127-32.
*7:136   ———. "Dryden's 'Heads of an Answer to Rymer': Notes Toward
   a Hypothetical Revolution." *RES* 19(1968):373-86.
*7:137   ———. "Dryden on Creation: 'Imagination' in the Later Crit-
   icism." *RES* 21(1970):295-314. Dryden did not develop his earlier
   ideas about the imagination, but instead retreated to a more conservative position which emphasized the restraining function of
   the judgment. *See* items 7:5, 7:30.
*7:138   ———. "Theory of Comedy in the Restoration." *MP* 70(1973):
   302-18. Surveys late seventeenth-century critical attitudes with
   the conclusion that in the Restoration there was no one definitive theory of comedy. *See* item 8/1:97.
7:139   Huntley, Frank L. "Dryden, Rochester, and the Eighth Satire of
   Juvenal." *PQ* 18(1939):269-84. Reprinted in [Swedenberg]:91-111.
7:140   ———. "Dryden's Discovery of Boileau." *MP* 45(1947):112-17.
   See items 7:4, 7:43.
*7:141   ———. *On Dryden's "Essay of Dramatic Poesy."* (University of
   Michigan Contributions in Modern Philology 16.) Ann Arbor: University of Michigan Press, 1951. Sees the essay as a fiction and
   thus minimizes the importance of the traditional historical iden-
   tifications for the different characters: focuses on Dryden's reliance upon the critical theories of Horace and Quintilian. *See*
   Samuel Holt Monk, *PQ* 32:269-70; James Kinsley, *RES* 3:398-99; John
   Sherwood, *CL* 4:375-77.
7:142   ———. "On the Persons in Dryden's *Essay of Dramatic Poesy*."
   MLN 63(1948):88-95. Reprinted in [Swedenberg]:83-90. *See* items
   7:14, 7:225.
7:143   ———. "The Unity of John Dryden's Dramatic Criticism, 1664-
   1681." Diss. Chicago, 1943.
7:144   ———. *The Unity of John Dryden's Dramatic Criticism: The Preface to Troilus and Cressida (1679)*. Chicago: Univeristy of Chicago Press, 1944.
7:145   Isles, Duncan. "Pope and Criticism." *Writers and their Background: Alexander Pope*, ed. Peter Dixon, pp. 250-85. Athens, Ohio:
   Ohio University Press, 1972.
7:146   Jameson, R. D. "Notes on Dryden's Lost Prosodia." *MP* 20(1923):
   241-53.
7:147   Jenkins, Ralph E. "Some Sources of Samuel Johnson's Literary
   Criticism." *DA* 30(1969):1528A(Austin, Texas).
7:148   Jensen, H. James. "A Glossary of John Dryden's Critical Terms."
   DA 28(1967):231A(Cornell).
*7:149   ———. *A Glossary of John Dryden's Critical Terms*. Minneapolis: University of Minnesota Press, 1969. Based on the editions
   of Scott-Saintsbury (2/1:11) and of Watson (2/4:17). *See* John M.
   Aden, *PQ* 49:343-44; *YWES* 50:47, 248-49; William Frost, *JEGP* 80:
   310-12.

7:150   Johnson, Charles F. *Shakespeare and His Critics*. Boston, New
York: Houghton Mifflin, 1909.

7:151   Jones, Claude E. "Dramatic Criticism in the *Critical Review*,
1756-1785." *MLQ* 20(1959):18-26, 133-44.

7:152   Jones, Richard Foster. "Science and Criticism in the Neo-
Classical Age of English Literature." *JHI* 1(1940):381-412. Reprinted in [17th Century]:41-74 and in [Schilling]:333-67.

7:153   ———. "Science and English Prose Style in the Third Quarter
of the Seventeenth Century." *PMLA* 45(1930):977-1009. Reprinted in
[17th Century]:75-110, in [Schilling]:66-102 and in *Literary English Since Shakespeare*, ed. George Watson, pp. 194-230. London:
Oxford University Press, 1970. The influence of the Royal Society
and Tillotson on Dryden's prose style.

7:154   Kallich, Martin. "The Association of Ideas and Critical Theory:
Hobbes, Locke, and Addison." *ELH* 12(1945):290-315. Dryden's and
Hobbes's figure of the "spaniel" for the fancy.

7:155   ———. *The Association of Ideas and Critical Theory in Eigh-
teenth-Century England: A History of a Psychological Method in
English Criticism*. (Studies in English Literature 55.) The Hague,
Paris: Mouton, 1970.

7:156   Kane, Sister Mary Franzita. "John Dryden's Doctrine of *Wit* as
Propriety: A Study of the Terms and Relations Involved in the Definition of 1677." *DA* 19(1959):1741(Notre Dame).

7:157   Kaplan, Charles. "Dryden's *An Essay of Dramatic Poesy*." *Expl*
8(1950): Item 36.

7:158   Ker, W. P. "Introduction [to Dryden's Essays]." *Essays of John
Dryden*, pp. xxvi-xxi. Oxford: At the Clarendon Press, 1900. Re-
printed in *Collected Essays*, London, 1925 and as "The Style of
Dryden's Prose" in *Literary English Since Shakespeare*, ed. George
Watson, pp. 231-35. London: Oxford University Press, 1970.

7:159   Klaver, Peter Roberts. "The Meaning of the Term *Wit* in English
Literary Criticism: 1680-1712." *DA* 27(1966):478A-79A(Mich.).

7:160   Koehler, G. Stanley. "Milton on 'Numbers,' 'Quantity,' and
Rime." *SP* 55(1958):201-17. Milton's prefatory note to *Paradise
Lost* is an attack on Dryden's position about rhyme. *See* item 7:
88.

7:161   Kolb, Gwin J. "Johnson Echoes Dryden." *MLN* 74(1959):212-13.

7:162   Korshin, Paul J. "The Evolution of Neoclassical Poetics: Cleveland, Denham, and Waller as Poetic Theorists." *ECS* 2(1968):102-37.
Dryden's criticism of all three is used.

7:163   Krupp, Kathleen M. "John Dryden on the Functions of Drama." *DA*
27(1967):2502A(Fla. State). In comedy Dryden stressed pleasure,
in tragedy instruction.

7:164   Ladriere, James C. "*Sarmoni Propivs*: A Study of the Horatian
Theory of the Epistle and of Dryden's Allusion to it in the Preface of *Religio Laici*." Diss. Michigan, 1938.

7:165   Lamar, Mary. *Dramatic Criticism by English Dramatists to 1750*.
Dallas: Lamar Press, 1930.

7:166   Lawlor, John. "Radical Satire and the Realistic Novel." *Essays
and Studies* 8(1955):58-75.

7:167   Lauber, John. "*Don Juan* as Anti-Epic." *SEL* 8(1968):607-19. Dryden's criticism of the heroic poem.

*7:168   LeClercq, Richard V. "The Academic Nature of the Whole Dis-
course of *An Essay of Dramatic Poesy*." *PLL* 8(1972):27-38. Dryden

was indebted to the Academy of Cicero for its development of a sceptical method of reasoning.

*7:169 ———. "Corneille and *An Essay of Dramatic Poesy*." *CL* 22 (1970):319-27. The use made of Corneille by the participants in the dialogue.

7:170 Lee, Rensselaer W. "*Ut pictura poesis*: The Humanistic Theory of Painting." *Art Bulletin* 22(1940):197-269.

7:171 Leeman, Richard K. "Corneille and Dryden: Their Theories of Dramatic Poetry." *DA* 22(1961):1158-59(Wis.).

7:172 Legouis, Pierre. "Corneille and Dryden as Dramatic Critics." *Seventeenth Century Studies Presented to Sir Herbert Grierson*, pp. 269-91. Oxford: At the Clarendon Press, 1938.

7:173 Leo, Brother, F. S. C. "Dryden as a Prose Writer." *Catholic University Bulletin* 20(1914):211-23. Dryden's prose is readable and frequently genial, but his critical attitudes were developed without consistency.

7:174 Locke, Louis G. *Tillotson: A Study in Seventeen-Century Literature*. (*Anglistica* 4.) Copenhagen: Rosenkilde and Bagger, 1954. Reformers of prose style: Tillotson, Dryden, Sprat, Temple.

7:175 Loftis, John. "Dryden's Criticism of Spanish Drama." *The Augustan Milieu: Essays Presented to Louis A. Landa*, eds. Henry Knight Miller, Eric Rothstein, and G. S. Rousseau, pp. 18-31. Oxford: At the Clarendon Press, 1970.

7:176 Loiseau, Jean. "The Age of Dryden." *Abraham Cowley's Reputation in England*. Paris: Didier, 1931.

7:177 Lounsbury, Thomas R. *Shakespeare as a Dramatic Artist: With an Account of His Reputation at Various Periods*. New Haven: Yale University Press, 1901. Reprinted New York: Ungar, 1965.

7:178 Love, H. H. R. "The Authorship of the Postscript of *Notes and Observations On The Empress Of Morocco*." *NQ* 13(1966):27-28.

*7:179 Love, Harold. "Dryden, Durfey, and the Standard of Comedy." *SEL* 13(1973):422-36. As a result of exchanges with Thomas Durfey, Dryden altered his theory of comedy.

7:180 Lovejoy, Arthur O. "'Nature' as Aesthetic Norm." *MLN* 42(1927): 444-50.

7:181 Lowens, Irving. "St. Evremond, Dryden, and the Theory of Opera." *Criticism* 1(1959):226-48.

7:182 Macdonald, Hugh. "Banter in English Controversial Prose after the Restoration." *Essays and Studies* 32(1946):21-39. Dryden gave prose a greater flexibility.

7:183 Mace, Dean T. "The Doctrine of Sound and Sense in Augustan Poetic Theory." *RES* 2(1951):129-39. Under the pressure of the New Science, poets had to reestablish the claims of poetry to seriousness.

*7:184 ———. "Dryden's Dialogue on Drama." *JWCI* 25(1962):87-112. Dryden brings two opposing views of art into conflict in the *Essay of Dramatick Poesy*: that which argues for a literal representation of nature and that which would present nature "wrought up to an higher pitch." *See* item 7:135.

7:185 ———. "*Ut pictura poesis*: Dryden, Poussin and the Parallel of Poetry and Painting in the Seventeenth Century." *Encounters: Essays on Literature and the Visual Arts*, ed. John Dixon Hunt, pp. 58-81. London: Studio Vista; New York: Norton, 1971.

7:186 Magnus, Laurie. *English Literature in its Foreign Relations 1300 to 1800*. London: Kegan Paul, Trench, Trubner; New York: E. P. Dutton, 1927.

7:187   Marks, Emerson R. "John Dryden." *The Poetics of Reason: English Neoclassical Criticism*, pp. 60-77. New York: Random House, 1968. An introductory essay.

7:188   ———. "Pragmatic Poetics: Dryden to Valéry." *BuR* 10(1962):213-23.

7:189   ———. *Relativist and Absolutist: The Early Neoclassical Debate in England*. New Brunswick, N.J.: Rutgers University Press, 1955. See Curt A. Zimansky, *PQ* 35:263-64.

7:190   Marsh, Robert H. "Major Conceptions of Criticism and Taste in England from Dryden to Hume." Diss. Johns Hopkins, 1956.

7:191   Martin, Mildred. "Influences on Dryden's Prose Style." Diss. Illinois, 1940.

7:192   Martin-Clarke, M. F. "Studies in Dryden's Criticism, with Particular Reference to His Critical Terminology and to Certain Aspects of His Dramatic Theory and Practice." *ASLIB* 16(1965-66):13 (Oxford).

7:193   Matteo, Gino John. "Shakespeare's *Othello*: The Study and the Stage, 1604-1904." *DA* 30(1969):689A-690A(Toronto). Dryden's criticism of Shakespeare.

7:194   Maurer, A. E. Wallace. "Dryden's Bad Memory and A Narrow Escape." *NQ* 5(1958):212-13. See ibid., 14(1967):345-46 ("Dryden's Memory Vindicated: Proceed with Bibliographical Caution") for a retraction. *Defense of the Paper Written by the Duchess of York*.

7:195   Maurocordato, Alexandre. "La Critique Classique Anglaise et la Fonction de la Tragédie (1660-1720)." *EA* 14(1961):10-24.

7:196   ———. *La critique classique en Angleterre de la Restauration à la mort de Joseph Addison*. Paris: Didier, 1964.

7:197   ———. "Positions de las critique dramatique chez Dryden." *Société des Anglicistes de l'Enseignement Supérieur: Acts du Congrès de Caen, 1966-67*, pp. 103-12. Paris: Didier, 1969.

7:198   Mazzeo, Joseph A. "Seventeenth-Century English Prose Style: The Quest for a Natural Style." *Mosaic* 6,iii(1973):107-44.

7:199   McAleer, John J. "John Dryden—Father of Shakespearean Criticism." *Shakespeare Newsletter* 19(1969):3.

7:200   McArthur, Herbert. "Romeo's Loquacious Friend." *SQ* 10(1959):35-44. Dryden's criticism of *Romeo and Juliet* and that of later critics such as Taine.

7:201   McNamara, Peter L. "Clothing Thought: Dryden on Language." *TSE* 20(1972):57-70. "To dress and set off design was the fundamental role of language." See item 7:135.

7:202   Merrill, Elizabeth. *The Dialogue in English Literature*. (Yale Studies in English 42.) New York: Yale University Press, 1911. Reprinted Hamden, Conn.: Archon Books, 1969. See item 7:237.

7:203   Miller, G. M. *The Historical Point of View in English Literary Criticism from 1570-1770*. (Anglistische Forschungen 35.) Heidelberg: C. Winter, 1913. Reprinted (Research Source Works Series 197.) New York: Burt Franklin, 1968. Following Bohn (7:30), Dryden is said to be ruled by events in the contemporary scene; when he is in favor with the Court, then he is conservative, when not, then he is nontraditional.

7:204   Miner, Earl. "Dryden as Prose Controversialist: His Rose in *A Defence of the Royal Papers*." *PQ* 43(1964):412-19.

7:205   ———. "Inclusive and Exclusive Decorums in Seventeenth-Century Prose." *Lang&S* 5(1972):192-203.

7:206 ———. "Patterns of Stoicism in Thought and Prose Styles, 1530-1700." *PMLA* 85(1970):1023-34. Conjectures on a revision of Croll's thesis about the connection of prose styles and philosophic concerns. *See* correspondence, John Freehafer, ibid., 86(1971): 1028-29; Franklin B. Williams, Jr., ibid., 1029-30; Ted-Larry Pebworth, ibid., 87(1972):101-02; William P. Williams, *MLR* 69(1974): 1-11.

7:207 ———. "Renaissance Contexts of Dryden's Criticism." *MQR* 12 (1973):97-115. Dryden's criticism is compared with that of his Renaissance predecessors.

7:208 ———. "Wit: Definition and Dialectic." *The Metaphysical Mode From Donne to Cowley*, pp. 118-58. Princeton: Princeton University Press, 1969. Reprinted in [Keast]:45-76.

*7:209 Monk, Samuel Holt. "Dryden and the Beginnings of Shakespeare Criticism in the Augustan Age." *The Persistence of Shakespeare Idolatry: Essays in Honor of Robert W. Babcock*, ed. Herbert M. Schueller, pp. 47-75. Detroit: Wayne State University Press, 1964. Dryden helped preserve English neoclassic criticism and literature from arid pedantry. *See* item 7:269.

7:210 ———. "Dryden's 'Eminent French Critic' in a Parallel of Poetry and Painting." *NQ* 2(1955):433. André Dacier.

7:211 Monroe, B. S. "An English Academy." *MP* 8(1910):107-22.

7:212 Deleted.

7:213 Moore, John L. "Tudor-Stuart Views of the Growth, Status, and Destiny of the English Language." *Studien zur englischen Philogie* 2(1910):1-173. Reprinted College Park: McGrath, 1970.

7:214 Morgan, P. "Fop Art: Dryden on Comedy." *ES* 53(1972):334-39. The difficulty in finding clearly defined theories about comedy in Dryden's criticism is due to the occasional and defensive nature of that criticism.

7:215 Munro, John, ed. *The Shakespeare Allusion-Book: A Collection of Allusions to Shakespeare from 1591 to 1700*. (The Shakespeare Library.) 2 vols. New York: Duffield; London: Chatto and Windus, 1909. Reprinted, with a Preface by Sir Edmund Chambers, London: Oxford University Press, 1932.

7:216 Murphee, A. A. "Wit and Dryden." *All These to Teach: Essays in Honor of C. A. Robertson*, eds. Robert A. Bryan, Alton C. Morris, A. A. Murphee and Aubrey L. Williams, pp. 159-70. Gainesville: University of Florida Press, 1965.

7:217 Nänny, Max. *John Drydens rhetorische Poetik: Versuch eines Aufbaus aus seinem kritischen Schaffen*. (Schweizer anglistische Arbeiten 49.) Bern: Winterthur, 1959. Dryden's poetic theory and practice are seen in the context of the European rhetorical tradition.

7:218 Nathanson, Leonard. "The Context of Dryden's Criticism of Donne's and Cowley's Love Poetry." *NQ* 4(1957):56-59, 197-98.

7:219 Nethercot, Arthur H. "Abraham Cowley's *Discourse Concerning Style*." *RES* 2(1926):385-404.

7:220 ———. "The Reputation of Abraham Cowley (1660-1800)." *PMLA* 38 (1923):588-641.

7:221 ———. "The Reputation of the 'Metaphysical Poets' during the Seventeenth Century." *JEGP* 23(1924):173-98.

7:222 ———. "The Term 'Metaphysical Poets' before Johnson." *MLN* 37 (1922):11-17. *See* item 7:266.

7:223 Niemeyer, Carl. "The Earl of Roscommon's Academy." *MLN* 49
        (1934):432–37. Discounts the idea that Dryden originated or
        played an important part in the formulation of the project.
7:224 Nitchie, Elizabeth. "Longinus and the Theory of Poetic Imita-
        tion in Seventeenth and Eighteenth Century England." *SP* 32(1935):
        580–97.
7:225 Noyes, George R. "'Crites' in Dryden's *Essay of Dramatic Po-
        esy*." *MLN* 38(1923):333–37. Identifies Crites as Roscommon. *See*
        items 7:14, 7:142.
7:226 ———. "Dryden as Critic." *Nation* 71(1900):231–33.
7:227 ———. "Dryden as Critic, with Special Reference to the French
        Influence." Diss. Harvard, 1898.
7:228 Padgett, Lawrence E. "Dryden's Edition of Corneille." *MLN* 71
        (1956):173–74.
7:229 Parkinson, Richard H. "The Epic in Five Acts." *SP* 43(1946):
        465–81.
7:230 Pechel, Rudolph, ed. *Christian Wernickes Epigramme*. (Palaestra
        71.) Berlin: Mayer and Müller, 1909.
*7:231 Pechter, Edward. *Dryden's Classical Theory of Literature*. Cam-
        bridge: Cambridge University Press, 1975.
7:232 ———. "John Dryden's Theory of Literature." *DAI* 30(1969):333A–
        34A(Calif., Berkeley).
7:233 Petsch, Robert. "Dryden und Rymer." *Germanisch-romanische
        Monatschrift* 7(1915–19):137–48.
7:234 Popson, Joseph John. The Collier Controversy: A Critical Basis
        for Understanding Drama of the Restoration Period." *DAI* 35(1974):
        3695A–96A(Fla.).
7:235 Pottle, Frederick A. "The Critic's Responsibility." *The Idiom
        of Poetry*, pp. 43–57. Ithaca: Cornell University Press, 1941. Rev.
        ed. 1946. 2nd ed., rev. and enl. Bloomington: Indiana University
        Press, 1963. Dryden would have been a good model of a critic, but
        he failed to fulfill his early promise.
7:236 Poyet, Albert. "A Humorous Pun in Dryden's *Epistle to the
        Whigs* (1682)." *Caliban* 7(1970):23–24.
7:237 Purpus, Eugene R. "The 'Plain, Easy, and Familar Way': The Di-
        alogue in English Literature, 1660–1725." *ELH* 17(1950):47–58. Es-
        tablishes the popularity of the dialogue in the Restoration. *See
        PQ* 30:250–51. *See also* item 7:202.
7:238 Ralli, Augustus. *A History of Shakespeare Criticism*. London:
        Oxford University Press, 1932. Reprinted New York: Humanities
        Press, 1959.
7:239 Ramsey, Paul, Jr. "Dryden's *Essay of Dramatic Poesy*." *Expl* 13
        (1955):Item 46. Comments on the opening scene.
*7:240 Randolph, Mary Claire. "The Structural Design of the Formal
        Verse Satire." *PQ* 21(1942):368–84. Reprinted in [Schilling]:262–
        80. Discusses the *Discourse of Satire*.
7:241 Read, Herbert. *English Prose Style*. New York: Holt, 1928.
7:242 Renner, Dick A. "The Poetic Theory of Sir William Davenant in
        Gondibert and Its *Preface*." *DA* 23(1963):2519(Missouri).
7:243 Ribner, Irving. "Dryden's Shakespearean Criticism and the Neo-
        Classical Paradox." *Shakespeare Association Bulletin* 21(1946):168–
        71. Dryden's influence on later Shakespearean critics.
7:244 Robertson, J. G. *Studies in the Genesis of Romantic Theory in
        the Eighteenth Century*. Cambridge: At the University Press, 1923.

7:245   Rose Marie, Sister. "Dryden's Prose." *CathW* 139(1934):432-38.
7:246   Rosenberg, Alfred. *Longinus in England bis zum Ende des 18. Jahrhunderts*. Berlin, 1917.
7:247   Ross, Carolyn C. "Dryden's Concept of Originality." *DAI* 35 (1974):2953A-54A(Ohio State).
7:248   Rothstein, Eric. "English Tragic Theory in the Late Seventeenth Century." *ELH* 29(1962):306-23. Dryden supported Rapin's critical theories in the preface to *Troilus and Cressida* and in *Heads of an Answer to Rymer*.
7:249   Routh, James. "The Classical Rule of Law in English Criticism of the Sixteenth and Seventeenth Centuries." *JEGP* 12(1913):612-30.
7:250   ───. "The Purpose of Art as Conceived in English Literary Criticism of the Sixteenth and Seventeenth Centuries." *EST* 48 (1914):124-44.
7:251   ───. *The Rise of Classical English Criticism: A History of the Canons of English Literary Taste and Rhetorical Doctrine, from the Beginning of English Criticism to the Death of Dryden*. New Orleans: Tulane University Press, 1915.
7:252   Rudd, Niall. "Dryden on Horace and Juvenal." *UTQ* 32(1963): 155-69. In the *Discourse of Satire* Dryden misrepresents the nature of Horace's and Juvenal's satires.
7:253   ───. *The Satires of Horace*. Cambridge: At the University Press, 1966. *Discourse of Satire*.
7:254   Rushton, Urban Joseph Peters. "The Development of Historical Criticism in England 1532-1700." *DA* 12(1952):308(Princeton). *See* item 7:329.
7:255   Saintsbury, George. "Augustan Prose." *A History of English Prose Rhythm*, pp. 227-92. London: Macmillan, 1912. Reprinted Bloomington: Indiana University Press, 1965.
7:256   ───. "Dryden and His Contemporaries." *A History of English Criticism*, pp. 105-46. Edinburgh, London: Blackwood, 1911. *See* items 7:16, 7:51.
7:257   Salerno, Luigi. "Seventeenth-Century English Literature on Painting." *JWCI* 14(1951):234-58. Dryden adapted the theme of *ut pictura poesis* to the drama. His translation of Du Fresnoy's *De Arte Graphica* influenced Shaftesbury's visual theory.
7:258   Salter, C. H. "Dryden and Addison." *MLR* 69(1974):29-39. Dryden had an important influence on Addison's critical attitudes.
7:259   Schulz, Max F. "Coleridge's 'Debt' to Dryden and Jonson." *NQ* 10(1963):189-91.
7:260   Seary, Peter. "Language Versus Design in Drama: A Background to the Pope-Theobald Controversy." *UTQ* 42(1972):40-63. Dryden's disagreements with Rymer as the background; Dryden, like Theobald, emphasizes verbal concerns, Rymer and Pope emphasize structural concerns.
7:261   Seegar, Oskar. *Die Auseinandersetzung zwischen Antike und Moderne in England bis zum Tode Dr. Samuel Johnsons*. Leipzig: Meyer and Müller, 1927.
7:262   Selden, Raman. "Hobbes, Dryden and the Ranging Spaniel." *NQ* 20 (1973):388-90.
7:263   Sellin, Paul R. "Heinsius and Dryden." *Daniel Heinsius and Stuart England: With a Short-Title Checklist of the Works of Daniel Heinsius*, pp. 178-99. Leiden: At the University Press; London:

Oxford University Press, for the Sir Thomas Browne Institute, 1968. The influence of Heinsius on Dryden.

7:264 ———. "The Poetic Theory of Daniel Heinsius and English Criticism of the Seventeenth Century: Jonson, Milton and Dryden." Diss. Chicago, 1963.

7:265 Shaaber, M. A. *Seventeenth Century English Prose*. New York: Harper, 1957.

7:266 Sharp, Robert L. "The Pejorative Use of *Metaphysical*." *MLN* 49 (1934):503–05. *See* item 7:222.

7:267 Sherbo, Arthur. "'Characters or Manners': Notes Toward the History of a Critical Term." *Criticism* 2(1969):343–47.

7:268 Sherwood, John C. "Dryden and the Critical Theories of Tasso." *CL* 18(1966):351–59. Parallels between Dryden's criticism and Tasso's *Discoursi*.

*7:269 ———. "Dryden and the Rules: The Preface to the *Fables*." *JEGP* 52(1953):13–26. Defends Dryden against the charge of inconsistency and praises his refusal to dogmatically apply the rules. *See* item 7:209.

*7:270 ———. "Dryden and the Rules: the Preface to *Troilus and Cressida*." *CL* 2(1950):73–83.

*7:271 ———. "Precept and Practice in Dryden's Criticism." *JEGP* 68 (1969):432–40. Dryden disregarded the rules when they conflicted with his appreciation of Shakespeare.

7:272 ———. "The Source of John Dryden's Critical Essays." Diss. Yale, 1944.

*7:273 Simon, Irène. "Dryden's Prose Style." *RLV* 31(1965):506–30. Dryden's prose is compared with that of Browne, Burton and Milton in a demonstration of his facility in duplicating conversation. *See* item 7:297.

*7:274 ———. "Dryden's Revision of the *Essay of Dramatic Poesy*." *RES* 14(1963):132–41. *See* items 2/4:21, 7:22, 7:38.

7:275 Singh, Sarup. "Dryden and the Unities." *IJES* 2(1961):78–90.

7:276 ———. "A Study of the Critical Theory of the Restoration Drama as Expressed in Dedications, Prefaces, Prologues, Epilogues and Other Dramatic Criticism of the Period." *ASLIB* 3(1952–53):9 (University College).

*7:277 ———. *The Theory of Drama in the Restoration Period*. Foreword by James R. Sutherland. Bombay: Orient Longmans; London: Longmans, Green, 1963. Collects critical opinions from a number of Restoration writers and arranges them under headings: Poetic Justice; Rhyme and the Language of Tragedy; the Opera; Tragi-Comedy; the Unities; the Comedy of Manners; Farce. *See* item 8/1: 205.

7:278 Smith, Constance I. "Hume: A Reference to Pope." *NQ* 7(1960): 115.

7:279 Smith, David Nichol, ed. *Eighteenth Century Essays on Shakespeare*. Glasgow: MacLehose, 1903. Reprinted Oxford: At the Clarendon Press, 1963. Dryden is the "father of Shakespearean criticism."

7:280 ———. *Shakespeare in the Eighteenth Century*. Oxford: At the Clarendon Press, 1928.

7:281 Smith, Herbert A. "Classicism and Criticism in English Literature from Dryden to Pope." Diss Yale, 1897.

7:282 Smith, John Harrington, "Dryden's Critical Temper." *Washington University Studies (Humanistic Series)* 12(1925):201–20. Defends

Dryden against the charge of inconsistency, but argues that his criticism was only part of a topical defense of his own writing and is thus of only minimal importance.

*7:283 Smith, R. Jack. "Shadwell's Impact on John Dryden." *RES* 20 (1944):29-44. Shadwell was foremost among Dryden's adversaries and important in the formation of his critical and dramatic ideas.

7:284 ———. "Dryden and Shadwell: A Study in Literary Controversy." *CU-AT* (1942):54-56.

7:285 Söderlind, Johannes. *Verb Syntax in John Dryden's Prose.* (Essays and Studies on English Language and Literature 10, 19.) 2 pts. Uppsala: Lundequistska Bokhandeln; Copenhagen: Ejnar Munksgaard; Cambridge, Mass.: Harvard University Press, 1951, 1958.

*7:286 Sorelius, Gunnar. *"The Giant Race Before the Food": Pre-Restoration Drama on the Stage and in the Criticism of the Restoration.* (Studia Anglistica Upsaliensia 4.) Uppsala: Almqvist and Wiksells, 1966. A good introductory survey of developments on the stage and in Restoration critical theory.

7:287 ———. "The Unities Again: Dr. Johnson and Delusion." *NQ* 9 (1962):466-67.

7:288 Spencer, Terence. "A Byron Plagiarism from Dryden." *NQ* 196 (1951):164. From the dedicatory epistle to *The Rival Ladies*.

7:289 Spingarn, Joel E. "Dryden's *Parallel of Poetry and Painting*." *MLR* 3(1908):75. Identifies André Dacier as the "eminent French critic."

7:290 ———. "Introduction." *Critical Essays of the Seventeenth Century.* 1:ix-cvi. Oxford: At the Clarendon Press, 1908. Reprinted Bloomington: Indiana University Press, 1957.

7:291 Spurgeon, Caroline F. *Five Hundred Years of Chaucer Criticism and Allusion: 1357-1900.* (Chaucer Society 2nd ser. 48-50, 52-56.) London: Chaucer Society, 1908-1917. Reprinted, 3 vols., Cambridge: Cambridge University Press, 1925; New York: Russell and Russell, 1960.

7:292 "Stage Speech." *TLS* 19 December 1929, pp. 1065-66. The Howard-Dryden controversy over the correct nature of speech in the drama. *See* item 2/1:1.

7:293 Steiner, Thomas R. "Precursors to Dryden: English and French Theories of Translation in the Seventeenth Century." *CLS* 7(1970): 50-81.

7:294 Strachan, L. R. M. "Dryden's 'Character of Polybius'." *NQ* (11th ser.) 9(1914):103-05. Corrects misprints in the Scott-Saintsbury ed. (2/1:11) of Dryden's works.

7:295 Strang, Barbara M. H. "Dryden's Innovations in Critical Vocabulary." *DUJ* 51(1959):114-23. Examines *OED* entries of critical terms and suggests Dryden's role in extending the range of literary criticism by creating a new, specialized terminology.

7:296 Sutherland, James. *The English Critic.* London: H. K. Lewis for University College London, 1953. *See TLS* 12 December 1952, p. 819.

7:297 ———. *On English Prose.* (The Alexander Lectureship.) Toronto: University of Toronto Press, 1957. Stresses the conversational quality of Dryden's prose and the fact that the prose was addressed to the aristocracy. *See* item 7:273.

7:298 ———. "Restoration Prose." *Restoration and Augustan Prose: Papers delivered by James R. Sutherland and Ian Watt at the Third Clark Library Seminar, 14 July 1956,* pp. 1-18. Los Angeles: Clark

Memorial Library, University of California, [1956]. Reprinted in
[Clark Library]:109-25.

7:299 Swain, Victor C. "On the Meaning of 'Wit' in Seventeenth-Century England." *DA* 22(1962):3189-90(Columbia).

7:300 Swedenberg, H. T., Jr. "Fable, Action, Unity, and Supernatural
Machinery in English Epic Theory, 1650-1800." *EST* 73(1938):39-48.

7:301 ———. "Rules and English Critics of the Epic, 1650-1800." *SP*
35(1938):566-87. Reprinted in [Schilling]:368-91 and in [Boys]:
281-303.

*7:302 ———. *The Theory of the Epic in England 1650-1800.* (University of California Publications in English 15.) Berkeley, Los Angeles: University of California Press, 1944. Establishes a context
for Dryden's criticism of the epic.

7:303 Thale, Mary. "Dryden's Critical Vocabulary: The Imitation of
Nature." *PLL* 2(1966):315-26. *See* item 7:135.

*7:304 ———. "Dryden's Dramatic Criticism: Polestar of the Ancients."
CL 18(1966):36-54. Dryden's use of classical critics in the development of his own theories.

*7:305 ———. "The Framework of *An Essay of Dramatic Poesy.*" *PLL* 8
(1972):362-69. Written two years after the dialogue section, the
framework of the *Essay* was used by Dryden to patriotically support King Charles.

7:306 ———. "John Dryden's Use of the Classics in his Literary Criticism." *DA* 22(1961):574(Northwestern).

7:307 Thomas, P. G. *Aspects of Literary Theory and Practice, 1550-
1870.* London: Heath, Cranton, 1931. Reprinted Port Washington,
N.Y.; London, Kennikat, 1971.

7:308 Thomas, Raymond L. "Neo-Classical, Romantic, and Twentieth-
Century Interpretations of Milton's Satan, 1695-1967." *DAI* 30
(1969):1185A-86A(Penn. State). Dryden's view that Satan is the
hero.

*7:309 Thorpe, Clarence DeWitt. "The Psychological Approach in Dry-
den." *The Aesthetic Theory of Thomas Hobbes*, pp. 189-220. (University of Michigan Publications Language and Literature 18.) Ann Arbor: University of Michigan Press, 1940. Reprinted New York: Russell and Russell, 1964. *See* item 4:100.

7:310 Thüme, Hans. *Beiträge zur Geschichte des Geniebegriffs in
England.* (Studien zur englischen Philologie 70.) Halle, 1927.

7:311 Tilley, A. A. "The Essay and the Beginning of Modern English
Prose." [Cambridge History]:421-46.

7:312 Tillyard, E. M. W. "A Note on Dryden's Criticism." [17th Cen-
tury]:330-38. Reprinted in *Essays Literary and Educational*, pp.
80-88. London: Chatto and Windus, 1962. A general, appreciative
essay.

7:313 Treadway, Thomas J. "The Critical Opinions of John Dryden." *DA*
2,ii(1940):49-50(St. Louis Univ.).

7:314 Trickett, Rachel. "The Augustan Pantheon: Mythology and Personification in Eighteenth-century Poetry." *Essay and Studies* 6(1953):
71-86.

7:315 Trimpi, Wesley. "The Meaning of Horace's *Ut Pictura Poesis.*"
JWCI 36(1973):1-34. An examination of what Horace meant by the
phrase, as distinct from how it was interpreted by later commenta-
tors.

*7:316 Trowbridge, Hoyt. "Dryden's *Essay on the Dramatic Poetry of
the Last Age.*" *PQ* 22(1943):240-50. Dryden's discussions of the
Elizabethan dramatists.

*7:317 ———. "The Place of Rules in Dryden's Criticism." *MP* 44(1946): 84-96. Reprinted in [Swedenberg]:112-34.

7:318 Tuveson, Ernest Lee. *The Imagination as a Means of Grace: Locke and the Aesthetics of Romanticism*. Berkeley, Los Angeles: University of California Press, 1960. Addison and Dryden on the use of the supernatural ("the fairy way of writing") in poetry.

7:319 Tyson, Gerald P. "Dryden's Dramatic Essay." *Ariel* 4,i(1973):72-86.

7:320 Underhill, John H. "Celebration in Eighteenth-Century English Criticism of Didactic Poetry." *DAI* 32(1972):6459A(Mich.).

7:321 Ustick, W. Lee, and Hoyt H. Hudson. "'Wit,' 'Mixt Wit,' and the Bee in Amber." *Huntington Library Bulletin* 8(1935):103-30.

7:322 Vetter, Dale B. "William Walsh's 'In Defence of Painting'." *MLN* 66(1951):518-23.

7:323 Vines, Sherard. *The Course of English Classicism From the Tudor to the Victorian Age*. (Hogarth Lectures on Literature Series 12.) London: The Hogarth Press, 1930.

7:324 Walcott, Fred G. "John Dryden's Answer to Thomas Rymer's *The Tragedies of the Last Age*." *PQ* 15(1936):194-214. *See* items 2/4:14, 7:135, 7:328.

7:325 Walder, Ernest. *Shakespearean Criticism, Textual and Literary, From Dryden to the End of the Eighteenth Century* [1895]. New York: AMS Press, 1972.

7:326 Walter, Ulrich. *Boileau Wirkung auf seine englischen Zeitgenossen*. Strassburg, 1911.

7:327 Wasserman, Earl R. *Elizabethan Poetry in the Eighteenth Century*. (University of Illinois Studies 32, ii-iii.) Urbana: University of Illinois Press, 1947.

7:328 Watson, George. "Dryden's First Answer to Rymer." *RES* 14(1963): 17-23. Establishes a reliable text for *Heads of an Answer to Rymer*. *See* items 2/4:14, 7:135.

7:329 ———. "John Dryden." *The Literary Critics: A Study of English Descriptive Criticism*, pp. 32-57. Baltimore: Penguin, 1962. Rev. ed. New York: Barnes and Noble, 1964. 2nd ed. Totowa, N.J.: Rowman and Littlefield, 1973. *Of Dramatick Poesie* was the first attempt at extended descriptive criticism. *See TLS* 8 June 1962, p. 430. *See also* items 7:135, 7:254.

7:330 Weimann, Robert. "Shakespeares Publikum and Plattformbühne im Spiegel Klassizistischer Kritik (bei Rymer, Dryden u. a.)." *SJ* 102(1966):60-96.

7:331 Weisinger, Herbert. "The Seventeenth-Century Reputation of the Elizabethans." *MLQ* 6(1945):13-20.

7:332 Welleck, René. "The Seventeenth Century." *The Rise of English Literary History*, pp. 14-44. Chapel Hill: University of North Carolina Press, 1941.

7:333 Wikeland, Philip R. "The Fettered Muse: Aspects of the Theory of Verse Translation in Augustan England, 1640-1750." Diss. U.C.L.A., 1948.

7:334 Wilcox, Angeline T. "The 'True Critic' in England in the Eighteenth Century." *SDD-NU* 19(1951):55-59.

7:335 Willey, Basil. "The Heroic Poem in a Scientific Age." *The Seventeenth Century Background: Studies in the Thought of the Age in Relation to Poetry and Religion*, pp. 205-63. London: Chatto and Windus, 1934. Reprinted New York: Columbia University Press, 1958. Dryden on *Paradise Lost* and heroic poetry.

7:336 Williams, Edwin E. "Dr. James Drake and Restoration Theory of Comedy." *RES* 15(1939):180-91.

7:337 Williamson, George. "Dryden as Critic." *University of California Chronicle* 32(1930):71-76.

*7:338 ———. "The Occasion of *An Essay of Dramatic Poesy*." *MP* 44 (1946):1-9. Reprinted in *Seventeenth Century Contexts*, pp. 272-88. London: Faber, 1960. Rev. ed. Chicago: University of Chicago, 1969. Also in [Swedenberg]:65-82. The *Essay* was, in part, a response to Samuel Sorbière's derogatory *Voyage to England*.

7:339 ———. *The Senecan Amble: A Study in Prose From Bacon to Collier*. Chicago: University of Chicago Press, 1951. Dryden wrote in the Senecan mode.

7:340 Wilson, F. P. *Seventeenth Century Prose*. (Ewing Lectures.) Berkeley, Los Angeles: University of California Press, 1960.

7:341 Wimsatt, William K., Jr., and Cleanth Brooks. *Literary Criticism: A Short History*. New York: Knopf, 1957. Dryden followed "probabilism," not scepticism.

7:342 Wollstein, Rose Heylbut. *English Opinion of French Poetry 1660-1750*. New York: Columbia University Press, 1923.

7:343 Wood, Paul Spencer. "The Opposition to Neo-Classicism in England Between 1600-1700." *PMLA* 43(1928):182-97. Reprinted in [Schilling]:402-18.

7:344 Woolf, Henry Bosley. "An Eighteenth-Century Allusion to Chaucer." *NQ* 192(1947):60.

7:345 Young, Mother Spalding. *The Element of Interpretation in Literary Criticism from the Greeks to the End of the Seventeenth Century*. [St. Louis?: St. Louis University?, 1932?.]

7:346 Zimansky, Curt A., ed. *The Critical Works of Thomas Rymer*. New Haven: Yale University Press, 1956. Includes a discussion of Dryden's relationship with Rymer and a comparison of their critical ideas.

See also items 1:29, 2/1:1, 2/1:5-7, 2/2:22, 2/2:32, 2/3:7, 2/4:1-3, 2/4:6-13, 2/4:15, 2/4:17-23, 2/5:1-2, 3:8, 3:33, 3:77, 3:172, 4:6, 4:61, 4:105, 4:135, 4:187, 4:199, 4:202-03, 4:214, 4:218, 4:232, 4:246, 4:263, 4:265, 4:283, 4:311, 4:323, 4:330, 4:344, 4:362, 4:403-04, 4:410, 4:419, 4:427, 4:429, 4:442, 4:446, 4:448, 4:450, 4:455, 4:464, 4:478, 4:483, 4:487, 4:489, 4:495, 4:506-07, 4:513, 4:533, 4:543, 4:551, 4:559-60, 5/4:9, 5/4:20, 5/5:4, 5/6:22, 5/6:25, 5/6:28, 5/12:5, 5/12:17, 5/12:21, 5/14:3, 6/1:2, 6/1:8, 6/1:18, 6/1:22, 6/2:6-7, 6/2:28, 6/2:69-70, 6/6:5, 8/1:58, 8/1:74, 8/1:125, 8/1:155-57, 8/1:206-07, 8/1:213, 8/2:1-2, 8/2:8, 8/2:25-28, 8/2:43, 8/2:51, 8/2:64, 8/2:71, 8/2:81, 8/2:100, 8/9:19, 8/9:28, 8/9:38, 8/9:66, 8/9:74, 8/10:26, 8/11:19, 9:17.

8. Dramatic Works

8/1. GENERAL STUDIES AND COMEDY

8/1:1 Alleman, Gilbert Spencer. *Matrimonial Law and the Materials of Restoration Comedy*. Philadelphia: University of Pennsylvania, 1942.

8/1:2 Allen, John. "Dryden and Congreve." *Masters of the British Drama*, pp. 103-18. London: Dobson, 1957.

*8/1:3   Allen, Ned Bliss. *The Sources of John Dryden's Comedies*. (University of Michigan Publications Language and Literature 16.) Ann Arbor: University of Michigan Press, 1935. *See* item 8/6:4.

8/1:4   Anthony, Sister Rose. *The Jeremy Collier Stage Controversy 1698-1726*. Milwaukee: Marquette University Press, 1937.

8/1:5   Archer, Stanley L. "The Epistle Dedicatory in Restoration Drama." *RECTR* 10,i(1971):8-13. *See* item 4:26.

8/1:6   Archer, William. *The Old Drama and the New: An Essay in Revaluation*. Boston: Small, Maynard, 1923.

8/1:7   Avery, Emmett L. *Congreve's Plays on the Eighteenth-Century Stage*. New York: The Modern Language Association, 1951.

8/1:8   ———, ed. *The London Stage 1660-1800*. Part 2: *1700-1729*. With a Critical Introd. 2 vols. Carbondale: Southern Illinois University Press, 1960. Lists performances of Dryden's plays.

8/1:9   ———. "A Tentative Calendar of Daily Theatrical Performances, 1660-1700." *RS* 13(1945):225-83.

8/1:10   ———, and A. H. Scouten. "A Tentative Calendar of Daily Theatrical Performances in London, 1700-1701 to 1704-1705." *PMLA* 63 (1948):114-80.

8/1:11   Baker, Sheridan. "Buckingham's Permanent *Rehearsal*." *MQR* 12 (1973):160-71.

8/1:12   Baldini, Gabriele. *Teatro inglese della restaurazione e del Settecento: Dryden, Otway, Congreve, Farquhar, Gay, Lillo, Goldsmith, Sheridan*. Firenze: Sansoni, [1955].

8/1:13   Ballein, Johannes. *Jeremy Collier's Angriff auf die englische Bühne*. Marburg: Karl Gleiser, 1910.

8/1:14   Banks, Wallace L. "Conventions of the French Romances in the Drama of John Dryden." Diss. Stanford, 1967.

8/1:15   Bateson, F. W. "Comedy of Manners." *EIC* 1(1951):89-93. Considers some terms popular with writers of dramatic criticism.

8/1:16   ———. "L. C. Knights and Restoration Comedy." *EIC* 7(1957): 56-67. Reprinted in [Loftis]:22-31. *See* items 8/1:88, 8/1:106, 8/1:241.

8/1:17   Berkeley, David S. "The Art of 'Whining' Love." *SP* 52(1955): 478-96.

8/1:18   ———. "The Penitent Rake in Restoration Comedy." *MP* 49 (1952):223-233.

8/1:19   ———. *The Précieuse, or Distressed Heroine of Restoration Comedy*. (Arts and Sciences Studies, Humanities Series 6.) Stillwater, Okla: Oklahoma State University, 1959.

*8/1:20   ———. "*Préciosité* and the Restoration Comedy of Manners." *HLQ* 18(1954):109-28. *Préciosité* is the context which gave meaning to the patterns of courtship in manners comedy. Restoration dramatists created mock-*précieuse* heroines, as did Dryden in Melantha.

8/1:21   ———. "Some Notes on Probability in Restoration Drama." *NQ* 2(1955):237-39, 342-44, 432.

8/1:22   Besing, Max. *Molière's Einfluss auf das englische Lustspiel bis 1700*. Leipzig: Noske, 1913.

8/1:23   Bevan, Allan R. "Dryden as a Dramatic Artist." Diss. Toronto, 1953.

8/1:24   Biggins, D. "Source Notes for Dryden, Wycherley and Otway." *NQ* 3(1956):298-301.

8/1:25   Blackwell, Herbert. "Some Formulary Characteristics of John Dryden's Comedies." *DA* 28(1968):2642A(Va.).

8/1:26   Blair, Thomas Marshall Howe. "John Banks: His Life and Works." *The Unhappy Favourite or The Earl of Essex" by John Banks*, pp. 3-29. New York: Columbia University Press, 1939. Dryden's influence on Banks.

8/1:27   Boas, Frederick S. *An Introduction to Eighteenth-Century Drama: 1700-1780*. Oxford: At the Clarendon Press, 1953.

8/1:28   Bode, Robert F. "A Study of the Development of the Theme of Love and Duty in English Comedy from Charles I to George I." *DAI* 31(1971):5351A(S.C.).

8/1:29   Bogorad, Samuel N. "The English History Play in Restoration Drama." Diss. Northwestern, 1947.

8/1:30   Bowers, Fredson. "Variants in Early Editions of Dryden's Plays." *HLB* 3(1949):278-88.

8/1:31   Bradbrook, M. C. "Prisoners and Politics: The Social Image from Shakespeare to Dryden." *English Dramatic Form: A History of Its Development*, pp. 100-19. London: Chatto and Windus, 1965.

8/1:32   Brewer, Gwendolyn W. "The Course of Mirth: Satiric Imagery in Selected Comedies of John Dryden." *DA* 29(1969):2206A-07A(Claremont). The imagery is used "organically."

8/1:33   Bronowski, Jacob. "John Dryden." *The Poet's Defence*, pp. 89-125. Cambridge: At the University Press, 1939. Reprinted Cleveland, New York: World, 1966. The importance of Jonson in Dryden's critical ideas.

8/1:34   Brooks, Cleanth. "A Note on the Death of Elizabethan Tragedy." *Modern Poetry and the Tradition*, pp. 203-18. Chapel Hill: University of North Carolina Press, 1939. Reprinted New York: Oxford University Press, 1965.

8/1:35   Canfield, Dorothea Frances. *Corneille and Racine in England: A Study of English Translations of the Two Corneilles and Racine, with Especial Reference to Their Presentation on the English Stage*. New York: Columbia University Press, 1904. Reprinted New York: AMS Press, 1966.

8/1:36   Carter, Albert Howard. "The Conception of Character in Dryden and Corneille" [Summary of a paper read to the SCMLA, November 1950]. *SCN* 9(1951):58.

8/1:37   Cazamian, Louis. *The Development of English Humor*. Parts I and II. Durham, N.C.: Duke University Press, 1952. Reprinted New York: AMS Press, 1965.

8/1:38   Cecil, C. D. "Libertine and *Précieux* Elements in Restoration Comedy." *EIC* 9(1959):239-53. *See* item 8/1:241.

8/1:39   Charlanne, Louis. *L'Influence française en Angleterre au XVIIe siècle*. Paris: Soc. Française d'Imprimerie et de Librairie, 1906. Reprinted Genève: Slatkine Reprints, 1971.

8/1:40   Child, Harold. "Revivals of English Dramatic Works, 1901-1918, 1926." *RES* 3(1927):169-85.

8/1:41   ——. "Revivals of English Dramatic Works, 1919-1925." *RES* 2(1926):177-88.

8/1:42   Clancy, James H. "Preliminaries to Restoration Comedy." *SM* 15 (1948):85-98.

8/1:43   Clark, William S. "Corpses, Concealments, and Curtains on the Restoration Stage." *RES* 13(1937):438-48.

8/1:44   Clinton-Baddeley, V. C. *The Burlesque Tradition in the English Theatre after 1660*. London: Methuen, 1952.

8/1:45   Corder, Jimmie Wayne. "The Restoration Way of the World: A Study of Restoration Comedy." *DA* 19(1959):1739(Okla.).

8/1:46   Courthope, W. J. "Dryden and the Romantic Drama after the Restoration." *A History of English Poetry*. 4:397-453. London, New
York: Macmillan, 1903. Reprinted New York: Russell and Russell,
1962.

8/1:47   Cunningham, John E. *Restoration Drama*. (Literature in Perspective Series.) London: Evans, 1966.

8/1:48   Darby, J. E. "An Examination of Some Restoration Versions of
Shakespeare's Plays." *ASLIB* 20(1969-70):16(Manchester).

8/1:49   Davenport, Warren W. "Private and Social Order in the Drama
of John Dryden." Diss. Florida, 1970.

8/1:50   Davis, Floyd H., Jr. "The Dramaturgical Functions of Song,
Dance, and Music in the Comedies of John Dryden." *DAI* 33(1972):
2888A(Ball State).

8/1:51   Deitz, Jonathan Eric. "The Designs of Plot: The New Direction
in Plot Resolution of Late Restoration Satiric Comedy." *DAI* 33
(1973):3640A(Penn.).

8/1:52   Dobrée, Bonamy. "Dryden and Shadwell." *Restoration Comedy
1660-1720*, pp. 102-20. Oxford: At the Clarendon Press, 1924. Reprinted London, New York: Oxford University Press, 1964. Praises
Dryden for presenting marriage in positive terms. *See* item 8/1:1.

8/1:53   Downes, John. *Roscius Anglicanus (1708)*, introd. John Loftis;
index of performers and plays by David S. Rodes. (ARS 134.) Los
Angeles: Clark Memorial Library, University of California, 1969.
A facsimile ed.

8/1:54   Eliot, T. S. "A Dialogue on Dramatic Poetry (1928)." *Selected
Essays*, pp. 31-45. Rev. ed. New York: Harcourt, Brace, 1950. A
loose imitation of Dryden's *Of Dramatick Poesy*

8/1:55   Ellehauge, Martin. *English Restoration Drama: Its Relation to
Past English and Past and Contemporary French Drama*. Copenhagen,
London: Levin and Munksgaard, 1933. Reprinted Folcroft, Pa.: Fol-
croft Press, 1970.

8/1:56   Elwin, Malcolm. *The Playgoer's Handbook to Restoration Drama*.
London: Macmillan, [1928].

8/1:57   Erlich, Richard D., and James Harner. "Pope's Annotations in
His Copy of Dryden's *Comedies, Tragedies, and Operas*: An Exercise
in Cryptography." *RECTR* 10,i(1971):14-24. Pope's interest in Dryden's versification.

8/1:58   Fetrow, Fred M. "Dryden's Dramatic Heroes: Conception and
Mode." *DAI* 31(1971):4117A(Neb.).

8/1:59   Forrester, Kent A. "Supernaturalism in Restoration Drama."
DAI 32(1971):1469A(Utah). *The Tempest* and *The Duke of Guise*.

8/1:60   Foster, George H. "British History on the London Stage, 1660-
1760." Diss. North Carolina, 1941.

8/1:61   Fujimura, Thomas H. *The Restoration Comedy of Wit*. Princeton:
Princeton University Press, 1952. Reprinted New York: Barnes and
Noble, 1968. *See* P. F. Baum, *SAQ* 52:312-13; Jacques Voisine, *RLC*
27:359-61; John Harold Wilson, *MLN* 68:511-12.

8/1:62   Gagen, Jean Elizabeth. *The New Woman: Her Emergence in English Drama, 1600-1730*. New York: Twayne Publishers, 1954.

8/1:63   Gaw, Allison. "Tuke's *Adventures of Five Hours* in Relation to
the 'Spanish Plot' and to John Dryden." *Studies in English Drama*
(Publications of the University of Pennsylvania Series in Philology and Literature 14), ed. Allison Gaw, pp. 1-61. New York: University of Pennsylvania, 1917.

8/1:64   Ghosh, J. C., ed. *The Works of Thomas Otway: Plays, Poems, and Love-Letters.* 2 vols. With an Introd. Oxford: At the Clarendon Press, 1932. *See* items 3:79, 3:181.

8/1:65   Gibb, Carson. "Figurative Structure in Restoration Comedy." *DA* 23(1963):4683-84(Penn.). The use of multiple plots in Restoration comedy; *The Spanish Fryar.*

8/1:66   Gibbons, Brian. "Congreve's *The Old Batchelour* and Jonsonian Comedy." *William Congreve*, ed. Brian Morris, pp. 1-20. (Mermaid Critical Commentaries.) Totowa, N.J.: Rowman and Littlefield, 1972. Dryden's influence on Congreve's ideas about comedy.

8/1:67   Gillet, J. C. "Molière en Angleterre, 1660-1670." *Mémoires de l'académie royale de Belgique, deuxième série, classe des lettres* 9(1913).

8/1:68   Gohn, Ernest S. "Seventeenth-Century Theories of the Passions and the Plays of John Dryden." Diss. Johns Hopkins, 1948.

8/1:69   Grace, John William. "Theory and Practice in the Comedy of John Dryden." *DA* 18(1958):2141(Mich.).

8/1:70   Granville-Barker, Harley. "Wycherley and Dryden." *On Dramatic Method*, pp. 113-55. London: Sidgwick and Jackson, 1931.

8/1:71   Graves, Thornton S. "The Stage Sword and Dagger." *SAQ* 20 (1921):201-12.

8/1:72   Gray, Philip H., Jr. "Lenten Casts and the Nursery: Evidence for the Dating of Certain Restoration Plays." *PMLA* 53(1938):781-94.

8/1:73   Griffin, Ernest G. "The Dramatic Chorus in English Literary Theory and Practice." *DA* 20(1959):3726-27(Columbia).

*8/1:74 Hagstrum, Jean H. "Dryden's Grotesque: An Aspect of the Baroque in His Art and Criticism." [Miner]:90-119. Heroic idealization and the grotesque are both part of neoclassic aesthetics.

8/1:75   Haraszti, Zoltán. "The Plays of John Dryden (with a facsimile)." *More Books* 8(1933):1-13, 45-59. A derogatory survey of the plays; discusses the Boston Public Library's holdings of first editions.

8/1:76   Harbage, Alfred. *Cavalier Drama: An Historical and Critical Supplement to the Study of the Elizabethan and Restoration Stage.* New York: Modern Language Association of America; London: Oxford University Press, 1936. Reprinted New York: Russell and Russell, 1964.

8/1:77   ———. "Elizabethan-Restoration Palimpsest." *Shakespeare Without Words and Other Essays*, pp. 170-218. Cambridge, Mass.: Harvard University Press, 1972. Adaptations and borrowings from Elizabethan plays by Restoration dramatists.

*8/1:78 Harris, Bernard. "The Dialect of those Fanatic Times." [Rest. Theatre]:11-40. Relates trends in the drama to historical events.

8/1:79   Hartnoll, Phyllis, ed. *The Oxford Companion to the Theatre.* 3rd ed. Oxford: Oxford University Press, 1967.

8/1:80   Harvey-Jellie, Wallace R. "John Dryden, Dramaturge." *L'Entente Littéraire: Etude de Littérature Comparée*, pp. 19-25. Montréal: [n.pub.], 1940.

8/1:81   ———. *Les Sources du théâtre anglais à l'époque de la Restauration.* Paris: Librairie générale de droit et de jurisprudence, 1906.

8/1:82   ———. *Le Théâtre Classique en Angleterre, dans l'âge de John Dryden.* Montréal: Librairie Beauchemin Limitée, [1932].

8/1:83   Hayman, John Griffiths. "Raillery during the Restoration Period and Early Eighteenth Century." *DA* 25(1965):4146-47(Northwestern).

8/1:84   Heldt, W. "A Chronological and Critical Review of the Appreciation and Condemnation of the Comic Dramatist of the Restoration
and Orange Periods." *Neophilologus* 8(1922):39-59, 109-28, 197-204.

8/1:85   Hill, Herbert W. "La Calprenède's Romances and the Restoration Drama." *University of Nevada Studies* 2,iii(1910):1-56; 3,ii
(1911):57-158.

8/1:86   Hogan, Charles Beecher, ed. *The London Stage 1660-1800.* Part
5: *1776-1800.* With a Critical Introd. 3 vols. Carbondale: Southern Illinois University Press, 1968. Lists performances of Dryden's plays.

8/1:87   Hogan, Floriana T. "Notes on Thirty-One English Plays and
Their Spanish Sources." *RECTR* 6,i(1967):56-59. *An Evening's Love;*
The Assignation.

8/1:88   Holland, Norman N. *The First Modern Comedies: The Signifi-*
cance of Etherege, Wycherley and Congreve. Cambridge, Mass.: Harvard University Press, 1959.

8/1:89   ———. "Restoration Comedy Again, II." *EIC* 7(1957):319-22.
See item 8/1:106.

8/1:90   Hook, Lucyle. "Portraits of Elizabeth Barry and Anne Brace-
girdle." *TN* 15(1960):129-37.

8/1:91   Hooker, Edward N., ed. *Epistle to a Friend concerning Poetry*
(1700) by Samuel Wesley. (Ser. 2 Essays on Poetry 2.) Ann Arbor:
Augustan Reprint Society, 1947. Praise of Dryden's plays.

8/1:92   Hotson, Leslie. *The Commonwealth and Restoration Stage.* Cambridge, Mass.: Harvard University Press, 1928. Reprinted New York:
Russell and Russell, 1962.

8/1:93   Howling, Robert T. "Moral Aspects of Restoration Comedy." *PSU-*
ADD 17(1954):479-83.

8/1:94   Hoy, Cyrus. "The Effect of the Restoration on Drama." *TSL* 6
(1961):85-91.

8/1:95   ———. *The Hyacinth Room: An Investigation into the Nature of*
Comedy, Tragedy, and Tragi-comedy. New York: Knopf, 1964.

8/1:96   Hughes, Leo. *The Drama's Patrons: A Study of the Eighteenth-*
Century London Audience. Austin: University of Texas Press, 1971.
See Lincoln B. Faller, *MP* 71:90.

*8/1:97   Hume, Robert D. "Diversity and Development in Restoration
Comedy 1660-1679." *ECS* 5(1972):365-97. Revaluates commonly held
assumptions about Restoration comedy. *See* items 7:138, 8/1:162.

8/1:98   Hunt, Hugh. "Restoration Acting." [Rest. Theatre]:179-92.

8/1:99   Irie, Keitaro. "The Auxiliary *Do* in John Dryden's Plays."
Anglica 5(1962):1-19.

8/1:100   Jackson, Allan S. "Restoration Scenery 1656-1680." *RECTR* 3,
ii(1964):25-38.

8/1:101   Jones, Virgil L. "Methods of Satire in the Political Drama
of the Restoration." *JEGP* 21(1922):662-69.

8/1:102   Ker, W. P. "On Comedy." *On Modern Literature: Lectures and*
Addresses, ed. Terence Spencer and James R. Sutherland, pp. 196-
209. Oxford: At the Clarendon Press, 1955.

8/1:103   Kerby, W. Moseley. "Molière and the Restoration Comedy in England." Diss. Rennes, 1907.

8/1:104   Kirsch, Arthur C. "An Essay on *Dramatick Poetry* (1681)." *HLQ*

28(1964):89-91. Contemporary praise of Dryden as the foremost dramatist of the day.

8/1:105   Knight, G. Wilson. *The Golden Labyrinth: A Study of British Drama*. New York: Norton, 1962.

8/1:106   Knights, L. C. "Restoration Comedy: The Reality and the Myth." *Scrutiny* 6(1937):122-43. Reprinted in *Explorations: Essays in Criticism*, pp. 131-49. London: Chatto and Windus, 1946. Also reprinted in [Loftis]:3-21. Restoration drama is not immoral; it is just dull. *See* items 8/1:16, 8/1:88-89, 8/1:115, 8/1:241.

8/1:107   Knipp, George W. "The State History of John Dryden's Plays." Diss. Johns Hopkins, 1938.

8/1:108   Kornbluth, Martin L. "Friendship in Fashion: The Dramatic Treatment of Friendship in the Restoration and Eighteenth Century." *DA* 17(1957):361-62(Penn. State).

8/1:109   Krutch, Joseph Wood. *Comedy and Conscience after the Restoration*. New York: Columbia University Press, 1924, 1949. Reprinted New York: Russell and Russell, 1967.

8/1:110   Langbaine, Gerard. *An Account of the English Dramatick Poets* [*1691*], pref. Arthur Freeman. (The English Stage: Attack and Defense, 1577-1730.) New York: Garland, 1973. A Facsimile ed.

8/1:111   ———. *Momus Triumphans: or, The Plagiaries of the English Stage (1688* [*1687*]), introd. David S. Rodes. (ARS 150.) Los Angeles: Clark Memorial Library, University of California, 1971. A facsimile ed.

8/1:112   Langhans, Edward A. "Restoration Manuscript Notes in Seventeenth Century Plays." *RECTR* 5,i(1966):30-39; ii(1966):2-17.

8/1:113   Larson, Richard L. "Studies in Dryden's Dramatic Technique: The Use of Scenes Depicting Persuasion and Accusation." Diss. Harvard, 1963.

8/1:114   Leech, Clifford. "Art and the Concept of Will." *DUJ* 48(1955): 1-7.

8/1:115   ———. "Restoration Comedy: The Earlier Phase." *EIC* 1(1951): 165-84. *See* item 8/1:106.

8/1:116   ———. *Shakespeare's Tragedies and Other Studies in Seventeenth Century Drama*. London: Chatto and Windus, 1950.

8/1:117   Lehmann, Elmar. "'If the People Have the Power': Zum Motiv des Volksaufstandes im Drama John Drydens." *Poetica* 4(1971):437-61. *See PQ* 51:675.

8/1:118   Lengefeld, W. Freiherr Kleinschmit von. "Ist Shakespeares Stil barock? Bemerkungen zur Sprache Shakespeares und Drydens." *Shakespeare-Studien: Festschrift für Heinrich Mutschmann*, eds. Walther Fischer and Karl Wentersdorf, pp. 88-106. Marburg: Elwert, 1951. Compares the language of Shakespeare and Dryden.

8/1:119   Lewis, Mineko S. "Humor Characterization in Restoration Comedy." *DAI* 34(1973):1247A(Tenn.).

8/1:120   Lewis, Peter. "*The Rehearsal*: A Study of its Satirical Methods." *DUJ* 62(1970):96-113.

8/1:121   Lill, James Vernon. "Dryden's Adaptations from Milton, Shakespeare, and Chaucer." *DA* 14(1954):1214(Minn.).

8/1:122   Loftis, John. *Comedy and Society from Congreve to Fielding*. (Stanford Studies in Language and Literature 19.) Stanford: Stanford University Press, 1959.

*8/1:123   ———. "Dryden's Comedies." [Miner]:27-57. A general survey.

8/1:124   ———. "The Hispanic Element in Dryden." *EUQ* 20(1964):90-100. *See* item 8/2:17.

*8/1:125 ———. "The Limits of Historical Veracity in Neoclassical Drama." [Culture and Society]:27-50. A revaluation of premises about the drama and a reconsideration of investigatory methodology.

*8/1:126 ———. *The Politics of Drama in Augustan England*. Oxford: Oxford University Press, 1963. Chap. 7 ("The Political Strain in Augustan Drama") reprinted in [Loftis]:229-35. Analyzes the relationship between political allegiances and aesthetic attitudes.

*8/1:127 ———. *The Spanish Plays of Neoclassical England*, New Haven, London: Yale University Press, 1973. *See* item 8/2:17.

8/1:128 Lott, James David. "Restoration Comedy: The Critical View, 1913-1965." *DA* 28(1968):2688A(Wis.).

*8/1:129 Love, Harold. "The Myth of the Restoration Audience." *Komos* 1(1967):49-56. Attacks the notion that the Restoration audience was dissolute and frivolous; rejects the Beljame, Macaulay and L. C. Knights view. *See* correspondence, A. S. Bear, ibid., 2(1969): 23-31; Harold Love, ibid., 2(1969):72-80.

8/1:130 Lynch, Kathleen M. *The Social Mode of Restoration Comedy*. (University of Michigan Publications Language and Literature 3.) New York: Macmillan, 1926. Reprinted New York: Octagon Books, 1965.

8/1:131 ———. "D'Urfe's L'Astrée and the 'Proviso' Scenes in Dryden's Comedy." *PQ* 4(1925):302-08.

8/1:132 Macaulay, T. C. "French and English Drama in the Seventeenth Century." *Essays and Studies* 20(1935):45-74. Each had developed in different directions; the English moved towards realism and a coarseness of humor and language.

8/1:133 Macqueen-Pope, Walter J. *Ladies First: The Story of Woman's Conquest of the British Stage*. London: Allen, 1952. Actresses on the Restoration stage.

8/1:134 ———. *Theatre Royal, Drury Lane*. London: Allen, [1945].

8/1:135 Mandach, André. *Molière et la comédie de moeurs en Angleterre (1660-68): Essai de littérature comparée*. Neuchatel: Baconnière, 1946.

8/1:136 Manifold, John Streeter. *The Music in English Drama from Shakespeare to Purcell*. London: Rockliff, 1956.

8/1:137 Martin, Lee J. "From Forestage to Proscenium: A Study of Restoration Staging Techniques." *ThS* 4(1963):3-28.

8/1:138 Martin, Leslie H., Jr. "Conventions of the French Romances in the Drama of John Dryden." *DA* 28(1967):1053A-54A(Stanford).

8/1:139 Maurer, David W. "The Spanish Intrigue Play on the Restoration Stage." *OSU-ADD* 18(1935):275-82.

8/1:140 McAfee, Helen. *Pepys on the Restoration Stage*. New Haven: Yale University Press; London: Oxford University Press, 1916.

8/1:141 McCall, John Joseph. "Gerard Langbaine's *An Account of the English Dramatick Poets* (1691): Edited with an Introduction and Notes." *DA* 18(1958):1788-89(Fla. State).

8/1:142 McDonald, Charles O. "Restoration Comedy as Drama of Satire: An Investigation into Seventeenth Century Aesthetics." *SP* 61 (1964):522-44.

8/1:143 McNamara, Peter Lance. "John Dryden's Contribution to the English Comic Tradition of Witty Love-Play." *DA* 25(1965):5910-11 (Tulane).

8/1:144 Meadley, T. D. "Attack on the Theatre: (*circa* 1580-1680)." *The London Quarterly and Holburn Review* 178(1953):36-41.

8/1:145 Merchant, W. Moelwyn. *Shakespeare and the Artist*. London, New York, Toronto: Oxford University Press, 1959. Theater production in the seventeenth century.

8/1:146 Merrin, James T., Jr. "The Theory of Comedy in the Restoration." Diss. Chicago, 1948.

8/1:147 Meyer, Paul. *Metrische Untersuchung über den Blankvers John Drydens*. Halle: Wischan and Wettengel, 1897.

8/1:148 Mignon, Elisabeth. *Crabbed Age and Youth: The Old Men and Women in the Restoration Comedy of Manners*. Durham, N.C.: Duke University Press, 1947.

8/1:149 Miles, Dudley H. *The Influence of Molière on Restoration Comedy*. New York: Columbia University Press, 1910.

8/1:150 Milhous, Judith, and Robert D. Hume. "Dating Play Premières from Publication Data." *HLB* 22(1974):374-405.

8/1:151 Milosevich, Vincent M. "Propriety as an Esthetic Principle in Dryden, Shakespeare and Wagner." *HAB* 21,i(1970):3-13.

8/1:152 Mincoff, Marco. "Fletcher's Early Tragedies." *RenD* 7(1964): 70-94. Fletcher's influence on Dryden's dramatic practice.

8/1:153 Mitchell, Eleanor R. "Pronouns of Address in English, 1580-1780: A Study of Form Changes as Reflected in British Drama." *DAI* 32(1972):4593A(Texas A&M).

8/1:154 Montgomery, Guy. "The Challenge of Restoration Comedy." *University of California Publications in English* 1(1929):133-51. Reprinted in [Loftis]:32-43. "Restoration Comedy has always, I think, needed protection."

8/1:155 Moore, Frank Harper. "Dryden's Theory and Practice of Comedy." Diss. North Carolina, 1953.

*8/1:156 ———. *The Nobler Pleasure: Dryden's Comedy in Theory and Practice*. Chapel Hill: University of North Carolina Press, 1963. *See* Arthur W. Hoffman, *MLQ* 25:498-99; Bruce King, *SR* 72:543-44; John Harold Wilson, *SAQ* 62:610-11; Donald G. Adam, *SCN* 21:63; *TLS* 23 January 1964, p. 69.

8/1:157 Moore, Robert Etheridge. *Henry Purcell and the Restoration Theatre*. London, Melbourne, Toronto: Heinemann; Cambridge, Mass.: Harvard University Press, 1961.

8/1:158 Muir, Kenneth. "John Dryden." *The Comedy of Manners*, pp. 41-54. London: Hutchinson University Library, 1970.

8/1:159 Mulert, Alfred. *Pierre Corneille auf der englischen Bühne und in her englischen Übersetzungsliteratur des siebzehnten Jahrhunderts*. Leipzig: Böhme, 1900.

8/1:160 Murrie, Eleanore Boswell. *The Restoration Court Stage (1660-1702)*. Cambridge, Mass.: Harvard University Press, 1932.

8/1:161 Nettleton, George H. *English Drama of the Restoration and Eighteenth Century (1642-1780)*. New York: Macmillan, 1921.

8/1:162 Nevo, Ruth. "Toward a Theory of Comedy." *JAAC* 21(1963):327-32. *See* items 7:138, 8/1:97.

8/1:163 Nicoll, Allardyce. *The Development of the Theatre: A Study of Theatrical Art from the Beginnings to the Present Day*. 5th ed. rev. New York: Harcourt, Brace and World, 1966.

8/1:164 ———. *A History of Early Eighteenth Century Drama: 1700-1750*. Cambridge: At the University Press, 1925. Reprinted as *A History of English Drama: 1660-1900*. Vol. 2. 3rd ed. Cambridge: At the University Press, 1955. Dryden's reputation in the early eighteenth century is examined, as are the dramatic forms used by Dryden and his contemporaries.

8/1:165 ———. *A History of Late Eighteenth Century Drama, 1750-1800.* Cambridge: At the University Press, 1927.

8/1:166 ———. *A History of Restoration Drama, 1660-1700.* Cambridge: At the University Press, 1923.

*8/1:167 ———. "Political Plays of the Restoration." *MLR* 16(1921): 224-42.

8/1:168 ———. "Scenery between Shakespeare and Dryden." *TLS* 15 August 1936, p. 658.

8/1:169 ———. *The Theatre and Dramatic Theory.* New York: Barnes and Noble, 1962.

8/1:170 Nolde, Johanna. *Die Bühnenanweisungen in John Drydens Dramen.* Münster: [n.p.], [1929?].

8/1:171 Norrell, Lemuel N. "The Cuckold in Restoration Comedy." *DA* 23(1963):3889(Fla. State Univ.).

8/1:172 Noyes, George R. "The Development of English Comedy of Manners." *Representative English Comedies*, eds. Charles Mills Gayley and Alwin Thaler. 4: *Dryden and His Contemporaries: Cowley to Farquhar*, pp. 538-48. New York, London: Macmillan, 1936. Reprinted New York: AMS Press, 1969.

8/1:173 Noyes, Robert Gale. "Ben Jonson on the English Stage, 1660-1776." Diss. Harvard, 1936.

8/1:174 ———. "Contemporary Musical Settings of the Songs in Restoration Drama." *ELH* 1(1934):325-44. Exclusive of Dryden.

8/1:175 ———. "Songs from Restoration Drama in Contemporary and Eighteenth-Century Poetical Miscellanies." *ELH* 3(1936):291-316. Exclusive of Dryden.

8/1:176 ———, and Roy Lamson, Jr. "Broadside-Ballad Versions of the Songs in Restoration Drama." *Harvard Studies and Notes in Philology and Literature* 19(1937):199-218.

8/1:177 Ohara, David M. "The Restoration Comic Perspective: A Study of the Comedy of Manners." *DA* 17(1957):3021-22(Penn.). The satiric scope of Restoration Comedy.

8/1:178 Paine, Clarence S. "The Comedy of Manners (1660-1700): A Reference Guide to the Comedy of the Restoration." *BB* 17(1941):25-27, 51-53, 70-72, 97-99, 116-17, 145-48.

8/1:179 Paul, Henry N. "Players' Quartos and Duodecimos of *Hamlet*." *MLN* 49(1934):369-75. Did Dryden prepare an acting version of *Hamlet*?

8/1:180 Payne, Rhoda. "Stage Direction During the Restoration." *TA* 20(1963):41-62.

8/1:181 Pfitzner, Käthe. *Die Ausländertypen im englischen Drama der Restorationszeit.* Breslau: Lebenslauf, 1931.

8/1:182 Porte, Michael S. "The Servant in Restoration Comedy." *DA* 21(1961):3093(Northwestern).

8/1:183 Praz, Mario. "Baroque in England." *MP* 61(1964):169-79.

8/1:184 ———. "Restoration Drama." *ES* 15(1933):1-14. Italian versions published in *La Cultura* 12(1933):62-82 and in *Studi e svaghi inglesi*. (Biblioteca italiana 4.) Firenze, 1937. Rev. art. *See* item 2/15:12.

8/1:185 Prior, Moody E. "Poetic Drama: An Analysis and a Suggestion." *English Institute Essays, 1949*, ed. Alan S. Downer, pp. 3-32. New York: Columbia University Press, 1950. Dryden's dramatic practice and critical position in the controversy over rhymed drama.

8/1:186 Rogal, Samuel J. "Thomas Lowndes' 1777 Listing of Dramatic Works." *RECTR* 13,i(1974):53-58. Dryden's plays are noted in works published by Lowndes.

8/1:187   Rosenfeld, Sybil. "Dramatic Advertisements in the Burney
Newspapers 1660-1700." *PMLA* 51(1936):123-52.

8/1:188   ——. "The Restoration Stage in Newspapers and Journal,
1660-1700." *MLR* 30(1935):445-59.

8/1:189   ——. "Some Notes on the Players in Oxford, 1661-1713." *RES*
19(1943): 366-75.

8/1:190   ——. *Strolling Players and Drama in the Provinces, 1660-
1765.* Cambridge: At the University Press, 1939.

8/1:191   Rubin, Barbara L. "The Dream of Self-Fulfillment in Restoration Comedy: A Study in Two Parts: The Heroic Pattern in Aristo-
phanic and Roman Comedy and Its Design and Decadence in English
Comedy from 1660 to 1700." *DAI* 30(1970):5419A-20A(Rochester).

8/1:192   Rundle, James U. "The Influence of the Spanish *Comedia* on
Restoration Comedy: A First Essay." Diss. Cincinnati, 1947.

8/1:193   Saxon, A. H. *Enter Foot and Horse: A History of Hippodrama
in England and France.* New Haven: Yale University Press, 1968.

8/1:194   Schelling, Felix B. "The Restoration Drama. I." [Cambridge
History]:131-65.

8/1:195   Schmidt, Karlerust. *Vorstudien zu einen Geschichte des
Komischen Epos.* Halle: Niemeyer, 1953.

8/1:196   Schneider, Ben Ross, Jr. *The Ethos of Restoration Comedy.*
Urbana, Chicago, London: University of Illinois Press, 1971. A
thematic analysis.

8/1:197   Schwarz, Janet L. "A Labyrinth of Design: A Study of Dryden's Dramatic Comedy." *DAI* 30(1970):4426A(Calif., Berkeley).

8/1:198   Scott, Florence R. "The Life and Works of Sir Robert Howard."
Diss. N.Y.U., 1943.

8/1:199   Scouten, Arthur H., ed. *The London Stage 1660-1800.* Part 3:
1729-1749. With a Critical Introd. 2 vols. Carbondale: Southern
Illinois University Press, 1961. Lists performances of Dryden's
plays.

8/1:200   ——. "Notes toward a History of Restoration Comedy." *PQ*
45(1966):62-70.

8/1:201   Seely, Frederick F. "Thomas Betterton, Dramatist." Diss.
Iowa, 1942.

8/1:202   Sellers, William H. "Literary Controversies Among Restoration Dramatists, 1660-1685." *DA* 20(1959):3306-08(Ohio State).

8/1:203   Shafer, Yvonne Bonsall. "The Proviso Scene in Restoration
Comedy." *RECTR* 9,i(1970):1-10.

8/1:204   Sharma, R. C. "Conventions of Speech in the Restoration Comedy of Manners." *IJES* 2(1961):23-38.

*8/1:205   ——. *Themes and Conventions in the Comedy of Manners.*
Foreword by Allardyce Nicoll. New York: Asia; Bombay: The Popular
Press, 1965. A very useful survey of common dramatic practices.
See item 7:277.

8/1:206   Sherwood, Margaret P. "Dryden's Dramatic Theory and Practice."
Diss. Yale, 1898.

8/1:207   ——. *Dryden's Dramatic Theory and Practice.* Boston, New
York, London: Lamson, Wolfee, 1898. Reprinted New York: Haskell
House, 1965. A disparaging view of Dryden and the age.

8/1:208   Silvette, Herbert. *The Doctor on the Stage: Medicine and
Medical Men in Seventeenth-Century England*, ed. Francelia Butler.
Knoxville: University of Tennessee Press, 1967.

8/1:209   Smith, Dane Farnsworth. *The Critics in the Audience of the
London Theatres from Buckingham to Sheridan: A Study of Neoclassi-

cism in the Playhouse 1671-1779. (University of New Mexico Publications in Language and Literature 12.) Albuquerque: University of New Mexico Press, 1953.

8/1:210 ———. *Plays About the Theatre in England from "The Rehearsal" in 1671 to the Licensing Act in 1737 or, the Self-Conscious Stage and its Burlesque and Satirical Reflections in the Age of Criticism.* London, New York: Oxford University Press, 1936.

8/1:211 Smith, John Harrington. *The Gay Couple in Restoration Comedy.* Cambridge, Mass.: Harvard University Press; London: Oxford University Press, 1948.

8/1:212 ———. "Shadwell, the Ladies, and the Change in Comedy." *MP* 46(1948):22-33. Shadwell's "exemplary drama" replaced the gay comedy of Dryden.

8/1:213 Snuggs, Henry L. "The Comic Humors: A New Interpretation." *PMLA* 62(1947):114-22.

8/1:214 Southern, Richard. *Changeable Scenery: Its Origin and Development in the British Theatre.* London: Faber, 1952.

8/1:215 Spencer, Hazelton. "Improving Shakespeare: Some Bibliographical Notes on the Restoration Adaptations." *PMLA* 41(1926):727-46.

8/1:216 Sprague, Arthur Colby. *Beaumont and Fletcher on the Restoration Stage.* Cambridge, Mass.: Harvard University Press, 1926. Reprinted New York: Blom, 1965.

*8/1:217 Staves, Sarah S. "Studies in the Comedy of John Dryden." *DA* 28(1968):2658A(Va.). Dryden changed dramatic forms not only in an attempt to appeal to his audience's changing taste, but also to find one form which suited his own point of view.

8/1:218 Stoll, Elmer Edgar. "The *Beau Monde* at the Restoration." *MLN* 49(1934):425-32. *See* item 8/2:47.

8/1:219 Stone, George Winchester, Jr., ed. *The London Stage 1660-1800.* Part 4: *1747-1776.* With a Critical Introd. 3 vols. Carbondale: Southern Illinois University Press, 1962. Lists performances of Dryden's plays.

8/1:220 Stroup, Thomas B. "Supernatural Beings in Restoration Drama." *Anglia* 61(1937):186-92. *See* item 8/2:25.

8/1:221 Summers, Montague. "Introduction." *The Complete Works of William Congreve*, pp. 3-64. Soho: The Nonesuch Press, 1923. Reprinted New York: Russell and Russell, 1964.

8/1:222 ———. *The Playhouse of Pepys.* New York: Macmillan, 1935. Reprinted New York: Humanities Press, 1964. A useful reference source for the study of Restoration drama.

8/1:223 ———, ed. *"The Rehearsal" by George Villiers, Duke of Buckingham (1625-1687).* Stratford-Upon-Avon: Shakespeare Head Press, 1914. Text of the 3rd ed., 1675.

8/1:224 ———. *The Restoration Theatre.* London: Routledge and Kegan Paul, 1934. Reprinted New York: Humanities Press, 1964.

8/1:225 ———, ed. *Roscius Anglicanus by John Downes.* With an Introd. London: Fortune Press, 1928. Reprinted New York: Blom, 1968.

8/1:226 Symons, Julian. "Restoration Comedy (Reconsideration II)." *KR* 7(1945):185-97. *See* Eric R. Bentley, ibid., 477-80.

8/1:227 Taylor, Aline Mackenzie. *Next to Shakespeare: Otway's "Venice Preserv'd" and "The Orphan" and Their History on the London Stage.* Durham, N.C.: Duke University Press, 1950.

8/1:228 Taylor, Charlene M. "Aspects of Social Criticism in Restoration Comedy." *DA* 26(1965):7301-02(Illinois). Censure of the figure of the social climber.

*8/1:229   Teeter, Louis. "The Dramatic Use of Hobbes's Political
Ideas." *ELH* 3(1936):140-69. Reprinted in [Swedenberg]:341-73.
See items 4:43, 8/2:32, 8/2:97. Dryden used, but did not accept
Hobbesian ideas.

8/1:230   Thaler, Alwin. *Shakespeare to Sheridan: A Book about the
Theatre of Yesterday and To-day*. Cambridge, Mass.: Harvard University Press, 1922.

8/1:231   Thorndike, Ashley H. "The Restoration, 1660-1680." *English
Comedy*, pp. 269-303. New York: Macmillan, 1929. Reprinted New
York: Cooper Square Publishers, 1965.

8/1:232   Tiermann, Hermann. "Die Bedeutung der 'Spanish Plots' für
das englischen Drama der Fruhrestauration." *RJ* 12(1961):278-311.

8/1:233   Tobin, Terence. "Plays Presented in Scotland 1660-1700."
RECTR 12,i(May 1973):51-53.

8/1:234   Traugott, John. "The Rake's Progress from Court to Comedy: A
Study in Comic Form." *SEL* 6(1966):381-407.

8/1:235   Underwood, Dale. *Etherege and the Seventeenth-Century Comedy
of Manners*. (Yale Studies in English 135.) New Haven: Yale University Press; London: Oxford University Press, 1957. *See* V. de Sola
Pinto, *PQ* 37:325-27; David M. Vieth, *JEGP* 58:127-31.

8/1:236   Van der Weele, Steven J. "The Critical Reputation of Restoration Comedy in Modern Times." *DA* 16(1956):344-45(Wis.).

8/1:237   Van Lennep, William, ed. *The London Stage 1660-1800*. Part I:
1660-1700. With a Critical Introd. by Emmett L. Avery and Arthur
H. Scouten. Carbondale: Southern Illinois University Press, 1965.
Lists performances of Dryden's plays.

8/1:238   ———. "Plays on the English Stage 1669-1672." *TN* 16(1961):
12-20.

8/1:239   Vernon, P. F. "Marriage of Convenience and the Moral Code of
Restoration Comedy." *EIC* 12(1962):370-87.

8/1:240   Visser, Colin W. "Dryden's Plays: A Critical Assessment." *DA*
29(1968):1520A-21A(Rochester).

8/1:241   Wain, John. "Restoration Comedy and its Modern Critics." *EIC*
6(1956):367-85. Reprinted in *Preliminary Essays*, pp. 1-35. London:
Macmillan; New York: St. Martin's, 1957. *See* item 8/1:38.

8/1:242   Wann, Louis. "The Oriental in Restoration Drama." *University
of Wisconsin Studies in Language and Literature* 2(1918):163-86.

8/1:243   Ward, A. W. "Dryden's Place in English Comedy." *Representative English Comedies*, eds. Charles Mills Gayley and Alwin Thaler.
4: *Dryden and His Contemporaries: Cowley to Farquhar*, pp. 105-31.
New York, London: Macmillan, 1936. Reprinted New York: AMS Press,
1969.

8/1:244   ———. "John Dryden." *A History of English Dramatic Literature to the Death of Queen Anne*. 3:346-92. 2nd rev. ed. London,
New York: Macmillan, 1899. A survey of the plays and an accusation of immorality.

8/1:245   Ward, Charles E. "Dryden's Drama 1662-1677: A Study in the
Native Tradition." Diss. Duke, 1934.

8/1:246   Watkin-Jones, A. "Langbaine's *Account of the English Dramatick Poets* (1691)." *Essays and Studies* 11(1936):75-85. Discusses
the extent to which critics have relied on Langbaine for their information about Restoration drama.

8/1:247   Weiss, Samuel Abba. "Hobbism and Restoration Comedy." *DA* 14
(1954):114(Columbia).

8/1:248   Wells, Staring B., ed. *A Comparison Between the Two Stages: A Late Restoration Book of the Theatre* [1702]. (Princeton Studies in English 26.) Princeton: Princeton University Press, 1942. Dryden's work is praised by Chagrin, the critic.

8/1:249   Wheatley, Katherine E. *Racine and English Classicism*. Austin: University of Texas Press, 1956. Dryden's use of Racine and his divergence from French theories about tragedy. *See* Bonamy Dobrée, *PQ* 36:338-39.

8/1:250   Whibley, Charles. "The Restoration Drama. II." [Cambridge History]:166-201.

8/1:251   White, Arthur F. "The Office of Revels and Dramatic Censorship during the Restoration Period." *Western Reserve University Bulletin: Studies in English Literature* 34(1931):5-45.

8/1:252   Whiting, George W. "The Condition of the London Theaters, 1679-83: A Reflection of the Political Situation." *MP* 25(1927): 195-206.

*8/1:253   ———. "Political Satire in London Stage Plays, 1680-83." *MP* 28(1930):29-43.

8/1:254   Wilcox, John. "John Dryden and Thomas Shadwell." *The Relation of Molière to Restoration Comedy*, pp. 105-26. New York: Columbia University Press, 1938. Reprinted New York: Blom, 1964.

8/1:255   Wilkinson, D. R. M. *The Comedy of Habit: An Essay on the Use of Courtesy Literature in a Study of Restoration Comic Drama.* (Leidse Germanistische en Anglistische Reeks van de Rijksuniversiteit te Leiden Deel 4.) Leiden: Universitaire Pers, 1964.

8/1:256   Wilson, John Harold. *All the King's Ladies: Actresses of the Restoration*. Chicago: University of Chicago Press, 1958.

8/1:257   ———. *The Influence of Beaumont and Fletcher on Restoration Drama*. Columbus, Ohio: Ohio University Press, 1928. Reprinted New York: Blom, 1968.

8/1:258   ———. *Mr. Goodman the Player*. Pittsburgh: University of Pittsburgh Press, 1964. Restoration state history seen from the perspective of Cardell Goodman.

8/1:259   ———. *Nell Gwyn: Royal Mistress*. London: Muller, 1952.

8/1:260   ———. *A Preface to Restoration Drama*. (Riverside Studies in Literature.) Boston: Houghton Mifflin, 1965.

8/1:261   ———. "Rant, Cant, and Tone on the Restoration Stage." *SP* 52(1955):592-98.

8/1:262   ———. "Six Restoration Play-Dates." *NQ* 9(1962):221-23. *The Mistaken Husband* and *Oedipus*.

8/1:263   ———. "A Theatre in York House." *TN* 16(1962):75-78. Foreign players in London in the early 1670's.

8/1:264   ———. "Theatre Notes from the Newdigate Newsletters." *TN* 15 (1961):79-84. Notes on *The Duke of Guise* (29 July and 28 November 1682) and a play "Englands deliverance from Popish Conspirators" (26 March 1696).

8/1:265   Woehl, Arthur L. "Some Plays in the Repertory of the Patent Houses." *Studies in Speech and Drama in Honor of Alexander M. Drummond*, pp. 105-22. Cornell: Cornell University Press, 1944.

8/1:266   Wright, Rose A. *The Political Play of the Restoration*. [Montesano, Washington: A. E. Veatch, 1916.]

8/1:267   Zamonski, John A. "Redemptive Love in the Plays of John Dryden: From *Wild Gallant* to *All for Love*." *DAI* 31(1971):4139A-40A (Ohio).

8/1:268   Zimbardo, Rose A. *Wycherley's Drama: A Link in the Development of English Satire.* (Yale Studies in English 156.) New Haven,
London: Yale Univeristy Press, 1965.

See also items 1:9, 1:29, 1:32, 1:39, 1:49-51, 1:56, 1:61, 1:92, 1:
104, 1:109, 2/2:22, 2/2:25, 2/2:29, 2/2:33, 2/5:1, 3:141, 3:179,
3:181, 4:19, 4:105, 4:138, 4:141, 4:218, 4:243, 4:245-46, 4:287,
4:348, 4:371, 4:448, 4:455, 4:478, 4:484-85, 4:520, 4:561, 5/13:1,
5/13:5, 5/13:11, 6/2:28, 7:23, 7:82, 7:99, 7:151, 7:234, 7:276-77,
7:286, 7:336, 9:7.

8/2. HEROIC PLAYS, TRAGEDY AND TRAGICOMEDY

8/2:1   Alssid, Michael W. "Dryden's Rhymed Heroic Tragedies: A Critical Study of the Plays and Their Place in Dryden's Poetry." *DA* 20
(1959):3281(Syracuse).

8/2:2   Anderberg, Gary T. "Idea and Passion: The Development of Dryden's Tragic Drama." *DAI* 33(1973):4327A(Stanford).

8/2:3   Ashby, Stanley R. "The Treatment of the Themes of Classic Tragedy in English Tragedy between 1660-1738." *HU-ST* 3(1927):141-43.

8/2:4   Auer, Otto. "Dryden's Heroic Play und Lee's Dramen." *Ueber
einige Dramen Nathaniel Lee's mit besonderer Berücksichtigung
seiner Beziehung zum französischen heroisch-galanten Roman*, pp.
12-25. (Berliner Beiträge zur germarischen und romanishcen Philologie 27. Germanische Abteilung 14.) Berlin: Ebering, 1904.

8/2:5   Baas, David. *Drydens heroische Tragödie: Eine ästhetische
Untersuchung.* Freiburg im Breisgau: C. A. Wagners, 1911.

8/2:6   Banks, Landrum. "Dryden's Baroque Drama." *Essays in Honor of
Esmond Linworth Marilla*, eds. Thomas Austin Kirby and William John
Olive, pp. 188-200. Baton Rouge: Louisiana State University Press,
1970.

8/2:7   ———. "The Imagery of Dryden's Rhymed Heroic Drama." *DA* 29
(1968):224-25A(Tenn.).

*8/2:8   Barbeau, Anne T. *The Intellectual Design of John Dryden's
Heroic Plays.* New Haven, London: Yale University Press, 1970. *See*
Arthur H. Scouten, *PQ* 50:422-23; K. E. Robinson, *NQ* 18:476-78;
George Falle, *ECS* 5:480-84; W. F. T. Myers, *RES* 22:346-48; Eric
Rothstein, *JEGP* 70:157-61.

8/2:9   ———. "John Dryden's Scheme of Values: A Study of His Heroic
Plays and Early Narrative Poems." *DA* 29(1968):559A(C.U.N.Y.).

8/2:10   Barber, C. L. *The Idea of Honour in the English Drama 1591-
1700.* (Gothenburg Studies in English 6.) Göteborg: Almqrist and
Wiksell, 1957. A semasiological study. *See* Barbara M. H. Strang,
MLR 54(1959):88-89; *JEGP* 57:125-26; *ES* 40:392-95.

8/2:11   Bartholomew, A. T. "The Restoration Drama. III." [Cambridge
History]:202-23.

8/2:12   Bernet, John W. "Toward the Restoration Heroic Play: The Evolution of Davenant's Serious Drama." *DAI* 30(1970):3423A-24A(Stanford).

8/2:13   Bleuler, Werner. *Das Heroische Drama John Drydens als Experiment dekorativer Formkunst.* Bern: Zürcher Dissertation, 1957.

8/2:14   Borinski, Ludwig. "Ideale der Restaurationszeit." *Festschrift
für Walther Fischer*, pp. 49-64. Heidelberg: Winter, 1959.

8/2:15   Broich, Ulrich. "Libertin und heroischer Held: das Drama der
englischen Restaurationszeit und seine Leitbilder." *Anglia* 85

(1967):34-57. Restoration comedy and the heroic play complement each other; they are the actuality and the ideal of the same ethical and sexual codes.

8/2:16 Burrows, Dorothy. "The Relation of Dryden's Serious Plays and Dramatic Criticism to Contemporary French Literature." Diss. Illinois, 1933.

8/2:17 Campbell, Dowling G. "Background and Applications of the Honor Code in Dryden's Four Spanish-Oriented Heroic Plays." *DAI* 35 (1974):1041A(Missouri, Columbia). *See* items 8/1:124, 8/1:127.

8/2:18 Chase, Lewis N. *The English Heroic Play: A Critical Description of the Rhymed Tragedy of the Restoration.* (Studies in Comparative Literature.) New York: Columbia University Press, 1903. Reprinted New York: Russell and Russell, 1965.

8/2:19 Child, C. G. "The Rise of the Heroic Play." *MLN* 19(1904):166-73.

*8/2:20 Clark, William S. "The Definition of the 'Heroic Play' in the Restoration Period." *RES* 8(1932):437-44. Defines the genre in contemporary terms. *See* item 8/2:47.

8/2:21 ——, ed. "Historical Preface" and "Critical Preface." *The Dramatic Works of Roger Boyle, Earl of Orrery.* 1:3-97. Cambridge, Mass.: Harvard University Press, 1937.

8/2:22 ——. "The Platonic Element in the Restoration Heroic Play." *PMLA* 45(1930):623-24. *See* item 8/2:47.

8/2:23 ——. "The Sources of the Restoration Heroic Play." *RES* 4 (1928):49-63. Although the French influence on Dryden was strong, he was too nationalistic to disregard native English traditions. *See* items 8/2:47, 8/2:85.

8/2:24 Cope, Jackson I. "Paradise Regained: Inner Ritual." *MiltonS* 1(1969):51-65. Milton's influence on Dryden's heroic plays.

8/2:25 Deane, Cecil V. *Dramatic Theory and the Rhymed Heroic Play.* London: Oxford University Press, 1931. Analyzes *The Indian Queen, The Rival Ladies* and *Tyrannick Love.* *See* item 8/1:220.

*8/2:26 Dobrée, Bonamy. *Restoration Tragedy 1660-1720.* Oxford: At the Clarendon Press, 1929. The heroic play was popular because the age was "hungry for heroism." Chap. on *All for Love.*

*8/2:27 Dutton, George B. "Theory and Practice in English Tragedy, 1650-1700." *EST* 49(1916):190-219. Explores the interrelationship between contemporary critical theory and dramatic practice.

8/2:28 Ebbs, John D. "The Principle of Poetic Justice Illustrated in Restoration Tragedy." *DA* 19(1959):2087-88(N.C.).

*8/2:29 Fujimura, Thomas H. "The Appeal of Dryden's Heroic Plays." *PMLA* 75(1960):37-45. *See* Arthur Sherbo, *PQ* 40:386. *See also* item 8/2:30.

*8/2:30 Gagen, Jean. "Love and Honor in Dryden's Heroic Plays." *PMLA* 77(1962):208-20. *See* items 8/2:29, 8/2:57.

8/2:31 Grübner, Willy. *Der Einfluss des Reims auf den Satzbau der englischen "Heroic Plays."* Königsberg, 1912.

*8/2:32 Hartsock, Mildred E. "Dryden's Plays: A Study in Ideas." *Seventeenth Century Studies (Second Series)*, ed. Robert Shafer, pp. 69-176. Princeton: Princeton University Press for the University of Cincinnati; London: Oxford University Press, 1937. *See* items 4:45, 8/1:229, 8/2:97.

8/2:33 Hecht, J. *Der heroische Frauentyp in Restaurationsdrama.* Leipzig, 1932.

8/2:34 Herrick, Marvin T. *Tragicomedy: Its Origin and Development in Italy, France, and England*. Urbana: University of Illinois Press, 1955.

8/2:35 Huneycutt, Melicent. "The Changing Concept of the Ideal Statesman as Reflected in English Verse Drama During the Reign of Charles II: 1660-1685." *DAI* 30(1969):685A-86A(N.C.). Montezuma, Maximin, Morat, Antony.

8/2:36 James, E. Nelson. "Drums and Trumpets." *RECTR* 9,ii(1970):46-55; 10,i(1971):54-57. The representation of battle scenes on stage.

*8/2:37 Jefferson, D. W. "The Significance of Dryden's Heroic Plays." *PLP-LS* 5(1940):125-39. Reprinted in [Loftis]:161-79 and in [Rest. Dramatists]:19-35. Develops a "comic" thesis to explain the heroic plays.

*8/2:38 King, Bruce. *Dryden's Major Plays*. London: Oliver and Boyd; New York: Barnes and Noble, 1966. *See* Pierre Legouis, *EA* 20:190-91; William Myers, *RES* 18:334-36; Eugene M. Waith, *YR* 17:123-26.

8/2:39 ———. "Dryden's Treatment of Ideas and Themes in His Dramatic Works, with Some Reference to the Intellectual Movement of His Time." *ASLIB* 10(1959-60):10(Leeds).

8/2:40 ———. "Heroic and Mock-Heroic Plays." *SR* 70(1963):514-17.

*8/2:41 Kirsch, Arthur C. "Dryden, Corneille, and the Heroic Play." *MP* 59(1962):248-64.

*8/2:42 ———. *Dryden's Heroic Drama*. Princeton: Princeton University Press, 1965. Chap. on *All for Love* reprinted in [20th Century Interpretations]:99-103. *See* Eugene M. Waith, *PQ* 45:554-55; Pierre Legouis, *EA* 20:191-92; Elizabeth Mackenzie, *RES* 18:336-37; Paul E. Parnell, *RECTR* 5,ii:59-62; *YWES* 46:219-20.

8/2:43 ———. "Dryden's Theory and Practice of the Rhymed Heroic Play." *DA* 22(1961):1979(Princeton).

8/2:44 Law, Richard A. "Admiration and Concernment in the Heroic Plays of John Dryden." *DAI* 35(1974):3688A-89A(Temple).

8/2:45 Leech, Clifford. "Restoration Tragedy: A Reconsideration." *DUJ* 42(1950):106-15. Reprinted in [Loftis]:144-60.

8/2:46 Lemly, John William. "Into Winter Quarters Gone: The Last Plays of Jonson and Dryden." *DAI* 34(1973):324A(Yale).

*8/2:47 Lynch, Kathleen M. "Conventions of Platonic Drama in the Heroic Plays of Orrery and Dryden." *PMLA* 44(1929):456-71. Argues for the English origin of the heroic play. *See* correspondence, William S. Clark, ibid., 45(1930):623-24; Kathleen M. Lynch, ibid., 625-26; R. S. Crane, *PQ* 9:178. *See also* items 8/1:218, 8/2:20, 8/2:22-23, 8/2:85.

8/2:48 Mann, Wolfgang. *Drydens heroische Tragödien als Ausdruck höfischer Barockkultur in England*. Württemberg: Gatzer and Hahn, 1932.

8/2:49 Martin, Leslie H., Jr. "The Imagery of Dryden's Rhymed Heroic Drama." Diss. Tennessee, 1967.

8/2:50 Miró, César. "México y Perú en la Tragedia Clásical Occidental." *CCLC* 100(1965):66-70.

8/2:51 Molinoff, Marlene S. "The *Via Media* of John Dryden's Tragicomedy." *DAI* 35(1974):1114A-15A(George Washington University). Dryden developed the Cavalier play under the influence of French *précieux* Platonism.

8/2:52 Moore, John Robert. "Political Allusions in Dryden's Later Plays." *PMLA* 73(1958):36-42.

8/2:53 Muller, Herbert J. *The Spirit of Tragedy*. New York: Knopf, 1956.

8/2:54 Newman, Robert Stanley. "The Tragedy of Wit: The Development of the Heroic Drama from Dryden to Addison." *DA* 25(1964):5262 (U.C.L.A.).

8/2:55 Nicoll, Allardyce. "The Origin and Types of the Heroic Tragedy." *Anglia* 44(1920):325-36. Distinguishes Orrery's species of heroic tragedy from that practiced by Dryden.

8/2:56 Noyes, Robert Gale. "Conventions of Song in Restoration Tragedy." *PMLA* 53(1938):162-88.

*8/2:57 Osborn, Scott C. "Heroical Love in Dryden's Heroic Drama." *PMLA* 73(1958):480-90. Uses Burton's *Anatomy* to establish a definition of love as a disease. *See* item 8/2:30.

8/2:58 Park, Hugh W. "Revenge in Restoration Tragedy." *DA* 20(1959): 1097-98(Utah).

8/2:59 Parsons, A. E. "The English Heroic Play." *MLR* 33(1938):1-14. Relates the heroic play to the heroic poem and the heroic prose romance.

8/2:60 Parsons, P. E. "*The Siege of Rhodes* and Restoration Tragedy: An Interpretation of Some Formal Developments in the Serious Drama of the Restoration." *ASLIB* 13(1962-63):9(Cambridge, Christ's).

*8/2:61 ———. "Restoration Melodrama and Its Actors." *Komos* 2(1970): 81-88. Almanzor, Antony and Cleopatra are used as examples of the way in which the stylized acting of the Restoration sought to convey passion, not to interpret character.

8/2:62 Pati, P. K. "Dryden's Heroic Plays: A Study of Their Theory and Practice." *IJES* 9(1968):87-95. The heroic play is not a tragedy but an epic in dramatic form.

8/2:63 Payne, F. W. "The Question of Precedence between Dryden and the Earl of Orrery with Regard to the English Heroic Play." *RES* 1(1925):173-81. Orrery developed the heroic play before Dryden.

8/2:64 Pendlebury, B[evis] J. *Dryden's Heroic Plays: A Study of the Origins* [1923]. New York: Russell and Russell, 1967.

8/2:65 Poston, Mervyn L. "The Origin of the English Heroic Play." *MLR* 16(1921):18-22. Dryden was influenced by Orrery.

*8/2:66 Prior, Moody E. "Tragedy and the Heroic Play." *The Language of Tragedy*, pp. 154-212. New York: Columbia University Press, 1947. Rev. ed. 1950. Reprinted Bloomington: Indiana University Press, 1966. Also in [Schilling]:95-114 and in [Critical Essays]: 95-114. Because of its connections with the epic, the heroic play, unlike tragedy, emphasizes admiration rather than pity or fear. *See PQ* 28:372-73.

8/2:67 Rasco, Kay Frances Dilworth. "Supernaturalism in the Heroic Play." *DA* 27(1967):3433A-34A(Northwestern).

8/2:68 Righter, Anne. "Heroic Tragedy." [Rest. Theatre]:135-57. The heroic plays are "essentially frivolous," a result of Charles II's influence on the drama.

8/2:69 Ristine, Frank Humphrey. *English Tragicomedy: Its Origin and History*. (Columbia University Studies in English.) New York: Columbia University Press, 1910. Reprinted New York: Russell and Russell, 1963.

8/2:70 Rodney, Caroline C. "Dryden's Tragicomedy." *DAI* 34(1973): 1253A(Cornell).

*8/2:71 Rothstein, Eric. *Restoration Tragedy: Form and the Process of Change*. Madison, Milwaukee, London: University of Wisconsin

Press, 1967. An important revaluation of Restoration drama. *See* Arthur C. Kirsch, *ELN* 6:55-56; Pierre Legouis, *EA* 21:310-11; Aline Taylor, *PQ* 47:342-44.

8/2:72   ——. "Unrhymed Tragedy, 1660-1702." *DA* 23(1962):1689(Princeton).

8/2:73   Schelling, Felix E. "Decadent Romance." *Elizabethan Drama: 1558-1642* [1908]. 2:307-70. New York: Russell and Russell, 1959.

8/2:74   Seward, Patricia M. "Was the English Restoration Theatre Significantly Influenced by Spanish Drama?" *RLC* 46(1972):95-125. *The Indian Emperour* and *The Assignation*; Dryden's comic style was not affected by his first-hand contact with Calderón.

8/2:75   Simpson, Friench, Jr. "The Relationship between Character and Action in Neo-classical Tragedy, with Special Reference to Some Tragedies by John Dryden." *AB-SU* 26(1951):141-42.

8/2:76   Speerschneider, Otto. *Metrische Untersuchungen über den heroischen Vers in J. Dryden's Dramen*. Halle: Wischan and Wettengel, 1897.

8/2:77   Spingarn, Edward. "The Restoration Heroic Play." *DA* 20(1959): 3732-33(Columbia).

8/2:78   Stalling, Donald L. "From Dryden to Lillo: The Course of English Tragedy 1660-1731." *DAI* 30(1970):2981A(Texas, Austin). Blames neoclassical critical theory and the rise of the middle class with its rejection of the nonutilitarian for the drama's failure to survive its own period.

8/2:79   Steiner, George. *The Death of Tragedy*. New York: Knopf, 1961.

8/2:80   Stroup, Thomas B. "Type Characters in the Serious Drama of the Restoration with Special Attention to the Plays of Davenant, Dryden, Lee, and Otway." Diss. Kentucky, 1956.

8/2:81   Thorndike, Ashley H. *Tragedy*. Boston, New York: Houghton Mifflin, 1908.

8/2:82   Tiedje, Egon. *Die Tradition Ben Jonsons in der Restaurationskomödie*. Hamburg: Gruyter, 1963.

8/2:83   Tisch, J. H. "Late Baroque Drama—A European Phenomenon?" *Proceedings of the Vth Congress of the International Comparative Literature Association (Belgrade 1967)*, pp. 125-36. Amsterdam: Swets and Zeitlinger, 1969.

8/2:84   Tritt, Carleton S. "Wit and Paradox in Dryden's Serious Plays." *DA* 29(1968):882A-83A(Wash.).

8/2:85   Tupper, James W. "The Relation of the Heroic Play to the Romances of Beaumont and Fletcher." *PMLA* 20(1905):584-621. The heroic play developed out of native English traditions. *See* items 8/2: 20, 8/2:47.

8/2:86   Verdurmen, John P. "Lee, Dryden and the Restoration Tragedy of Concernment." *DAI* 33(1973):6887A-88A(Stanford). A study of the interaction and subsequent collaboration of Dryden and Lee.

*8/2:87   Waith, Eugene M. "Dryden and the Tradition of Serious Drama." [Miner]:58-89. A survey of Dryden's serious plays, with an emphasis on his conception of the hero.

*8/2:88   ——. *The Herculean Hero in Marlowe, Chapman, Shakespeare and Dryden*. New York: Columbia University Press; London: Chatto and Windus, 1962. Sections on *The Conquest of Granada*, *Aureng-Zebe* and *All for Love*. "*All for Love*" section reprinted [Rest. Dramatists]:51-62 and in [20th Century Interpretations]:72-82. *See* Irving Ribner, *Criticism* 5:183-85; *NQ* 10:354-55; *DUJ* 24:152-53.

*8/2:89 ———. *Ideas of Greatness: Heroic Drama in England*. New York: Barnes and Noble, 1971. *See* Robert D. Hume, *PQ* 51:365.

8/2:90 ———. "Spectacles of State." *SEL* 13(1973):316-30. Masques and the heroic drama were used to educate the monarch who watched the performance.

8/2:91 ———. "Tears of Magnanimity in Otway and Racine." *French and English Drama of the Seventeenth Century: Papers read at a Clark Library Seminar, March 13, 1971*, introd. Henry Goodman, pp. 1-22. Los Angeles: Clark Memorial Library, University of California, 1972. Dryden on "pity."

*8/2:92 ———. "The Voice of Mr. Bayes." *SEL* 3(1963):335-43. Dryden's attitude toward his heroes, his audience and his patrons is seen through the dedicatons to the plays.

8/2:93 Wasserman, Earl R. "The Pleasures of Tragedy." *ELH* 14(1947): 283-307.

*8/2:94 West, Michael. "Dryden and the Disintegration of Renaissance Heroic Ideals." *Costerus* 7(1973):193-222. Dryden's heroic plays are "best explained as the final stage in the decay of Renaissance ideals of Christian heroism." *See* items 4:484, 8/2:95.

*8/2:95 Winterbottom, John A. "The Development of the Hero in Dryden's Tragedies." *JEGP* 52(1953):161-73. Dryden's development as an artist and an intellectual is characterized by increasing disillusionment, which is reflected in his treatment of the iconoclastic hero. *See* items 8/2:94, 8/7:7.

8/2:96 ———. "Patterns of Piety: Studies in the Intellectual Background of Dryden's Tragedies." Diss. Yale, 1948.

*8/2:97 ———. "The Place of Hobbesian Ideas in Dryden's Tragedies." *JEGP* 57(1958):665-83. Reprinted in [Swedenberg]:374-94. After Dryden's ideas have been separated from those of his characters, he is seen to be closer philosophically to Filmer than to Hobbes. *See* item 8/2:32.

8/2:98 ———. "Stoicism in Dryden's Tragedies." *JEGP* 61(1962):868-83.

8/2:99 Youngren, Mary Ann. "The Marks of Sovereignty: Authority and Force in Dryden's Heroic Dramas." Diss. Harvard, 1968.

8/2:100 Zebouni, Selma Assir. *Dryden: A Study in Heroic Characterization*. (Louisiana State University Studies Humanities Series 16.) Baton Rouge: Louisiana State University Press, 1965. *See* Victor M. Hamm, *Renascence* 18:110-11; Arthur C. Kirsch, *CE* 27:644; Pierre Legouis, *TLS* 15 July 1966, p. 602; V. de Sola Pinto, *CritQ* 7:288-89; Eugene M. Waith, *PQ* 45:556-57; James Black, *MLR* 62:115-17; William Frost, *JEGP* 66:151-53; Jean Gagen, *MP* 65:162-64.

8/2:101 ———. "The Hero In Dryden's Heroic Tragedy: A Revaluation." *DA* 24(1963):2467(Louisiana State).

See also items 1:99-100, 2/5:2, 4:19, 4:187, 4:212, 4:223, 4:242, 4: 388, 4:396, 4:417, 4:429, 4:444, 4:506, 4:508, 4:520, 6/1:20, 6/2: 79, 6/4:5, 7:30, 7:65, 7:89, 7:104-05, 7:116, 7:135, 7:138, 7:163, 7:277, 7:286, 8/1:74-75, 8/1:97, 8/1:126, 8/1:184, 8/1:240, 8/4:5, 8/9:74, 9:16-17.

8/3. *THE WILD GALLANT; THE RIVAL LADIES;*

SECRET-LOVE; AN EVENING'S LOVE

8/3:1 Allen, Ned B. "The Sources of Dryden's *The Mock Astrologer*." *PQ* 36(1957):435-64. Scudéry, Corneille, Molière, Quinault.

8/3:2 Biggins, D. "Source Notes for Dryden, Wycherley and Otway." *NQ* 3(1956):298-301. *The Rival Ladies* and *The Indian Emperour*.

8/3:3 Bowers, Fredson. "The First Edition of Dryden's *Wild Gallant*, 1669." *Library* (5th ser.) 5(1950):51-54.

8/3:4 Cooke, Arthur L. "Two Parallels between Dryden's *Wild Gallant* and Congreve's *Love for Love*." *NQ* 1(1954):27-28.

8/3:5 Croissant, DeWitt C. "Early Sentimental Comedy." *Essays in Dramatic Literature: The Parrott Presentation Volume*, ed. Hardin Craig, pp. 47-71. Princeton: Princeton University Press, 1935. Reprinted New York: Russell and Russell, 1967. *The Wild Gallant* and *The Rival Ladies*.

8/3:6 Harbage, Alfred. "Elizabethan-Restoration Palimpsest." *MLR* 35 (1940):287-379. *The Wild Gallant* is an adaptation of a lost play by Brome.

8/3:7 Hume, Robert D. "Dryden, James Howard, and the Date of *All Mistaken* [1665?]." *PQ* 51(1972):422-29. Dryden's *Secret Love* may be indebted to Howard's comedy. *See* item 8/3:16.

8/3:8 Martin, Leslie H. "Dryden and the Art of Transversion." *CompD* 6(1972):3-13. Dryden adapted the "History of Cleobuline, Queen of Corinth" in writing *Secret Love*.

8/3:9 Moore, Frank Harper. "Dr Pelling, Dr Pell, and Dryden's Lord Nonsuch." *MLR* 49(1954):349-51. *The Wild Gallant*.

8/3:10 Oppenheimer, Max. "Supplementary Data on the French and English Adaptations of Calderón's *El astrólogo fingido*." *RLC* 24 (1948):547-60.

8/3:11 O'Regan, M. J. "Two Notes on French Reminiscences in Restoration Comedy." *Hermathena* 93(1959):63-70. Dryden borrowed from Corneille in *An Evening's Love*.

8/3:12 Perkinson, Richard H. "Lady du Lake." *NQ* 168(1935):260-61. *The Wild Gallant*.

8/3:13 Scott, Florence R. "Lady Honoria Howard." *RES* 20(1944):158-59. Honoria in *The Rival Ladies*. *See* items 3:44, 3:194.

8/3:14 Seaton, Ethel. "Two Restoration Plays." *TLS* 18 October 1934, p. 715. *The Rival Ladies*.

8/3:15 Smith, John Harrington. "Tony Lumpkin and the Country Booby Type in Antecedent English Comedy." *PMLA* 58(1943):1038-49. *The Wild Gallant*. *See* A. Friedman, *PQ* 23:166-67.

8/3:16 Sutherland, James R. "The Date of James Howard's *All Mistaken, or, The Mad Couple*." *NQ* 11(1964):339-40. Dates Howard's comedy in 1665 and argues that *Secret Love* is derived from it. *See* item 8/3:7.

The Wild Gallant: *See also* items 2/5:9, 3:34, 5/13:22, 8/1:1, 8/1:3, 8/1:62-63, 8/1:77, 8/1:156, 8/1:167, 8/1:196, 8/1:203, 8/1:255, 8/1:267.

The Rival Ladies: *See also* items 5/13:12, 8/2:25, 8/2:51, 8/2:69.

Secret Love: *See also* items 2/2:31, 2/5:1, 2/5:4, 3:172, 5/13:7, 8/1: 177, 8/1:267, 8/2:70, 8/5:6.

An Evening's Love: *See also* items 2/5:5, 2/5:22, 4:190, 5/6:13, 8/1: 87.

8/4. *THE INDIAN-QUEEN; THE INDIAN EMPEROUR;*

TYRANNICK LOVE; THE CONQUEST OF GRANADA

8/4:1 Adams, Henry Hitch. "A Prompt Copy of Dryden's *Tyrannic Love*." *SB* 4(1951-52):170-74. The Folger copy of the 2nd ed. quarto of 1672 (Macdonald 74b).

8/4:2 Alssid, Michael W. "The Perfect Conquest: A Study of Theme, Structure and Characters in Dryden's *The Indian Emperour*." *SP* 59 (1962):539-59.

8/4:3 Arnold, Denis. "Purcell's *Indian Queen*." *The Listener* 1 March 1973, p. 285.

8/4:4 Ball, Alice D. "An Emendation of Dryden's *Conquest of Granada*, Part One." *ELH* 6(1939):217-18. Attributes the speech beginning 1. 151 to Selin instead of to Zulema.

8/4:5 Biddle, Evelyn Q. "A Critical Study of the Influence of the Classical and Christian Traditions upon the Character of the Hero as Revealed Through the Concepts of 'Love' and 'Honor' in Three Restoration Heroic Tragedies." *DA* 27(1967):3969A-70A(U.S.C.). *The Conquest of Granada*.

8/4:6 Bowers, Fredson. "The 1665 Manuscript of Dryden's *Indian Emperour*." *SP* 48(1951):738-60.

8/4:7 Compton, Gail H. "The Metaphor of Conquest in Dryden's *The Conquest of Granada*." *DAI* 30(1969):274A(Fla.).

8/4:8 Coshow, Betty Gay. "Dryden's 'Zambra Dance'." *Expl* 16(1957): Item 16. *See* reply, Bruce King, ibid., 18(1959):Item 18. *The Conquest of Granada*.

8/4:9 Dey, E. Merton. "Drydeniana." *NQ* (9th ser.) 3(1899):165. Stage directions in the *Indian Emperour*.

8/4:10 Freehafer, John. "Dryden's *Indian Emperour*." *Expl* 27(1968): Item 24.

8/4:11 Jaquith, William G. "Dryden's *Tyrannic Love* and *All for Love*: A Study of Comic and Tragic Dialects." *DAI* 34(1973):3345A-46A (U.C.L.A.).

8/4:12 King, Bruce. "Dryden, Tillotson, and *Tyrannic Love*." *RES* 16 (1965):364-377. *See* items 7:38, 7:274.

8/4:13 Kinsley, James. "A Dryden Play at Edinburgh." *Scottish Historical Review* 33(1954):129-32. *The Indian Emperour*.

8/4:14 Loftis, John. "Exploration and Enlightenment: Dryden's *The Indian Emperour* and Its Background." *PQ* 45(1966):71-84.

8/4:15 ———. "*El príncipe constante* and *The Indian Emperour*: A Reconsideration." *MLR* 65(1970):761-67. *See* item 8/4:23.

8/4:16 MacMillan, Dougald. "The Sources of Dryden's *The Indian Emperour*." *HLQ* 13(1950):355-70. *Purchass his Pilgrims* (1625) and Davenant's *The Cruelty of the Spaniards in Peru*.

8/4:17 Nettleton, George H. "Author's Changes in Dryden's *Conquest of Granada*, Part I." *MLN* 50(1935):360-64. A study of the five quartos in the Yale Library.

8/4:18 Novak, Maximillian E. "The Demonology of Dryden's *Tyrannick Love* and 'Anti-Scott'." *ELN* 4(1966):95-98.

8/4:19 Perkins, Merle L. "Dryden's *The Indian Emperour* and Voltaire's *Alzire*." *CL* 9(1957):229-37.

8/4:20 Ringler, Richard N. "Two Sources for Dryden's *The Indian Emperour*." *PQ* 42(1963):423-29. Donne's *First Anniversarie* and Spenser's *Faerie Queene*.

8/4:21 Schweitzer, Jerome W. "Another Note on Dryden's Use of Georges de Scudéry's *Almahide*." *MLN* 62(1947):262-63.

8/4:22 ———. "Dryden's Use of Scudéry's *Almahide*." *MLN* 54(1939): 190-92.

8/4:23 Shergold, N. D., and Peter Ure. "Dryden and Calderón: A New Spanish Source for *The Indian Emperour*." *MLR* 61(1966):369-83. *El príncipe constante*. *See* items 8/1:127, 8/4:15.

*8/4:24 Smith, John Harrington. "The Dryden-Howard Collaboration."

SP 51(1954):54–74. Considers the question of authorship from the perspective of Howard's work. *The Indian Queen.*

8/4:25   Spector, Robert Donald. "A Dryden Echo in Tennyson." *NQ* 197 (1952):520. *Indian Emperour.*

*8/4:26   Steck, James S. "Dryden's *Indian Emperour*: The Early Editions and their Relation to the Text." *SB* 2(1949–50):139–52. Establishes the genealogical order of the 13 editions of the play, appearing between 1667 and 1697. *See* items 1:10–11, 1:65, 1:83, 8/4:6.

8/4:27   Stroup, Thomas B. "Scenery for *The Indian Queen.*" *MLN* 52 (1937):408–09.

8/4:28   Wallace, Leonard DeLong. "A New Date for the *Conquest of Granada.*" *MP* 16(1919):271–72.

8/4:29   Ward, Charles E. "Massinger and Dryden." *ELH* 2(1935):263–66. Dryden's debt to Massinger in the influence of *The Virgin Martyr* on *Tyrannick Love.*

8/4:30   Wilson, John Harold. "The Duchess of Portsmouth's Players." *NQ* 10(1963):106–07. *Indian Emperour.*

The Indian Queen: *See also* items 1:51, 2/5:3, 2/5:9, 3:44, 3:141, 8/1:157, 8/2:8, 8/2:19, 8/2:25, 8/2:30, 8/2:50, 8/2:57, 8/2:61, 8/2:63, 8/2:100.

The Indian Emperour: *See also* items 1:10–11, 1:96, 2/1:1, 2/5:2, 2/5:4, 2/5:25, 8/2:1, 8/2:17, 8/2:50, 8/2:74, 8/3:2.

Tyrannick Love: *See also* items 2/5:5, 4:16, 4:27, 7:38, 8/1:74, 8/2:1, 8/2:25, 8/2:38.

The Conquest of Granada: *See also* items 2/5:6–8, 5/13:20, 8/2:1, 8/2:17, 8/2:28, 8/2:30, 8/2:38.

8/5. *MARRIAGE A-LA-MODE*

8/5:1   Beall, Chandler B. "A Quaint Conceit From Guarini to Dryden." *MLN* 64(1949):461–68. The sexual pun of "die" in "Whil'st Alexis lay prest."

8/5:2   Brooks, Harold. "Some Notes on Dryden, Cowley, and Shadwell." *NQ* 168(1935):94–95. Contemporary praise of *Marriage A-la-Mode.*

8/5:3   Hume, Robert D. "The Date of Dryden's *Marrage A-la-Mode.*" *HLB* 21(1973):161–66. Probably acted by early December 1671.

*8/5:4   King, Bruce. "Dryden's *Marriage a la Mode.*" *DramS* 4(1965):28–37. Dryden's only perfect comedy.

8/5:5   Kronenberger, Louis. "Dryden: *The Spanish Friar, Marriage à la Mode.*" *The Thread of Laughter: Chapters on English Stage Comedy from Jonson to Maugham*, pp. 81–92. New York: Knopf, 1952.

8/5:6   Krüger, Wilhelm. *Das Verhältnis von Colley Cibbers Lustspiel "The Comical Lovers" zu John Drydens "Marriage A La Mode" und "Secret Love; or, the Maiden Queen."* Halle: Wischan and Wettengel, 1902.

8/5:7   Martin, Leslie Howard. "The Source and Originality of Dryden's Melantha." *PQ* 52(1973):746–53. Berisa from Scudéry's *Grand Cyrus* is the source for Melantha.

8/5:8   Okerlund, Arlene N. "Literature and Its Audience: The Reader in Action in Selected Works of Spenser, Dryden, Thackeray, and T. S. Eliot." *DAI* 30(1969):1991A(Calif., San Diego).

8/5:9 Reichert, John "A Note on Buckingham and Dryden." *NQ* 9(1962): 220-21

See also items 2/2:31, 2/5:1, 2/5:6-8, 2/5:18, 2/5:32, 8/1:1, 8/1:20, 8/1:52, 8/1:62, 8/1:156, 8/1:177, 8/1:196, 8/1:203, 8/1:234, 8/1: 255, 8/2:38, 8/2:51, 8/2:69-70, 8/6:7.

8/6. *THE ASSIGNATION; AMBOYNA; THE KIND KEEPER,*

OR MR. LIMBERHAM

*8/6:1 Baker, Van R. "Heroic Posturing Satirized: Dryden's *Mr. Limberham*." *PLL* 8(1972):370-79. Dryden satirizes the licentiousness of Woodall, Aldo and Limberham.

*8/6:2 Bredvold, Louis I. "Political Aspects of Dryden's *Amboyna* and *The Spanish Fryar*." *University of Michigan Publications, Language and Literature* 8(1932):119-32. Reprinted [Swedenberg]:300-13.

8/6:3 de Beer, E. S. "Dryden: 'The Kind Keeper': The 'Poet of Scandalous Memory'." *NQ* 179(1940):128-29. Andrew Marvell.

*8/6:4 Moore, Frank Harper. "Heroic Comedy: A New Interpretation of Dryden's *Assignation*." *SP* 51(1954):585-98. The play is Dryden's attempt to mingle high comedy with heroic comedy. *See* item 8/1:3.

8/6:5 Rundle, James Urvin. "The Source of Dryden's 'Comic Plot' in *The Assignation*." *MP* 45(1947):104-11. Calderón's *Con quien vengo vengo*.

8/6:6 Staves, Susan. "Why Was Dryden's *Mr. Limberham* Banned?: A Problem in Restoration Theatre History." *RECTR* 13,i(1974):1-11. The available evidence does not conclusively prove that the play was banned either for its licentiousness or for political reasons.

8/6:7 Ward, Charles E. "The Dates of Two Dryden Plays." *PMLA* 51(1936): 786-92. *Amboyna* (before June, 1672); *Marriage A-la-Mode* (before the end of 1671 and the publication of *The Rehearsal*).

8/6:8 Zamonski, John A. "The Spiritual Nature of Carnal Love in Dryden's *Assignation*." *ETJ* 25(1973):189-92.

The Assignation: *See also* items 8/1:1, 8/1:156, 8/2:38, 8/2:74.

Amboyna: *See also* items 4:528, 8/1:126.

The Kind Keeper, or Mr. Limberham: *See also* items 8/1:167, 8/1:196.

8/7. *AURENG-ZEBE*

*8/7:1 Alssid, Michael W. "The Design of Dryden's *Aureng-Zebe*." *JEGP* 64(1965):452-69. An analysis of the imagery, characterization and design.

8/7:2 Brooks, Harold F. "Dryden's *Aureng-Zebe*: Debts to Corneille and Racine." *RLC* 46(1972):5-34.

8/7:3 Dixon, Peter. "Pope and Dryden." *NQ* 13(1966):460-61. A parallel to *Epistle to a Lady*.

*8/7:4 Kirsch, Arthur C. "The Significance of Dryden's *Aureng-Zebe*." *ELH* 29(1962):160-75. Reprinted in [Loftis]:180-94 and in [Rest. Dramatists]:37-49. The play reflects changes taking place in Restoration serious drama. *See* item 8/7:7.

8/7:5 LeComte, Edward S. "*Samson Agonistes* and *Aureng-Zebe*." *EA* 11 (1958):18-22. Verbal borrowings.

8/7:6 Martin, Leslie Howard. "*Aureng-Zebe* and the Ritual of the Persian King." *MP* 71(1973):169-71. Offers a possible source for the allusion to "the Persian King."

*8/7:7 ———. "The Consistency of Dryden's *Aureng-Zebe*." *SP* 70(1973): 306-28. The play does not signal Dryden's disenchantment with the heroic tradition, but rather it indicates his turning to alternatives which had long existed within the epic tradition. *See* items 8/2:94-95, 8/7:4.

8/7:8 Morton, Richard. "'By No Strong Passion Swayed': A Note on John Dryden's *Aureng-Zebe*." *ESA* 1(1958):59-68. Aureng-Zebe is not wholly exemplary, for while he is politically admirable, his love is less than ideal.

*8/7:9 Newman, Robert S. "Irony and the Problem of Tone in Dryden's *Aureng-Zebe*." *SEL* 10(1970):439-58. Dryden is hopeful, yet sceptical about idealized love and honor. *See* items 8/2:37-38, 8/7:1.

See also items 2/5:2, 2/5:7-8, 2/5:17, 2/5:20, 2/5:28, 3:56, 8/2:1, 8/2:8, 8/2:30, 8/2:38, 8/2:41-42, 8/2:62, 8/2:66, 9:10.

8/8. POST-1667 COLLABORATIONS: *SIR MARTIN MAR-ALL;*

THE MISTAKEN HUSBAND; OEDIPUS; THE DUKE OF GUISE

8/8:1 Albrecht, L. *Dryden's "Sir Martin Mar-All" in Bezug auf seine Quellen.* Rostock: Adlers Erben, 1906.

8/8:2 Bachorik, Laurence L. "*The Duke of Guise* and Dryden's *Vindication*: A New Consideration." *ELN* 10(1973):208-12.

8/8:3 Bentzien, Werner. *Studien zu Drydens "Oedipus."* Rostock: Carl Boldt'sche, 1910.

8/8:4 Cross, Gustav. "Ovid Metamorphosed: Marston, Webster, and Nathaniel Lee." *NQ* 3(1956):244-45, 508-09. The Dryden-Lee *Oedipus* is indebted to the Golding translation of Ovid.

8/8:5 Hinnant, Charles H. "The Background of the Early Version of Dryden's *The Duke of Guise*." *ELN* 6(1968):102-06.

8/8:6 Hirt, A. "A Question of Excess: Neo-Classical Adaptations of Greek Tragedy." *Costerus* 3(1972):55-119.

8/8:7 Kallich, Martin. "Oedipus: From Man to Archetype." *CLS* 3 (1966):33-46.

8/8:8 King, Bruce. "Anti-Whig Satire in *The Duke of Guise*." *ELN* 2 (1965):190-93.

8/8:9 Maxwell, J. C. "Dryden's Epilogue to *Oedipus*, ll. 5-6." *NQ* 9 (1962):384-85.

8/8:10 Moore, Frank Harper. "The Composition of *Sir Martin Mar-All*." *Essays in English Literature of the Classical Period Presented to Dougald MacMillan*, eds. Daniel W. Patterson and Albrecht B. Strauss, pp. 27-38. (*SP* Extra Series 4.) Chapel Hill: University of North Carolina Press, 1967. The Duke of Newcastle co-authored the play with Dryden.

8/8:11 Rangno, Melanie Collins. "Nathaniel Lee's Plays of the Exclusion Crisis." *DAI* 34(1974):4215A(U.C.L.A.). *The Duke of Guise*.

8/8:12 Swinburne, Algernon Charles. "A Relic of Dryden." *Complete Works* (Bonchurch Edition), eds. Sir Edmund Gross and Thomas James Wise. 14:411-21. London: Heinemann; New York: Gabriel Wells, 1926. *The Mistaken Husband*.

Sir Martin Mar-All: See also items 1:78, 2/5:1, 2/5:4, 8/1:1, 8/1:156, 8/1:196.

Oedipus: See also items 3:79, 8/1:262, 8/2:86, 8/11:9.

The Duke of Guise: See also items 2/5:10, 3:183, 4:16, 4:190, 4:265-66, 4:299, 4:302, 4:444, 4:457, 4:535, 5/4:3, 8/1:59, 8/1:101, 8/1:126, 8/1:167, 8/1:252-53, 8/1:264.

8/9. PLAYS BASED ON SHAKESPEAREAN ORIGINALS: *THE TEMPEST;*
ALL FOR LOVE; TROILUS AND CRESSIDA

8/9:1 "All for Love." *CathW* 175(1952):393.

8/9:2 Atkins, G. Douglas. "The Function and Significance of the Priest in Dryden's *Troilus and Cressida*." *TSLL* 13(1971):29-37. *See* item 3:52.

8/9:3 Aycock, Wendell M. "The Irrepressible Characters of Shakespeare's *The Tempest*: Sequels and Re-Creations." *DAI* 31(1970): 351A(S.C.).

8/9:4 Bailey, John. "Dryden and Shakespeare." *TLS* 1 April 1904, p. 97. Reprinted in *Poets and Poetry*, pp. 72-79. Oxford: At the Clarendon Press, 1911. Also reprinted in [20th Century Interpretations]:14-18. Rev. art. *See* item 2/5:8.

8/9:5 Beauchamp, Virginia W. "Dramatic Treatment of *Antony and Cleopatra* in the Sixteenth and Seventeenth Centuries: Variations in Dramatic Form upon a Single Theme." Diss. Chicago, 1956.

8/9:6 Bernhardt, W. W. "Shakespeare's *Troilus and Cressida* and Dryden's *Truth Found Too Late*." *SQ* 20(1969):129-41.

8/9:7 Boase, T. S. R. "The Danger of Unity." *New Statesman* 11 February 1922, p. 531. *All for Love.*

8/9:8 Boatner, Janet W. "Criseyde's Character in the Major Writers from Benoît Through Dryden: The Changes and Their Significance." *DAI* 31(1971):4705A(Wis.).

8/9:9 Caracciolo, Peter. "Dryden and the *Antony and Cleopatra* of Sir Charles Sedley." *ES* 50(1969: Anglo-American Supplement): 1-1v. *See* item 8/9:25.

8/9:10 ——. "Some Unrecorded Variants in the First Edition of Dryden's *All for Love*, 1678." *BC* 13(1964):498-500.

8/9:11 Casanave, Don S. "Shakespeare's *The Tempest* in a Restoration Context: A Study of Dryden's *The Enchanted Island*." *DAI* 33(1973): 6303A(Mich.).

8/9:12 Clarke, Sir Ernest. "'The Tempest' as an 'Opera'." *Athenaeum* 4113(25 August 1906):222-23. *See* item 8/9:50.

8/9:13 Cook, Dorothy. "Dryden's Adaptation of Shakespeare's *Troilus and Cressida*." *ConnR* 7,i(1973):66-72.

8/9:14 Cooke, M. G. "The Restoration Ethos of Byron's Classical Plays." *PMLA* 79(1964):569-78. *Sardanapalus's* indebtedness to *All for Love.*

8/9:15 Corvesor, D. "Shakespeare Adaptations from Dryden to Garrick." Diss. London, Birkbeck College, 1926.

8/9:16 Davies, H. Neville. "Dryden's *All for Love* and Sedley's *Antony and Cleopatra*." *NQ* 14(1967):221-27.

8/9:17 ——. "Dryden's *All for Love* and Thomas May's *The Tragedie of Cleopatra Queen of Ægypt*." *NQ* 12(1965):139-44.

8/9:18 ——. "Shakespeare's Sonnet LXVI Echoed in *All for Love*." *NQ* 15(1968):262-63.

*8/9:19 Dillon, George L. "The Seventeenth-Century Shift in the Theory and Language of Passion." *Lang&S* 4(1971):131-43. In accordance with changed ideas about passion and character, Restoration adaptations of Shakespeare altered the diction of the tragedies.

*8/9:20 Dobrée, Bonamy. "Cleopatra and 'That Criticall Warr'." *TLS* 11 October 1928, pp. 717-18. Reprinted in *Restoration Tragedy 1660-1720*, pp. 66-90. Oxford: At the Clarendon Press, 1929. Also reprinted in [20th Century Interpretations]:19-31. An important early revaluation of *All for Love*.

8/9:21 Dunkin, Paul S. "The Dryden *Troilus* and *Cressida* Imprint: Another Theory." *SB* 2(1949-50):185-89.

8/9:22 Eich, Louis M. "Alterations of Shakespeare 1660-1710: And an Investigation of the Critical and Dramatic Principles and Theatrical Conventions which Prompted These Revisions." *DA* 8,i(1948):90-91(Mich.).

8/9:23 Emerson, Everett H., Harold E. Davis, and Ira Johnson. "Intention and Achievement in *All for Love*." *CE* 17(1955):84-87. Reprinted in [20th Century Interpretations]:55-60. *See* item 8/9:44.

8/9:24 Everett, William. "Six Cleopatras." *Atlantic Monthly* 95(1905): 252-63.

8/9:25 Faas, K. E. "Some Notes on Dryden's *All for Love*." *Anglia* 88 (1970):341-46. Dryden's indebtedness to Sedley. *See* item 8/9:9.

8/9:26 Forker, Charles R. "*Romeo and Juliet* and the 'Cydnus' Speech in Dryden's *All for Love*." *NQ* 9(1962):382-83.

8/9:27 Freedman, Morris. "*All for Love* and *Samson Agonistes*." *NQ* 3 (1956):514-17. Milton's influence on Dryden.

*8/9:28 Goggin, L. P. "This Bow of Ulysses." *Essays and Studies in Language and Literature (DSPS)* 5(1964):49-86.

8/9:29 Hannmann, Friedrich. *Dryden's tragödie "All for Love or the World well Lost" und ihr verhältnis zu Shakespeare's "Antony and Cleopatra."* Rostock: Carl Boldt'sche, 1903.

8/9:30 Harrison, T. P., Jr. "*Othello* as a Model for Dryden in *All for Love*." *Studies in English* (University of Texas) 7(1927):136-43. Criticizes Dryden for increasing the importance of Alexas's role.

8/9:31 Hennings, Thomas P. "The Glorious and Loving Hero: Intellectual and Dramatic Backgrounds of Dryden's *All for Love*." *DAI* 32 (1971):966A(Wis.).

8/9:32 Hook, Lucyle. "Shakespeare Improv'd, or A Case for the Affirmative." *SQ* 4(1953):289-99. Restoration adaptations of Shakespeare afforded women better acting parts than did the originials.

8/9:33 Hooker, Helene M. "Dryden's and Shadwell's *Tempest*." *HLQ* 6 (1943):224-28.

8/9:34 Hope, A. D. "*All for Love*, or Comedy as Tragedy." *The Cave and the Spring*, pp. 144-63. Adelaide: Rigby, 1965. The play is a comedy because the characters are ruled by a merchantile mentality.

8/9:35 Hope-Wallace, Philip. "The Enchanted Island." *Time and Tide* 40(1959):708. A rev. of a performance of *The Tempest*.

*8/9:36 Hughes, Derek W. "The Significance of *All for Love*." *ELH* 37 (1970):540-63. By studying the imagery, the play is shown to focus on conflict, subjectivism and instability.

8/9:37 Hughes, R. E. "Dryden's *All for Love*: The Sensual Dilemma." *Drama Critique* 3,ii(1960):68-72.

8/9:38 Hyman, Stanley Edgar. *Poetry and Criticism: Four Revolutions in Literary Taste.* New York: Atheneum, 1961. Dryden's modifications of *Antony and Cleopatra* are in accord with neoclassical theories, which Dryden himself, in the Preface, established. *See* Robert Martin Adams, *HudR* 14:311-12.

8/9:39 Ibershoff, C. H. "Dryden's *Tempest* as a Source of Bodmer's *Noah*." *MP* 15(1917):247-53.

*8/9:40 Jackson, Wallace. "Dryden's Emperor and Lilio's Merchant: The Relevant Bases of Action." *MLQ* 26(1965):536-44. *All for Love* questions the value of heroic energy and passion in a world of "duty and contractural obligations."

8/9:41 Johnson, James William. "John Dryden, His Times, and *All for Love*." *Essays in Honor of Richebourg Gaillard McWilliams*, ed. Howard Creed, pp. 21-28. (Birmingham-Southern College Bulletin 63,ii.) Birmingham: Birmingham-Southern College, 1970.

*8/9:42 Kearful, Frank J. "'Tis Past Recovery': Tragic Consciousness in *All for Love*." *MLQ* 34(1973):227-46. The play's tragedy of the consciousness of time is felt by the audience as much as by the characters.

8/9:43 Kilbourne, Frederick W. *Alterations and Adaptations of Shakespeare*. Boston: Poet Lore, 1906.

*8/9:44 King, Bruce. "Dryden's Intent in *All for Love*." *CE* 24(1963): 267-71. Dryden's stated moral intent in the Preface is not his true one.

8/9:45 ———. "Dryden, Tillotson, and *Tyrannic Love*." *RES* 16(1965): 364-77. Dryden was influenced by Tillotson while he was writing *Tyrannic Love*.

8/9:46 Klima, S. "Some Unrecorded Borrowings from Shakespeare in Dryden's *All for Love*." *NQ* 10(1963):415-18.

8/9:47 Knight, L. H. "Stage Adaptations of Shakespeare, 1660-1900." Diss. University of Wales, Swansea, 1961.

8/9:48 Kossman, H. "A Note on Dryden's 'All for Love,' V. 165ff." *ES* 31(1950):99-100.

8/9:49 Lavine, Anne R. "This Bow of Ulysses: Shakespeare's *Troilus and Cressida* and Its Imitation by Dryden." *DA* 22(1962):3186-88 (Bryn Mawr).

8/9:50 Lawrence, W. J. "Did Thomas Shadwell Write an Opera on 'The Tempest'?" *Anglia* 27(1904):205-17; 29(1906):539-41. Rev. ed., reprinted in *The Elizabethan Playhouse and Other Studies*, pp. 193-206. Stratford-upon-Avon: [n.pub.], [1912]. Reprinted New York: Russell and Russell, 1963. *See* items 8/9:12, 8/9:88.

8/9:51 Leavis, F. R. "'Antony and Cleopatra' and 'All for Love': A Critical Exercise." *Scrutiny* 5(1936):158-69. After comparing the language of the two plays, Leavis concludes that Dryden's play is neither tragedy nor poetry.

8/9:52 Levison, William S. "Restoration Adaptations of Shakespeare as Baroque Literature." *DAI* 34(1973):730A(Ill.).

8/9:53 Loofbourow, John W. "Robinson Crusoe's Island and the Restoration *Tempest*." *EnlE* 2(1971):201-07.

8/9:54 Macey, Samuel L. "Duffet's *Mock Tempest* and the Assimilation of Shakespeare During the Restoration and Eighteenth Century." *RECTR* 7,i(1968):44-52.

8/9:55 Marsh, Robert. "Historical Interpretation and the History of Criticism." *Literary Criticism and Historical Understanding*, ed. Phillip Damon, pp. 1-24. (Selected Papers from the English Institute.) New York, London: Columbia University Press, 1967. Using a comparison of *All for Love* and *Antony and Cleopatra*, the point is made that superficial resemblances of kind may actually obscure important differences in conception. *See* item 8/9:80.

8/9:56 Maurer, A. E. Wallace. "From Renaissance to Neo-Classic." *NQ* 5(1958):287. *Troilus and Cressida*.

8/9:57 McCollum, John I., Jr. "Dryden's 'Adaptations': The Tragedies." Diss. Duke, 1956.

8/9:58 Mellers, Wilfrid. *Harmonious Meeting: A Study of the Relationship between English Music, Poetry and Theatre, c. 1600-1900*. London: Dobson, 1965. The Dryden-Davenant *Tempest* ruins the original by the introduction of realism; Purcell's music, however, is closer to Shakespeare's design.

*8/9:59 Merchant, W. Moelwyn. "Shakespeare 'Made Fit'." [Rest. Theatre]:195-219. A strongly worded rebuke to those who continue to interpret and evaluate the Shakespearean adaptations of Dryden and others in Elizabethan and modern terms.

8/9:60 Milton, William M. "*Tempest* in a Teapot." *ELH* 14(1946):207-18.

8/9:61 Monk, Samuel Holt. "A Note in Montague Summers's Edition of *The Way of the World*, Corrected." *NQ* 7(1960):70. *The Tempest*.

8/9:62 Morton, Richard. "'Silver at the Bottom of the Melting-Pot': Dryden's Troilus and Shadwell's Timon." *Stratford Papers on Shakespeare, 1963*, ed. B. W. Jackson, pp. 126-50. Toronto: W. J. Gage for McMaster University, 1964. Sees the two plays as adapting Shakespeare to the taste of the age.

8/9:63 Muir, Kenneth. "The Imagery of *All for Love*." *PLPLS* 5(1940): 140-47. Reprinted in [20th Century Intrepretations]:32-42. Establishes that Dryden does not use "iterative imagery" and concludes that the images of the play are merely decorative. *See* item 8/9: 74.

8/9:64 ———. "Three Shakespeare Adaptations." *PLPLS-LHS* 8(1959):233-40. *Troilus and Cressida*.

8/9:65 Nazareth, Peter. "*All for Love*: Dryden's Hybrid Play." *ESA* 6 (1963):154-63. The play is flawed because Dryden slavishly followed neoclassical critical principles.

8/9:66 Newell, Rosalie. "*Troilus and Cressida, or Truth Found Too Late*: A Study of External and Internal Form in Dryden's Critical Theory and Dramatic Practice." *DAI* 33(1973):5739(U.C.L.A.).

8/9:67 Nicoll, Allardyce. *Dryden as an Adapter of Shakespeare*. (Shakespeare Association Papers 8.) London: Shakespeare Association, 1922.

8/9:68 Noble, Richard. "Shakespeare Adaptations." *TLS* 23 March 1922, p. 196.

8/9:69 Nojima, Hidekatsu. "Four Cressidas—A Heroine in Eclipse: Part I, Chaucer's Cressida." *Essays* 17(1963):50-81. Chaucer's, Henryson's, Shakespeare's and Dryden's Cressida are compared. *See AES* 7:272-73.

8/9:70 Novak, Maximilian E. "Elkanah Settle's Attacks on Thomas Shadwell and the Authorship of the 'Operatic Tempest'." *NQ* 15(1968): 263-65.

8/9:71 Odell, George C. D. *Shakespeare from Betterton to Irving*. 2 vols. New York: Scribner, 1920. Reprinted New York: Blom, 1963. *Troilus and Cressida*.

8/9:72 Palmer, D. J. *Shakespeare: "The Tempest." A Casebook*. London: Macmillan, 1968.

8/9:73 Palmer, Roderick. "Treatments of Antony and Cleopatra." *CEA* 27, iv(1965):8-9. "Dryden transformed the great Roman tragedy into a mere love tragedy."

*8/9:74 Reinert, Otto. "Passion and Pity in *All for Love*: A Reconsideration." *The Hidden Sense and Other Essays*, pp. 159-95. (Norwegian Studies in English 9.) Oslo: Universitetsforlaget, 1963. Reprinted in an abridged form in [20th Century Interpretations]:83-98. A defense of the play in a demonstration of its unified design. *See* item 8/9:63.

8/9:75 Ringler, Richard N. "Dryden at the House of Busirane." *ES* 49 (1968):224-29.

8/9:76 Schlueter, Anne R. "John Drydens *All for Love*: Eine Interpretation." Diss. Göttingen, 1963.

8/9:77 Sloman, Judith. "Dryden, Caliban, and Negative Capability." *Transactions of the Samuel Johnson Society of the Northwest* 6 (1973):45-57.

8/9:78 Smith, Denzell S. "Dryden's Purpose in Adapting Shakespeare's *Troilus and Cressida*." *BSUF* 10,iii(1969):49-52.

8/9:79 Spencer, Hazelton. "Dryden's Adaptations." *Shakespeare Improved: The Restoration Versions in Quarto and on the Stage*, pp. 192-240. Cambridge, Mass.: Harvard University Press, 1927. Reprinted New York: Ungar, 1963.

8/9:80 Stallman, R. W. "The Scholar's Net: Literary Sources." *CE* 17 (1955):20-27. A debate on the nature of literary indebtedness: Stallman attacks F. W. Bateson's articles in *Scrutiny* 4(1935): 181-185 and in *EIC* 4(1954):436-40, arguing that while *All for Love* has *Antony and Cleopatra* as its source, it differs entirely from the latter in its meaning, technique and conception. *See* reply, F. W. Bateson, *CE* 17(1955):131-35.

8/9:81 Starnes, D. T. "Imitation of Shakespeare in Dryden's *All for Love*." *TSLL* 6(1964):39-46. Cites other Shakespeare plays "imitated" in the play.

8/9:82 ———. "More about Dryden as an Adapter of Shakespeare." *Studies in English* (University of Texas) 8(1928):100-06. Dryden's use of passages from *As You Like It*, *Julius Caesar*, *Hamlet* and *Macbeth* in *All for Love*.

8/9:83 Stratman, Carl J., "John Dryden's *All for Love*: Unrecorded Editions." *PBSA* 56(1963):77-79. 15 eds. published between 1710 and 1793.

8/9:84 Suckling, Norman. "Dryden in Egypt: Reflections on *All for Love*." *DUJ* 45(1952):2-7. Reprinted in an abridged form in [20th Century Interpretations]:46-54. Dryden's play is of a different genre (spoken opera) than Shakespeare's and, therefore, neither should be used to evaluate the other.

8/9:85 Traub, Walther. "Dryden und der Klassizismus: Verklärung und Verbürgerlichung." *Auffassung und Gestaltung der Cleopatra in der englischen Literatur*, pp. 48-61. Würzburg: Triltsch, 1938.

8/9:86 Tritt, Carleton S. "The Title of *All for Love*." *ELN* 10(1973): 273-75.

*8/9:87 Wallerstein, Ruth. "Dryden and the Analysis of Shakespeare's Techniques." *RES* 19(1943):165-85. Reprinted in [Swedenberg]:551-75. The different types of passion "imitated" by Dryden in *All for Love*.

8/9:88 Walmsley, D. M. "Shadwell and the Operatic *Tempest*." *RES* 2 (1926):463-66. Debating the attribution of the play. *See* correspondence, George Thorn-Drury, ibid., 3(1927):204-08; D. M. Walmsley, ibid., 451-53. *See also* items 3:188, 8/9:50, 8/9:89.

8/9:89 Ward, Charles E. "*The Tempest*: A Restoration Opera Problem."
        ELH 13(1946):119-30. Shadwell is not the author of the operatic
        Tempest.

8/9:90 Warmington, E. L. "A Dryden Misprint." *London Mercury* 14
        (1926):188.

8/9:91 Weinbrot, Howard D. "Alexas in *All for Love*: His Genealogy
        and Function." *SP* 64(1967):625-39.

8/9:92 Witt, Otto. "The Tempest or The Enchanted. Island. A Comedy by
        John Dryden. 1670. The Sea Voyage. A Comedy by Beaumont and
        Fletcher. 1647. The Goblin's Tragi-Comedy by Sir John Suckling.
        1646. in ihrem Verhältnis zu Shakespeares 'Tempest' und den
        übrigen Quellen." Diss. Rostock, 1899.

8/9:93 Zenke, Hermann. "Drydens Troilus und Cressida im Verhältnis
        zu Shakespeares Drama und die übrigen Bearbeitungen des Stoffes
        in England." Diss. Rostock, 1904.

The Tempest: *See also* items 2/5:5, 2/5:24, 2/5:27, 2/5:30-31, 2/5:33,
        2/5:35, 4:350, 4:468, 5/6:33, 5/6:39, 8/1:59, 8/1:157, 8/1:210,
        8/11:9.

All for Love: *See also* items 2/1:7, 2/5:2-3, 2/5:6, 2/5:11, 2/5:13,
        2/5:16, 2/5:19, 2/5:21, 2/5:23, 2/5:26, 2/5:29, 2/5:36-37, 2/5:
        39, 3:188, 4:16, 4:39, 4:105, 4:155, 4:167, 4:197, 4:342, 4:367,
        4:403, 4:464, 4:507, 5/13:8, 7:82, 8/1:48, 8/1:156, 8/1:183-84,
        8/1:215, 8/1:267, 8/2:26, 8/2:28, 8/2:38, 8/2:61, 8/2:66, 8/2:
        100, 8/4:11, 8/9:1, 9:19.

Troilus and Cressida: *See also* items 2/5:34, 4:444.

8/10. *THE STATE OF INNOCENCE*

8/10:1 Bowers, Fredson. "The Pirated Quarto of Dryden's *State of In-
        nocence*." *SB* 5(1952-53):166-69. Macdonald 81c. *See* item 8/10:9.

8/10:2 Churchill, George B. "The Relation of Dryden's 'State of Inno-
        cence' to Milton's 'Paradise Lost' and Wycherley's 'Plain Dealer,'
        an Inquiry into Dates." *MP* 4(1906):381-88.

8/10:3 Evans, G. Blakemore. "Dryden's 'State of Innocence'." *TLS* 21
        March 1942, p. 144. Discusses the genealogy of the text.

8/10:4 ———. "Edward Ecclestone: His Relationship to Dryden and
        Milton." *MLR* 44(1949):550-52.

8/10:5 ———. "Milton and Lee's *The Rival Queens* (1677)." *MLN* 64
        (1949):527-28.

8/10:6 Fletcher, Harris F. "Nathaniel Lee and Milton." *MLN* 44(1920):
        173-75. Verses contributed by Lee.

8/10:7 Freedman, Morris. "The 'Tagging' of Paradise Lost: Rhyme in
        Dryden's *The State of Innocence*." *MiltonQ* 5(1971):18-22.

8/10:8 Hamilton, Marion H. "Dryden's *The State of Innocence*: An Old-
        Spelling Edition with a Critical Study of the Early Printed Texts
        and Manuscripts." *UV-AD* (1952):8-10.

8/10:9 ———. "The Early Editions of Dryden's *State of Innocence*."
        SB 5(1952-53):163-66. The chronology of the pre-1701 quarto eds.
        See item 8/10:1.

8/10:10 ———. "The Manuscripts of Dryden's *The State of Innocence*
        and the Relation of the Harvard MS to the First Quarto." *SB* 6
        (1954):237-46. Establishes Q1 as the text of highest substantive
        authority.

*8/10:11   Harris, Bernard, "'That Soft Seducer, Love': Dryden's *The
State of Innocence and Fall of Man*." *Approaches to "Paradise
Lost": The York Tercentenary Lectures*, ed. C. A. Patrides, pp.
119-36. Toronto: University of Toronto Press, 1968. Dryden's dif-
ficulties in adapting Milton's poem to a dramatic setting.

*8/10:12   Havens, P. S. "Dryden's 'Tagged' Version of 'Paradise
Lost'." *Essays in Dramatic Literature: The Parrott Presentation
Volume*, ed. Hardin Craig, pp. 383-97. Princeton: Princeton University Press, 1935. Reprinted New York: Russell and Russell, 1967.
The play is not an arrogant attempt to improve *Paradise Lost*;
rather, it is an experiment in epic writing, which was only published reluctantly.

8/10:13   Havens, Raymond D. "An Adaptation of One of Dryden's Plays."
RES 4(1928):88. Cites an announcement in the 15 February 1712
Spectator for a performance of *The State of Innocence*.

8/10:14   Howell, A. C. "*Res et verba*: Words and Things." *ELH* 13(1964):
131-42.

8/10:15   King, Bruce. "The Significance of Dryden's *State of Innocence*." *SEL* 4(1964):371-91. The treatment of free will and deter-
minism, with reference to the Hobbes-Bishop Bramhall debate.

8/10:16   Legouis, Pierre. "Dryden plus Miltonien que Milton?" *EA* 20
(1967):370-77.

8/10:17   Manuel, M. "The Seventeenth-Century Critics and Biographers
of Milton." Diss. Ohio State, 1956. Includes a discussion of *The
State of Innocence*.

*8/10:18   McFadden, George. "Dryden's 'Most Barren Period'—and Mil-
ton." *HLQ* 24(1961):283-96. During the period 1672-1676 Dryden
studied other writers, notably Milton, from whom he learned the
Virgilian technique of intensifying sound.

8/10:19   Roston, Murray. "Dryden's *State of Innocence*." *Biblical Drama in England: From the Middle Ages to the Present Day*, pp. 175-
81. London: Faber, 1968. A general survey.

8/10:20   Scott, Anna M. "Uber das Verhältnis von Drydens *State of Innocence* zu Miltons *Paradise Lost*." Diss. Halle, 1900.

8/10:21   Shaw, Arthur Marvin. "Dryden's Handling of *Paradise Lost*"
[Abstract of a paper delivered at Centenary College]. *SCN* 11
(1953):22.

8/10:22   Stephenson, William E. "Religious Drama in the Restoration."
PQ 50(1971):599-609.

8/10:23   Tyler, Henry. "Milton and Dryden." *TLS* 12 April 1947, p. 171.

8/10:24   White, H. O. "Dryden and Descartes." *TLS* 19 December 1929,
p. 1081. *See* Louis I. Bredvold, ibid., 2 January 1930, p. 12.

8/10:25   Whiting, G. W. "The Ellesmere MS of the *State of Innocence*."
TLS 14 January 1932, p. 28.

*8/10:26   Williamson, George. "Dryden's View of Milton." *Milton and
Others*, pp. 103-21. London: Faber, 1965. Dryden's conception of
heroic poetry.

See also items 1:51, 3:61-62, 3:167, 4:47, 4:155, 4:168, 4:377, 4:464-
65, 4:487, 4:493, 4:507, 7:80, 8/1:196, 8/2:38, 8/11:9.

8/11. OPERAS: *KING ARTHUR; ALBION AND ALBANIUS*

8/11:1   Aldridge, Alfred Owne. "Dryden Song and Wesley Hymn." *Saturday Review of Literature* 25(30 May 1942):15. Wesley may have bor-

rowed from Dryden's "Song of Venus" in *King Arthur* when he wrote "Love Divine."

8/11:2 Brinkley, Roberta Florence. *Arthurian Legend in the Seventeenth Century.* (Johns Hopkins Monographs in Literary History 3.) Baltimore: Johns Hopkins Press, 1932.

8/11:3 Chisholm, Duncan. "The English Origins of Handel's 'Pastor fido'." *Musical Times* 115(1974):650-54.

8/11:4 Davies, H. Neville. "Dryden's Libretti in the Light of Seventeenth-Century Ideas About Words and Music." *ASLIB* 15(1964-65):13 (Liverpool).

8/11:5 Dent, Edward J. *Foundations of English Opera: A Study of Musical Drama in England During the Seventeenth Century,* introd. Michael M. Winesanker. Cambridge: At the University Press, 1928. Reprinted New York: Da Capo Press, 1965.

8/11:6 Gottesman, Lillian. "The Arthurian Romance in English Opera and Pantomime, 1660-1800." *RECTR* 8,ii(1969):47-53.

8/11:7 Graham, Colin, ed. and adapter. *King Arthur, His Magical History.* With music by Purcell, realized by Philip Ledger. London: Faber, 1970.

8/11:8 H. "A British Worthy." *Saturday Review* 145(25 February 1928): 219-20. A rev. of a Cambridge University performance of *King Arthur.*

8/11:9 Haraszti, Zoltán. "Dryden's Adaptations and Operas (with a facsimile)." *More Books* 8(1939):89-99.

8/11:10 Haun, Eugene. *But Hark! More Harmony: The Libretti of Restoration Opera in English.* Ypsilanti, Mich.: Eastern Michigan University Press, 1971. *See PQ* 51:163.

8/11:11 ———. "The Libretti of the Restoration Opera in English: A Study in Theatrical Genres." *DA* 14(1954):1395(Penn.).

8/11:12 Heisch, Elizabeth A. "The Problem of Prosody in the Early English Opera: 1660-1700: A Study of the Setting of Words to Music." *DAI* 32(1972):6377A(U.C.L.A.).

8/11:13 Henigan, Robert H. "English Dramma per Musica: A Study of Musical Drama in England from *The Siege of Rhodes* to the Opening of the Haymarket Theater." *DA* 22(1961):1609-10(Missouri). *King Arthur.*

8/11:14 Hitchman, Percy J. "*King Arthur* at Nottingham: A Notable Revival." *TN* 11(1957):121-28.

8/11:15 Holland, A. K. *Henry Purcell: The English Musical Tradition.* London: G. Bell, 1932.

8/11:16 Kinsley, James. "The Music of the Heart." *RMS* 8(1964):5-52. Dryden's work as a librettist for Purcell and his critical theories about musical drama.

8/11:17 Kliger, Samuel. *The Goths in England; A Study in Seventeenth and Eighteenth Century Thought.* Cambridge, Mass.: Harvard University Press, 1952.

8/11:18 Lawrence, W. J. "Dryden's Abortive Opera." *TLS* 6 August 1931, p. 606. *See* correspondence, Montague Summers, ibid., 13 August 1931, p. 621; Bernard M. Wagner, ibid., 1 October 1931, p. 757; George W. Whiting, ibid., 24 December 1931, p. 1041.

8/11:19 Mace, Dean Tolle. "English Musical Thought in the Seventeenth Century: A Study of an Art in Decline." *DA* 12(1952):620 (Columbia). *King Arthur.*

8/11:20 Mark, Jeffrey. "Dryden and the Beginnings of Opera in England." *Music and Letters* 5(1924):247-52.

8/11:21   Mathieu-Arth, Françoise. "La 'Psyche' de Thomas Shadwell d'
après Moilière." *Dramaturgie et Société: Rapports entre l'oeuvre
théâtrale*, ed. Jean Jacquot, assisted by Elie Konigson and Marcel
Oddon. 1:373-93. (Colloques internationaux due centre national de
las recherche scientifique: Sciences humaines.) Paris: Editions
du centre national de la recherche scientifique, 1968. Shadwell's
experiments with operatic form prepared the way for *King Arthur*.

8/11:22   Maynadier, Howard. "The Age of Prose and Reason." *The Arthur
of the English Poets*, pp. 295-313. Boston, New York: Houghton
Mifflin, 1907. Reprinted New York, London: Johnson Reprint, 1969.
Dryden made rational what was romantic in the Arthurian Legend.

8/11:23   Merriman, James Douglas. "Dryden's Arthur." *The Flower of
Kings: A Study of the Arthurian Legend in England between 1485
and 1835*, pp. 60-64. Lawrence: University of Kansas Press, 1973.

8/11:24   ———. "The Flower of Kings: A Study of the Arthurian Legend in England Between 1485 and 1835." *DA* 23(1963):3354-55(Columbia).

8/11:25   Moore, Robert Etheridge. *Henry Purcell and the Restoration
Theatre*. Cambridge, Mass.: Harvard University Press, 1961.

8/11:26   Myers, Clara L. "Opera in England from 1656 to 1728." *Western Reserve University Bulletin* 9,v(1906):129-56.

8/11:27   Noyes, Robert Gale. "Contemporary Musical Settings of the
Songs in Restoration Dramatic Operas." *Harvard Studies and Notes
in Philology and Literature* 20(1938):99-121.

8/11:28   Parry, C. H. H. "English Music after the Commonwealth." *Oxford History of Music*. Vol. 3. Oxford: Oxford University Press,
1902.

8/11:29   Pulver, Jeffrey. "Purcell and Dryden." *Musical Opinion and
Musical Trade Review* 59(1936):589-90.

8/11:30   Reid, Margaret J. C. "Arthur in the Sixteenth, Seventeenth
and Eighteenth Centuries: Spenser, Milton, Dryden." *The Arthurian
Legend: Comparison of Treatment in Modern and Medieval Literature*, pp. 30-41. Edinburgh, London: Oliver and Boyd, 1938. Reprinted New York: Barnes and Noble, 1961. Brief notes on *King Arthur*.

8/11:31   Squire, William Barclay. "The Music of Shadwell's 'Tempest'."
MusQ 8(1921):565-78.

8/11:32   ———. "Purcell's Dramatic Music." *Sammelbände der Musik-
gesellschaft* 5(1904):489-564.

8/11:33   Summers, Montague. "A Note on Purcell's Music." *Dryden: The
Dramatic Works*. I:cxxxi-iv. London: The Nonesuch Press, 1931.

8/11:34   Walmsley, D. M. "The Influence of Foreign Opera on English
Operatic Plays of the Restoration Period." *Anglia* 52(1928):37-50.

8/11:35   White, Eric Walter. "Early Theatrical Performances of Purcell's Operas: with a Calendar of Recorded Performances, 1690-
1710." *TN* 13(1958-59):43-65.

8/11:36   ———. *The Rise of English Opera*, introd. Benjamin Britten.
London: Lehman, 1951.

Operas: See also items 1:49, 4:348, 4:532, 4:563, 5/12:17, 7:181, 7:
277, 8/1:136, 8/1:210, 8/1:253, 8/2:71, 8/2:90.

King Arthur: See also items 2/5:14, 3:23, 4:142, 4:297, 4:439, 8/1:
157, 8/2:52, 8/2:28, 8/2:90.

Albion and Albanius: See also items 2/1:4, 2/5:7, 4:267, 8/1:101, 8/1:
126, 8/1:167.

8/12. *THE SPANISH FRYAR; DON SEBASTIAN; AMPHITRYON;*

CLEOMENES; LOVE TRIUMPHANT; THE SECULAR MASQUE

8/12:1   Archer, Stanley. "A Performance of Dryden's *Cleomenes*." *NQ* 18 (1971):460–61.

8/12:2   Barden, Thomas E. "Dryden's Aims in *Amphytryon*." *Costerus* 9 (1973):1–8. Dryden's play is compared with those by Plautus and Molière.

8/12:3   Bondurant, Alexander. "The *Amphitruo* of Plautus, Molière's *Amphitryon*, and the *Amphitryon* of Dryden." *SR* 33(1925):455–68.

8/12:4   Brossman, Sidney W. "Dryden's Cassandra and Congreve's Zara." *NQ* 3(1956):102–03. Dryden's influence on Congreve; *Cleomenes*.

8/12:5   ———. "Dryden's *Cleomenes* and Fletcher's *Bonduca*." *NQ* 4(1957): 66–68.

8/12:6   Dearing, Bruce. "Some Views of a Beast." *MLN* 71(1956):326–29. Includes a discussion of "Thy chase had a beast in view" from *The Secular Masque*. *See* item 8/12:15.

8/12:7   Golden, Samuel A. "Dryden's *Cleomenes* and Theophilus Parsons." *NQ* 13(1966):380.

*8/12:8   Jefferson, D. W. "'All, all of a piece throughout': Thoughts on Dryden's Dramatic Poetry." [Rest. Theatre]:159–76. *Don Sebastian* is Dryden's best play.

*8/12:9   King, Bruce. "*Don Sebastian*: Dryden's Moral Fable." *SR* 70 (1962):651–70.

8/12:10   Legouis, Pierre. "Quinault et Dryden: Une source de *The Spanish Fryar*." *RLC* 11(1931):398–415.

8/12:11   Lindberger, Örjan. *The Transformation of Amphitryon*. (Stockholm Studies in the History of Literature 1.) Stockholm: Almquist and Wiksell, 1958.

8/12:12   Merzbach, Margaret Kober. "The Third Source of Dryden's *Amphitryon*." *Anglia* 73(1955):213–14. Thomas Heywood's *The Silver Age*.

8/12:13   Meyerstein, E. H. W. "Dryden and 'The Soldier'." *TLS* 8 March 1923, p. 160. A borrowing by Rupert Brooks from *Don Sebastian*?

8/12:14   Moore, John Robert, "Dryden and Rupert Brooke." *MLR* 54(1959): 266.

*8/12:15   Roper, Alan. "Dryden's 'Secular Masque'." *MLQ* 23(1962):29–40. *See* item 8/12:6.

8/12:16   Schröder, Edwin. *Dryden's letztes Drama: "Love Triumphant or Nature will Prevail*." Rostock: Adlers Erben, 1905.

8/12:17   Ward, Charles E. "Dryden's *Spanish Friar* and a Provincial Touring Company." *NQ* 176(1939):96–97.

8/12:18   Wilson, John Harold. "The Duke's Theatre in March, 1680." *NQ* 9(1962):385–86. *The Spanish Fryar*.

The Spanish Fryar: *See also* items 2/5:6–7, 2/5:11, 2/5:38, 4:16, 4: 267, 4:362, 4:522, 8/1:1, 8/1:65, 8/1:126, 8/1:156, 8/1:167, 8/1: 196, 8/1:253, 8/2:38, 8/2:46, 8/2:51, 8/2:69–70, 8/2:100, 8/5:5, 8/6:2.

Don Sebastian: *See also* items 2/5:2, 4:444, 8/2:26, 8/2:28, 8/2:46, 8/2:52, 8/2:71, 8/12:14.

Amphitryon: *See also* items 4:562, 8/1:157, 8/1:203, 9:12.

Cleomenes: *See also* items 2/5:15, 3:54, 8/1:101, 8/2:26.

Love Triumphant: *See also* items 1:40, 8/2:38.

The Secular Masque: *See also* items 2/1:7, 4:79.

9. Foreign Reputation

9:1   Baumgartner, Milton D. "Dryden's Relation to Germany." *UNS* 14 (1914):289–375.

9:2   ———. *On Dryden's Relation to Germany in the Eighteenth Century.* Lancaster, Pennsylvania: University of Chicago, 1914.

9:3   Brown, Andrew F. "Shakespeare in Germany: Dryden, Langbaine, and the *Acta Eruditorum.*" *GR* 40(1965):87–95.

9:4   Crinò, Anna Maria, ed. *Fatti e figure del Seicento anglo-toscano: Documenti inediti sui rapporti letterari, diplomatici, culturali fra Toscana e Inghilterra.* Firenze: Olschki, 1957.

9:5   Eichler, Albert. "Christian Wernickes Hans Sachs und sein Dryden-sches Vorbild." *Zeitschrift für vergleichende Litteraturgeschichte* 17(1909):208–24.

9:6   Fenger, Henning. "Voltaire et le Theatre Anglais." *Orbis Litterarum* 7(1949):161–287.

9:7   Golden, Samuel A. "Benjamin Furly's Library: An Intermediary Source in Anglo-Dutch Literary Relations." *Hermathena* 96(1962):16–20. Dryden's plays, dated 1710, in Furly's library.

9:8   Hunter, Alfred C. "Le 'Conte de la femme de Bath' en Français au XVIIIe siècle." *RLC* 9(1929):117–40.

9:9   Jeune, Simon. "*Hamlet* d'Otway, *Macbeth* de Dryden ou Shakespeare en France en 1714." *RLC* 36(1962):560–64.

9:10   Kies, Paul P. "A Possible Source of Lessing's *Horoskop.*" *Research Studies, State College of Washington* 6(1938):126–28. *Aureng-Zebe* is the source.

9:11   Maillet, Albert. "Dryden et Voltaire." *RLC* 18(1938):272–86.

9:12   Merzbach, Margaret Kober. "Kleist and Dryden." *SCB* 21,iv(1961): 11–16. Heinrich von Kleist's debt to Dryden and Molière in writing his own version of *Amphitryon*.

9:13   Parra, Anton Ranieri. "Considerazioni sulla fortuna di John Dryden nell'Italia del Settecento." *RLMC* 22(1969):17–46.

9:14   Price, Lawrence M. *The Reception of English Literature in Germany.* Berkeley: University of California Press, 1932. Reprinted New York, London: Blom, 1968.

9:15   Price, Mary B., and Lawrence M. Price. "The Publication of English Literature in Germany in the Eighteenth Century." *University of California Publications in Modern Philology* 17(1934):82–84.

9:16   Russell, Trusten W. "Voltaire, Dryden and Heroic Tragedy." Diss. Columbia, 1947.

9:17   ———. *Voltaire, Dryden, and Heroic Tragedy.* New York: Columbia University Press, 1946. Reprinted New York: AMS Press, 1966. Investigates the effect of Dryden's epic theory and dramatic practice on Voltaire's critical writings and plays. *See* H. C. Lancaster, *MLN* 62:492–95.

9:18   ———. "Dryden, Inspirateur de Voltaire." *RLC* 22(1948):321–28. Voltaire's opinion of Dryden's verse and plays.

9:19   Sgard, Jean. "Une Image de Prévost: Marc-Antoine aux Portes du Tombeau." *RHL* 68(1968):605-09.

9:20   Vetter, Theodore. "J. J. Bodmer und die englische Litteratur." *Bodmer Denkschrift*, pp. 315-86. Zurich, 1900.

9:21   Waterhouse, Gilbert. *The Literary Relations of England and Germany in the Seventeenth Century*. Cambridge: At the University Press, 1914.

See also item 8/9:39.

INDEXES

Index of Authors,

Proper Names and Titles

Index of Topics

Acting, 2/5:9, 3:102, 8/1:98,
8/1:258, 8/2:61, 8/9:32
Actresses, 8/1:90, 8/1:133, 8/1:
256
Adaptations, p. 10; 1:49, 8/1:77.
See also under Sec. 8/9
Anglican Church, the, 4:29-30,
4:211, 5/7:16, 5/7:24
Animal lore. *See under* Sec. 5/11
Apologetics, Roman Catholic, 4:
43, 4:131, 4:211, 5/7:3, 5/7:
12, 5/11:15
Arthurian legend. *See under* Sec.
8/11
Audience, theater, 5/13:5, 8/1:
96, 8/1:129, 8/1:209, 8/2:92
Augustan, 4:95, 4:184, 4:247, 4:
515, 4:524

Baroque, 4:14, 4:464-65, 4:468,
4:518, 4:539, 5/5:4, 5/10:1,
5/12:12, 6/2:33, 8/1:74, 8/1:
118, 8/1:183-84, 8/2:6-7, 8/2:
48, 8/2:83, 8/9:52
Beast fable, p. 12. *See also under* Sec. 5/11
Beatus-ille theme, 4:280, 4:375,
5/14:11, 6/2:68

Catholicism, pp. 6-7; 3:14, 3:45,
3:161, 3:166, 3:180, 3:200, 4:

30, 4:34, 4:110, 4:131, 4:158,
4:337, 4:502, 4:535, 5/7:12,
5/11:15. *See also under* Apologetics, Roman Catholic, Sec. 5/7
and 5/11
Censorship, 4:276, 6/2:18, 8/1:
251, 8/6:6
Character-writing, 4:116, 4:159,
4:198, 4:202, 4:221, 4:444,
5/4:37, 7:319
Classical education, 4:446
Classical orations, 5/4:75
Classical poetry, 4:153, 4:181
Classical rhetoric, 4:153-54, 5/1:
3
Concordance. *See under* Tabular
views
Court wits, the, 3:156, 3:202.
See also under Rochester and
Sedley
Critical approaches, pp. 8-14; 4:
60, 4:175, 4:288, 4:307, 4:336,
4:340, 4:422, 4:467, 4:489-91,
4:509, 4:544, 4:559, 5/4:9, 5/4:
28, 5/6:34, 5/8:2, 8/1:97, 8/1:
125, 8/9:59

Davidic King, the, 4:256, 4:320,
4:470, 5/4:3, 5/4:9, 5/4:45
Decorum, 7:82, 7:166, 7:205, 7:
207

7:36, 8/2:22, 8/2:30, 8/2:47,
8/2:51, 8/2:57. *See also under*
Eleonora, Orrery, *Précieuse*,
Sec. 8/1 and 8/2
Poems on Affairs of State, 2/1:
4-5, 2/2:20, 2/2:27, 2/2:46, 4:
369, 4:80, 5/11:12
Poet as spokesman for established
authority, 3:183, 4:7, 4:55, 4:
65, 4:178, 4:223, 4:232, 4:299,
4:348, 4:380, 4:417-18, 4:481,
4:498, 4:551, 4:564-65, 5/1:3,
5/4:9, 5/5:4
Poetry of praise, 4:17, 4:36, 4:
40, 4:46, 4:114, 4:178, 4:203,
4:211, 4:222, 4:269, 4:280, 4:
291, 4:369, 4:380, 4:417-18, 4:
534, 5/1:6, 7:8, 8/2:90
Poetry of statement, pp. 9, 11;
4:22, 4:65, 4:136, 4:187, 4:
202, 4:242, 4:306, 4:464, 4:
506, 4:542, 4:544, 4:560, 5/5:
8, 5/7:17, 5/7:23
Popish Plot, pp. 5, 9, 12; 2/2:
32, 3:183, 4:34, 4:43, 4:106,
4:260, 4:266, 4:272, 4:357, 4:
392, 4:535, 5/4:5, 5/13:33, 8/1:
126, 8/1:253, 8/8:11. *See also*
under The History of the League,
Sec. 5/4 and 5/5
Précieuse, 8/1:17, 8/1:19-20,
8/1:38, 8/2:51, 8/2:64, 8/2:87,
8/7:7, 8/9:31
Probability, 7:72, 7:97, 7:105,
7:231, 7:317, 7:341, 8/1:21
Progress-piece, 4:290, 4:341-42,
4:344, 4:348, 4:483, 5/11:27,
5/14:12, 7:207
Psychological approach, 7:32, 7:
61, 7:63, 7:154-55, 7:309, 8/1:
31

Rhyme-blank verse controversy,
the, 2/4:2, 3:61-62, 3:141, 7:
88, 7:102, 7:135, 7:160, 7:231,
7:277, 8/1:185, 8/1:198, 8/2:
18, 8/2:24, 8/2:55, 8/2:64, 8/2:
71, 8/9:28. *See also under A*
Defence of An Essay, *Of Dramat-*
ic Poesy and Sir Robert Howard
Royal Society, p. 6; 3:26, 3:107,
3:160, 4:43, 4:133, 4:158, 4:
523, 7:42, 7:153, 7:341. *See*
also under Science
Rules, pp. 14, 15; 7:28, 7:93,

7:104-05, 7:127, 7:135, 7:231,
7:269-71, 7:275, 7:277, 7:287,
7:300-02, 7:317, 7:346, 8/2:25,
8/2:27, 8/9:28

Satire, p. 14; 2/2:9, 2/2:23, 2/2:
43, 3:183, 4:4, 4:42, 4:77, 4:
101-02, 4:110, 4:115, 4:168, 4:
170, 4:198, 4:202, 4:208, 4:214,
4:221, 4:235, 4:237-39, 4:242-
43, 4:263, 4:265, 4:272, 4:276,
4:278-79, 4:283, 4:305, 4:345,
4:369-70, 4:383-84, 4:390, 4:
394-95, 4:433, 4:440-42, 4:444,
4:446, 4:452, 4:479, 4:510, 4:
525, 4:536, 4:540-41, 4:547-48,
4:553, 4:559, 5/4:7-10, 5/4:20,
5/6:2, 5/6:24, 5/6:34, 5/6:43,
5/11:14, 5/11:28, 6/2:32, 6/2:
43, 6/2:69, 7:71, 7:74, 7:94-
95, 7:107, 7:166, 7:240, 7:253,
8/1:32, 8/1:51, 8/1:101, 8/1:
142, 8/1:253
Scandinavia, 4:439
Science, p. 6; 4:43, 4:72, 4:118,
4:130, 4:133, 4:158, 4:190, 4:
253, 4:373, 4:523, 4:560, 5/14:
5, 7:10, 7:97, 7:152-53, 7:183,
7:198, 7:335. *See also under*
Royal Society, Sec. 5/2 and 5/3
Spaniel, nimble, 7:86, 7:122, 7:
154-55, 7:262, 7:303. *See also*
under Fancy
Specula principum, 4:40
Staging in the Restoration theater, 2/5:9, 5/13:11, 8/1:43,
8/1:71, 8/1:100, 8/1:137, 8/1:
145, 8/1:168, 8/1:180, 8/1:214,
8/2:36, 8/4:9, 8/4:27. *See also*
under Acting and *The London*
Stage
Stoicism, 7:206, 8/2:98

Tabular views (includes dictionary and concordance formats),
pp. 14, 18; 1:75, 4:81, 4:221,
4:334, 4:419, 5/6:2, 6/2:73-74,
7:3, 7:63, 7:148-49, 7:313
Translatio studii. *See under* Progress piece
Typology, p. 11; 4:274, 4:288, 4:
320, 4:342, 4:409, 4:564-65,
5/1:6, 5/4:45, 5/14:3, 7:106

Unities. *See under* Rules

ADDENDUM

Drydeniana

Garland Publishing's series on *The Life & Times of Seven Major British Writers: Dryden, Pope, Swift, Richardson, Sterne, Johnson, Gibbon* constitutes a major contribution to the study of Dryden and the eighteenth century. Although I received notice of this series of facsimiles while the bibliography was already in press, I was convinced that it is of such importance as to deserve a separate addendum section. Regrettably, the material of the series has not been indexed. Under the heading of *Drydeniana*, Garland in 1974-75 published a fourteen-volume collection which includes the following items:

1. *Early Career—1668 to 1671*: Sir Robert Howard's *The Great Favourite, or the Duke of Lerma* (1668); R. A. F's *A Letter from a Gentleman to the Honourable E. Howard Esq; Occasioned by a Civiliz'd Epistle of Mr. Dryden's* (1668); Richard Flecknoe's *Epigrams of All Sorts, Made at Several Times, On Several Occasions* (1671).

2. *On Heroic Love I*: S. L.'s *Remarques on the Humours and Conversations of the Town* (1673); *Remarks upon Remarques: or, a Vindication of the Conversations of the Town* (1673).

3. *On Heroic Love II*: *Reflexions on Marriage, and the Poetick Discipline* (1673); *Animadversions on Two Late Books, One Called Remarques, &c. . . . the Other Called Reflections on Marriage* (1673); *Raillerie à la Mode Consider'd: or the Supercilious Detractor* (1673).

4. *On Heroic Love III*: William Ramsey's *Conjugium Conjurgium, or Some Serious Considerations on Marriage* (1673); *Marriage Asserted: In Answer to a Book Entituled Conjugium Conjurgium* (1674).

5. *The Censure of the Rota; Elkanah Settle*: Richard Leigh's *The Friendly Vindication of Mr. Dryden from the Censure of the Rota* (1673); Charles Blount's *Mr. Dreyden Vindicated, in a Reply to the Friendly Vindication of Mr. Dreyden* (1673); *A Description of the Academy of the Athenian Virtuosi: with a Discourse Held there in Vindication of Mr. Dryden's Conquest of Granada* (1673); Elkanah Settle's *The Empress

of Morocco. A Tragedy (1673); Joseph Arrowsmith's *The Reformation. A Comedy* (1673); Elkanah Settle's *Notes and Observations on the Empress of Morocco Revised* (1674).

6. *On Absalom and Achitophel*: Christopher Nesse's *A Key (With the Whip) to Open the Mystery & Inquiry of the Poem Called, Absalom & Achitophel* (1682); Samuel Pordage's [or Elkanah Settle's] *Azaria and Hushai, a Poem* (1682); Samuel Pordage's *The Medal Revers'd. A Satyre against Persecution* (1682); Thomas Shadwell's *The Medal of John Bayes: A Satyr against Folly and Knavery* (1682); Thomas Shadwell's *Satyr to his Muse. By the Author of Absalom & Achitophel* (1682); *The Tory Poets: A Satyr* (1682); *Poeta de Tristibus: or, the Poet's Complaint. A Poem* (1682); *Directions to Fame, About an Elegy on . . . Thomas Thynn, Esq.* (1682).

7. *On the Duke of Guise*: Thomas Hunt's *A Defence of the Charter, and Municipal Rights of the City of London* (1683); Thomas Shadwell's *Some Reflections upon the Pretended Parallel in the Play Called The Duke of Guise* (1683); *The True History of the Duke of Guise* (1683); Charles Blount's *Religio Laici. Written in a Letter to John Dryden, Esq.* (1683).

8. *The Hind and the Panther, and Other Works*: *The Laurel, a Poem on the Poet-Laureat* (1685); Thomas Shadwell's *The Tenth Satyr of Juvenal, English and Latin* (1687); Matthew Prior and Charles Montague's *The Hind and the Panther Transvers'd* (1687); *The Revolter. A Trage-comedy Acted between the Hind and the Panther, and Religio Laici* (1687); Thomas Heyrick's *The New Atlantis. A Poem, in Three Books. With some Reflections upon The Hind and the Panther* (1687); Martin Clifford's *Notes upon Mr. Dryden's Poems* (1687).

9. *Mr. Bays and his Religion*: Thomas Brown's *The Reasons of Mr. Bays Changing his Religion* (1688); Thomas Brown's *The Late Converts Exposed: or the Reasons of Mr. Bays Changing his Religion* (1690); Thomas Brown's *The Reasons of Mr. Joseph Hains the Player's Conversion & Re-conversion* (1690).

10. *Late Criticism*: J. R.'s *Religio Laici, or a Laymans Faith . . . by a Convert of Mr. Bay's* (1688); *Rabshakeh Vapulans: or, an Answer to the Tribe of Levi . . . a Poem* (1691); Charles Gildon's *Miscellaneous Letters and Essays, on Several Subjects . . . Directed to John Dryden, Esq; etc.* (1694); *The Fatal Discovery; or, Love in Ruines. A Tragedy . . . with a Preface in Answer to a Scandalous Copy of Verses, Written by Mr. Dryden* (1698).

11. *Blount on Poetry*: Sir Thomas Pope Blount's *De re poetica: or, Remarks upon Poetry* (1694).

12. *On Dryden's Virgil*: Luke Milbourne's *Notes on Dryden's Virgil*.

13. *Folio Verse Relating to Dryden*: Henry Care's *Towser the Second a Bull-dog. Or a Short Reply to Absalom and Achitophel* (1681); George Villiers, Duke of Buckingham's *Poetical Reflections on a Late Poem Entituled, Absalom and Achitophel* (1681); *A Panegyrick on the Author of Absalom and Achitophel* (1681); *Absolon's IX Worthies: or, a Key to a Late Book or Poem, Entituled A.B. & A.C.* (1682); Edmund Hickeringill's *The Mushroom: or, A Satyr . . . in Answer to a Satyr against Sedition called the Meddal* (1682); Elkanah Settle's *Absalom Senior: or, Achitophel Transpros'd. A Poem* (1682); *The Royal Medal Vindicated. A Poem* (1682); *An Epode to his Worthy Friend Mr. John Dryden, to Advise him not to Answer Two Malicious Pamphlets against his Tragedy Called, The Duke of Guise* (1683); *Sol in Opposition to Saturn. Or a Short Return to a Late Tragedy called, The Duke of Guise*

(1683); Thomas Shadwell's *A Lenten Prologue Refus'd by the Players*
(1683); Robert Gould's *The Laureat. Jack Squabbs History* (1687); *A
Poem in Defence of the Church of England; in Opposition to The Hind
and the Panther* (1688); *An Epistle to Mr. Dryden* (1688); *The Address
of John Dryden, Laureat to his Highness the Prince of Orange* (1689);
Urania's Temple: or, a Satyr upon the Silent Poets (1698); *A. B.'s An
Ode Occasion'd by the Death of the Queen, with a Letter from the Au-
thor to Mr. Dryden* (1695); *The Mourning Poets: or, an Account of the
Poems on the Death of the Queen* (1695); Edward Howard's *An Essay Upon
Pastoral* (1695); George Stepney's *A Poem Dedicated to the Blessed Mem-
ory of her Late Gracious Majesty Queen Mary* (1695); William Pittis'
An Epistolary Poem to John Dryden, Esq. (1699).

14. On the Death of *Dryden: Folio Verse: The Patentee: or, Some Reflections in Verse on Mr. R----'s Forgetting the Design of his Majesty's Bear-Garden . . . on the Day When Mr. Dryden's Obseques Were
Perform'd* (1700); Charles Brome's *To the Memory of Mr. Dryden. A Poem*
(1700); *Luctus Britannici: or the Tears of the British Muses; for the
Death of John Dryden, Esq.* (1700); Thomas Brown's *A Description of
Mr. D----n's Funeral. A Poem* (1700); Alexander Oldys' *An Ode, by Way
of Elegy, on the Universally Lamented Death of the Incomparable Mr.
Dryden* (1700); Edward Ward's *The London Spy. For the Month of April,
1700. The Second Volume. Part VI* (1700); *The Nine Muses. Or, Poems
Written by Nine Severall Ladies upon the Death of the Late Famous
John Dryden, Esq.* (1700); *A New Session of the Poets, Occasion'd by
the Death of Mr. Dryden* (1700); *An Epistle to Sr. Richard Blackmore,
Occasion'd by the New Session of the Poets* (1700).